PREMARITAL SEXUAL STANDARDS

IN AMERICA

By Gis and by Saint Charity,
    Alack, and fie for shame!
Young men will do't, if they come to't;
    By Cock they are to blame.
Quoth she, before you tumbled me,
    You promis'd me to wed.
He Answers:
So would I ha' done, by yonder sun,
    An thou hadst not come to my bed.

Ophelia in Act IV,
Hamlet.

Premarital Sexual Standards in America

A Sociological Investigation of the Relative Social and
Cultural Integration of American Sexual Standards

BY IRA L. REISS

The Free Press of Glencoe, Illinois

To Harriet, My Wife

Whose Kindness and Understanding Mean So Much to Me

Acknowledgments

THIS BOOK HAS BEEN A DOZEN YEARS IN THE making. The original impetus was in good measure a consequence of the intellectual curiosity aroused by my friends in college. Since that time my research has centered on the studies of other sociologists and my own work with young people. My debt to these persons is documented in this book. More recently, I am indebted to my former colleagues at the College of William and Mary for their help in my writing. My gratitude goes to R. Wayne Kernodle, Edwin Rhyne, and Christopher Waters, all of whom read the manuscript and gave me the benefit of their comments. My special thanks go to the Institute for Sex Research and in particular to Dr. Gebhard and Dr. Martin who were kind enough to assemble some important calculations for me. Finally, my greatest debt is to my wife, Harriet, who gave much of her time and effort in helping to improve the form of the work and who gave innumerable insights regarding its content.

IRA L. REISS

March 12, 1960
Kingston, New York

7

Contents

Contents

Introduction

THIS BOOK IS NOT INTENDED TO BE A SPECIAL
plea for one particular premarital sexual standard—be it con-
ventional or otherwise; rather, it is an attempt to analyze all
our sexual standards in terms of their integration with the
major trends and values of our society.

The basic source of documentary evidence is the major
researches undertaken in this area. Research, such as that of
Kinsey, Ehrmann, Burgess and Wallin, and Terman, is uti-
lized extensively. I also refer to my own researches with young
people regarding their sexual standards.

Although there have been numerous studies of premarital
sexual *behavior,* there has never been an attempt to objectively describe and fully analyze our premarital sexual *standards.* Knowledge of sexual standards can yield a degree of
understanding that knowledge about sexual behavior alone
cannot. By studying standards of sexual behavior, one can see
more fully the role of society and culture in sexual behavior.

The groundwork for analysing premarital sexual standards must be put forth carefully, and this is the purpose of
chapters one and two. Chapter one examines the physiological
and learned bases of our sexual codes. Comparisons are made
between our own behavior and that of other species and other

13

societies, in order to clarify this situation. Chapter two describes briefly segments of our historical past relevant to the explanation of present-day sexual standards. Hebrew, Greek, and Roman cultures are examined for customs which we have inherited. The romantic love, urban-industrial, and feminist revolutions are also examined briefly to show how these movements have affected our older sexual standards and created new ones which are only now emerging. The remainder of the book focuses more directly on the degree to which present-day sexual standards are integrated in American society.

Throughout the book, evidence and reasoning are used to document the major points and to suggest hypotheses for further investigation. My effort aims at improving our conceptualization of this area, by analyzing the characteristics, consequences, and trends of our sexual standards and, in this way, clarifying the integration of these standards in our society and culture.

Our sexual standards are of increasing concern to my fellow sociologists, and they are of prime interest to the intelligent nonprofessional who is curious to know more about his society. I have tried to write this book so that it would be understandable to all who have such intellectual curiosity.

PREMARITAL SEXUAL STANDARDS

IN AMERICA

Chapter One

The Sexual Nature of Man

IN ORDER TO UNDERSTAND THE SEXUAL
standards in America, or in any society, one must have some
knowledge of the ways in which our social existence shapes
our sexual nature. One must know something about the sexual similarities and differences existing between man and
other animals, between men and women, and among various
societies in the world today. Let us dwell briefly on these
topics in this chapter, and, in this fashion, begin the quest
for understanding America's sexual standards.

The similarities between man and the other animals in
physiological areas are easily seen.[1] The human embryo and
fetus in its various stages of development resembles many
other embryos, e.g., it appears almost identical to that of

1. For gaining insight into the story of evolution, see George Gaylord
Simpson, *The Meaning of Evolution* (New Haven: Yale University Press,
1951) and Theodosius Dobzhansky, *Evolution, Genetics and Man* (New
York: John Wiley and Sons, 1955). For understanding the role sex has
played in evolution, see Norman J. Berrill, *Sex and the Nature of Things*
(New York: Dodd, Mead and Company, 1954). Another book by Berrill
may prove most interesting to those who want an informal introduction to
the evolution of man: *Man's Emerging Mind* (New York: Dodd, Mead
and Company, 1955).

17

many fishes at first; then for a short time it resembles that of some reptiles, then other mammals as the rabbit or monkey, and it is only after a few months of pregnancy that the untrained observer can be sure to what animal the fetus belongs. This similarity to other prenatal forms is further evidence of the evolutionary connections among all creatures. This, of course, is not in itself sufficient evidence or explanation of the development from one-celled creatures to man, but for that, the reader must go to the biological literature; my purpose here is mainly to establish man's roots in the animal kingdom.

SIGNS OF RELATION

Before pointing out how our sexual life differs from that of other animals, let us focus on some similarities. These examples will only be similarities, not identities. But by making such analogies, we will have more of a basis of comparison between men and other animals. Many of us are somewhat familiar with a polygamous-type family and even more familiar with a male-dominated family system. See how similar this sea elephant family is to its human counterpart:

> A female left a herd and headed for the sea. As soon as she entered the water, five subordinate males hovering outside the surf converged upon her under forced draft, then reared and blew their horns in an effort to drive one another off by vocal challenge alone. The noise attracted the harem master who, without taking time to send a warning blast, charged full speed down the beach toward the turmoil in the water. The subordinates all drew off without a gesture and the harem bull caught up with the female and mated with her.[2]

It is quite conceivable that many a sheik had similar diffi-

---

2. Berrill, *Sex and the Nature of Things,* p. 234.

culties with his human harem. The dominance, the lust, the aggressiveness, in the roles played by the sea elephants, could fit well into many a human drama. Of course, there are also many important differences in the case of man, but these shall be dealt with later.

One finds other similarities in the area of female restraints. The female moth casts an odor into the air which attracts male moths. However, it is predominantly the virgin moth alone who is able to cast this odor, so the experienced female is "punished" and, therefore, ignored. Again, the female firefly is a "modest" creature. She never winks first—the male firefly must wink at her and then she will respond.

Courtship is well developed in the Empidae fly family. The male fly hovers near the female, vibrating his wings; she responds by similar vibrations, and then he approaches her with his front legs uplifted. The female fly lifts up her front legs and the two flies embrace! The exchange of sexual favors for valuable gifts is also common among this species of fly. The male fly will capture an insect and wrap it in silk threads. He presents this "gift" to the female, and while she is busily unwrapping the gift, the male mates with her.[3]

The female is not always the submissive one with the male the aggressor. For example, the female spider quite often will literally eat up her puny mate after the sex act is finished. Such female dominance and aggressiveness is not unusual. Bee societies have existed for almost one hundred million years and the queen bee is as tyrannical and all-powerful as the male sea elephant. She is upper caste and picks the most able male for a mate. She is constantly guarded and fed by the lower-caste bees that wait on her.

The laughing gulls on the islands off Cape Cod present a good illustration of behavior which, *on the surface*, appears quite similar to our own:

---

3. Dobzhansky, *op. cit.*, p. 279.

In a small group the first problem of a lusty male, after running at a female and recognizing her by her standing firm, is to get rid of any nearby competitors. So, one at a time he charges them as well, and those that are males retreat and fly away. This leaves him, as a rule, with more than one female, too much for his monogamous personality. One female, therefore, drives the rest away and only the pair are left. . . . More and more, the two indulge in a mutual courtship feeding of a purely symbolic kind, while the male issues long, plaintive sex moans. When at last they seem to be so well acquainted that they can distinguish each other from all of their neighbors, they go off on their own. The male goes first to select the site and then calls the female to him. . . . After mating, both birds share in building the nest, the male collecting, the female constructing, later on, they take turns in brooding the eggs.[4]

The *superficial* similarities to our own customs are obvious. The courtship process builds up emotional attachments in birds such as the laughing gulls, and many birds stay together for a long period of time. In fact, geese often mate for a full lifetime with one partner only. This is true of other animals also, such as the wild fox.

In all these cases, there appears to be some similarity to man's sexual behavior. But, more importantly, there is a basic difference between man's sexual behavior and that of these other creatures. This difference lies in the concept of learned behavior.

The male sea elephant does not have to be taught that it desires a harem, how to mate, and so forth. These responses seem fairly well established at birth in the hormone structure and other physiological ways, and, given a typical environment, they will evidence themselves. The laughing gull does not have to learn over the years how to "court" a female gull— he is born with certain physiological mechanisms which usually guarantee these responses when the proper situation

---

4. Berrill, *Sex and the Nature of Things,* pp. 138, 139.

arises. The female firefly does not have to learn that it is "impudent" of her to "wink" first—she simply does not wink first because of her inherited characteristics.

Now, of course, there is some learned aspect in many of these responses, e.g., I imagine that the male sea elephant does learn from practice how better to manage a harem, even though the original impetus to obtaining the harem is based on unlearned mechanisms. However, learning, per se, does not seem vital for the animal courtship patterns I have discussed; they are based predominantly on inborn tendencies.

Now, what is the case with man? When a man courts a woman in a particular way or has particular desires for a type of sexual relation, is it similarly based almost exclusively on inherited tendencies? I think not, for unlike other animal species, men, in different societies, court in many different ways and desire many different types of sexual relations. Of course, there is a biological or inherited aspect to man's sexual standards; but in determining specific characteristics, learning is the dominant factor, and the inherited aspect only a minor limitation. To substantiate this important point, let us now examine man's sexual standards in the many non-literate cultures of the world.

ARE WE CIVILIZED?

There is a tendency for Americans to think of non-literate people (people who have no written language, such as the South Sea Islanders) as "savages," as "uncivilized," and as therefore being sexually promiscuous. It is somewhat surprising to find such erroneous beliefs so widespread in this day and age. The non-literate person, as far as we know, has the same intellectual capacity as the literate American; the non-literate person has some customs which are more complex than ours and some which are simpler. The non-literate does not lack sexual standards. His sexual behavior is regulated by numerous standards—some of them less demanding than ours, but always there are rules and regulations.

Unlike many other living creatures, man's sexual drives are ever present and thus are vital in terms of relating the men and women who make up society. Sexual behavior is so ever present that it has great possibilities for increasing or decreasing social integration. It is aways socially regulated in some fashion or another, because it involves such important factors as love, jealousy, social position, and pleasure.

Many a nineteenth-century anthropologist had the typical bias of his time; when he discovered people who lived differently than he did, he immediately interpreted this difference to mean inferiority. For the nineteenth-century intellectual, in many cases, the logic was simply that if the non-literate were intelligent and moral, he would be living as Europeans did. Today, science makes no such extravagant claims regarding intellectual inferiority or primitive promiscuity, for we know that there is no evidence to support such a position.

Let us not prejudge the worth of these customs or people. Instead, let us look at some of the customs in order to illustrate the learned aspect in the human animal's sexual standards.

a) Man, the Aggressive Sex? The human female has a unique distinction among female animals. As far as can be discerned, only the human female is capable of orgasm, or reaching a sexual climax. Some other female animals, when they are in estrus ("heat") seem to enjoy sexual behavior, but they do not evince any clear indication of orgasmic climax to their pleasure. Furthermore, the human female does not seem to have regular periods of estrus during which she desires intercourse much more than at other times. I am not talking here of moods or individual differences but of a biological trait. There are studies which seem to show that the woman still has traces of periodicity, in that she most desires sexual relations just before and just after her menstrual period.[5] This contention has not been fully supported. Even if such regularity were fully substantiated, it might be explained by learning rather than biological factors, i.e., perhaps the thought that for several days she will not be able to have sexual intercourse makes a woman more easily aroused before her menses, and perhaps the relief that those days of waiting are over also makes a woman more responsive shortly after her menses. If there are biological factors operative, then nature has, in one sense, gone amiss, for immediately before and after the menses is the most infertile time to have coitus. Regardless of the particular aspect of this situation, one can say that women, unlike other female animals, are capable of being sexually aroused at almost any time, even though they may be more desirous at certain times.[5a]

Many Americans think that women are by nature less sexually aggressive than men, and point out the presence of such a pattern in our country as evidence for their contention. But these people are looking at only one case— America. As soon as one looks at other cultures, he clearly perceives that the lack, or presence, of aggressiveness in woman is vitally affected by learning, by what her culture teaches

5. K. B. Davis, *Factors in the Sex Life of Twenty-Two Hundred Women* (New York: Harper and Brothers, 1929). L. M. Terman, *Psychological Factors in Marital Happiness* (New York: McGraw-Hill Book Co., 1938). See also A. C. Kinsey, W. B. Pomeroy, C. E. Martin, and P. H. Gebhard, *Sexual Behavior in the Human Female* (Philadelphia: W. B. Saunders Company, 1953), pages 608-10 and Part III which is a full physiological comparison of male and female. This book will be hereafter referred to as follows: Kinsey, *Human Female*. The other Kinsey study with W. B. Pomeroy and C. E. Martin, *Sexual Behavior in the Human Male* (Philadelphia: W. B. Saunders Company, 1948), will be referred to as follows: Kinsey, *Human Male*. On pp. 628-31 of *Human Female*, Kinsey presents evidence which indicates that, on occasions, females of other species may reach orgasm.

5a. Kinsey believes that females of other species may at times be sexually arousable even when estrus is not present. *Human Female*, pp. 736-38.

her. The Hopi Indians, in our own Southwest, and the Trukese and Trobriander, in other parts of the world, all afford examples of cultures where the woman is as aggressive as the man and apathetic women are scorned.

I might add here that there are societies where women are not only equal to men as sexual aggressors but where they definitely outdo the men. Kwoma, Maori, and Mataco societies are good examples of female sexual aggressiveness. In this connection, it should be clear that the widespread belief that males of all animal species play the more active role in initiating sex can be seriously questioned. Furthermore, in man's nearest relatives, the chimpanzees, orangutans, gorillas, and gibbons, it has often been reported that females in estrus initiate sexual activity more than males.[6] Our own experience tends to make us think that everyone else in the world is just like us, or, if they are not, they must be abnormal. Both such ethnocentric assumptions are quite often in error.

To further illustrate the initiation of sex activities by women, there is a custom in Lesu, Dahomean, and Kurtatchi cultures which entails exposure of the female genital area to entice a male to have coitus. Ford and Beach describe sexual customs in other areas as follows:

> On Bali, girls commonly make overtures to boys or give encouragement to a shy suitor. At a ceremonial dance the Goajiro woman is permitted to trip a man; and if she succeeds he is duty-bound to have intercourse with her. In theory the Lepcha woman should never make direct sexual advances; but in point of fact nearly every boy has his first complete sexual experience with the wife of an "elder brother" or "uncle" and this occurs as a result of the woman's direct invitations.
>
> A few societies make little or no distinction between the

6. Clellan S. Ford and Frank A. Beach, *Patterns of Sexual Behavior* (New York: Harper and Brothers, 1953), pp. 102-3; an excellent account of sexual customs in 190 non-literate societies.

sexes in the matter of initiating sexual affairs. Among the Tro-
brianders, Lesu and Kurtatchi either the boy or the girl is permitted by custom to take the first steps in soliciting intercourse.
In these societies lovemaking is said to be as spontaneous on
the part of one sex as of the other.

There are a few societies in which the girl generally begins
all love affairs. Among the Kwoma the girl makes the first advances.[7]

This should make it quite clear that, if so trained, women will
initiate sex activity as easily as men. There may be some
physiological differences. The male sex organs, due to their
externality, may have some initial advantage for the sexual development of the male, due to ease of location and
manipulation. I am not proposing an identity but am merely
pointing out that whatever initial differences there may be
are greatly modifiable by cultural training.[8]

b) *Mirror, Mirror on the Wall.* . . . Many of us also tend
to think that our standards of sexual beauty are universal.
One would think that the memory of the "flat-chested, narrow-
hipped" twenties would be enough to convince us of the
changing standards of beauty.[9] Ford and Beach found in the

---

7. *Ibid.*, p. 102.

8. Kinsey, *Human Female*. Part III has an elaborate discussion of
differences between men and women. The position taken by Kinsey in this
section is somewhat anomolous. He admits the power of learning in sexual
behavior and shows that there are no conclusive male-female differences in
anatomy and physiology of sexual response and that hormonal differences
are speculative. Yet he maintains in chap. xvi that males are basically more
easily conditioned to sexual stimuli than females. Kinsey himself presents
in other places evidence from other cultures to refute this belief. He also
mentions similar differences in sensitivity to sexual stimuli among different
classes of men (*Human Male*, p. 363) but in this case he accepts such differences as learned! In light of all this, I find it easier to explain male-
female differences by reference predominantly to differences in cultural
upbringing, although I shall also speak of biological factors in this chapter and in chapter iv.

9. For a pictorial demonstration of such change in the last few thousand
years, see Madge Garland, *The Changing Face of Beauty* (New York:
M. Barrows Co., 1957).

societies they studied that the only female sexual characteristic almost unanimously preferred was wide hips; all other characteristics varied in order of preference, e.g., some societies preferred plump body builds, others slim builds, some pendulous breasts, others upright breasts. In a few societies, the size of the clitoris or the labia majora are considered major beauty characteristics, e.g., this is the case respectively among the Easter Islanders and the Dahomeans. Since what appeals to men in one society does not necessarily appeal to men in other societies, it seems that much of what is sexually attractive is learned.

Other examples of the preponderant role of learned behavior in human sexual standards are not hard to find. For example, instead of our comparatively subtle methods of sexual seduction, the Alorese solicit young women by touching their breasts. This supposedly arouses the woman so much that she cannot resist. Choroti women show their excitement during sexual intercourse by spitting in the lover's face! The lover does not resent this any more than the American male resents the scratches and bites he may receive on his back and neck. The locale for intercourse also varies a great deal. In our society it is customary to copulate in private, but in other societies, such as the Formosan, the natives often engage in coitus outdoors, providing there are no children around.

c) *Premarital and Extramarital Intercourse.* Although the majority of non-literate cultures are opposed to most forms of extramarital sex (adultery), the vast majority are in favor of premarital sexual intercourse. Murdock's examination of non-literate cultures revealed that 70 per cent allowed premarital coitus for both males and females, but only about 20 per cent allowed full extramarital coitus.[10] Many people seem

---

10. George Peter Murdock, *Social Structure* (New York: The Macmillan Company, 1949), p. 265. It should be clear that this taboo on adultery

to feel that if a society allows premarital coitus, it cannot prevent extramarital coitus, but the record of these societies indicates that it is possible to allow premarital coitus and refuse to permit extramarital coitus. Again, the human being seems a most pliable creature, capable of learning many modes of living.

It may well be that for most, not all, societies casual adultery is more disruptive of social order than casual premarital intercourse, since such adultery disturbs an established family structure. This is possibly the reason for such a common taboo on adultery. However, in some cultures, as the Eskimo, adultery seems to fit quite well. Some of the Eskimos while away the bleak winter months by playing a game called "putting out the lamps," in which married and single couples put out the oil lamps and scramble for a new partner for the night.[11]

There are many different standards of premarital sex in the cultures that allow such relationships. There are cultures that allow premarital coitus, providing neither partner is

---

refers primarily to adultery with an unrelated person. Adultery with one's brother- or sister-in-law is accepted in many societies, for these in-laws are possible future mates. Both Murdock and Ford and Beach used the files on preliterate cultures at Yale for their research. These files cover over 250 cultures and are the best of their sort in the world. Nevertheless, information on sexual customs is most often quite limited. Ford and Beach studied 190 cultures and found slightly higher percentages of those who accept adultery (39 per cent). See: Ford and Beach, *op. cit.,* pp. 113-15. Kinsey lists 50 per cent of all societies forbidding adultery for women, 40 per cent forbidding it except on special occasions and 10 per cent allowing adultery. Restrictions on men were minimal. Kinsey, *Human Female,* p. 436.

11. Incest taboos are much more universal, but may have a similar "practical" reason for being. Incest would prevent the addition of wealth from other families and introduce sexual competition within each family. This line of reasoning seems probable since biological explanations of incest are not valid, i.e., many island groups are quite inbred over thousands of years and still forbid incest although their ordinary marriages are genetically just about as "close." For a brief discussion, see Ralph Beals and Harry Hoijer, *Introduction to Anthropology* (New York: The Macmillan Company, 1953), pp. 416-24. See also H. L. Shapiro (ed.), *Man, Culture and Society* (New York: Oxford, 1956), chap. xii by Claude Levi-Strauss. See also Murdock, *op. cit.,* chap. x.

married and they both are of a similar age group. Most cultures place many additional restrictions on the occurrence of premarital coitus, e.g., some societies give the girl the right to pick one of her lovers as her husband if she becomes pregnant. Samoa is one such culture. Other cultures, such as the Hopi, require premarital coitus to be limited to "steady boyfriends" or "fiances."[12]

The few cultures which fully restrict premarital coitus vary in the nature of their restriction. In many of them, the restriction is a "double standard" type, i.e., the male is allowed to have sexual freedom, but the female is severely condemned if she engages in premarital coitus. This is similar to the situation in America today, where the female is more severely condemned for her premarital sexual behavor than is the male. In a few societies, the harsher penalties apply to the male, and the female is given sexual privileges—just about the reverse of our practice! In other societies, both male and female are closely guarded and equally restricted in their premarital behavior.[13]

Comparatively speaking, our society is a highly restrictive one in terms of sexual behavior, but in practice most people seem to break the formal rules we set up. Theoretically, we restrict sexual intercourse to marriage. Nevertheless, Kinsey found that the majority of the men and women in his sample had engaged in premarital sexual intercourse.[14] Thus,

---

12. For a brief but interesting account of eighteen cultures, see George P. Murdock, *Our Primitive Contemporaries* (New York: The Macmillan Company, 1954). See also Elman R. Service, *A Profile of Primitive Culture* (New York: Harper and Brothers, 1957).

13. Ford and Beach, *op. cit.,* chap. vi.

14. Kinsey, *Human Male,* p. 550. The percentage of males who engaged in premarital coitus varied from 67 per cent for college-educated to 98 per cent for eighth-grade educated men. See p. 330 in *Human Female* for the summary findings on female premarital intercourse. Fifty per cent of the married women had premarital coitus. These permissive people are not all violating their beliefs—in many cases they are abiding by more liberal sexual standards. See my chapter three. It should be stressed here that I

it is important to keep in mind the difference between the code a society *formally* or *ideally* holds to and the *informal* or *operational* code which is much closer to actual behavior. A society may have a *formal* standard of abstinence for all and an *informal* standard of freedom for men. Actual behavior will likely entail intercourse which is very much in line with the informal standard.[15]

d) Homosexuality. The restrictiveness of the American sexual code is apparent when we examine attitudes towards homosexuality. Of the seventy-six non-literate societies on which Ford and Beach were able to gather material, forty-nine of them had a permissive attitude towards homosexuality. This does not mean that all forty-nine of them approved of homosexuality for all males. Rather, it means a great many things —from approval for *some* males to engage in homosexuality, to approval for *all* men to engage in homosexuality at certain times.But in all cases, the attitude was a permissive one and thus more liberal than our own attitude toward homosexuality.

> Among the Siwans of Africa, for example, all men and boys engage in anal intercourse. They adopt the feminine role only in strictly sexual situations and males are singled out as peculiar if they do not indulge in these homosexual activities. Prominent Siwan men lend their sons to each other and they talk about their masculine love affairs as openly as they discuss their love of women. Both married and unmarried males are expected to have both homosexual and heterosexual affairs. Among many of the aborigines of Australia this type of coitus is a recognized custom between unmarried men and uninitiated boys . . .

am not proposing, and neither was Kinsey, that these percentages are applicable to all groups of Americans; they are to be taken always with qualifications. Kinsey's figures are most representative of the Northeastern, well-educated, upper- or middle-class person. Many of Kinsey's 12,000 interviews come from this segment.

15. The distinction between formal and informal culture is virtually the same as the common distinction between overt and covert culture or explicit and implicit culture. I use these terms (formal and informal) for simplicity's sake.

Keraki bachelors of New Guinea universally practice sodomy
and in the course of his puberty rite, each boy is initiated into
anal intercourse by the older males. After his first year of playing the passive role, he spends the rest of his bachelorhood
sodomizing the newly initiated.[16]

The evidence for female homosexuality is more difficult
to locate, but Ford and Beach found clear evidence for such
practices being accepted in seventeen societies. Mutual masturbation seems to be the most common form of homosexual
practice among women. Both male and female homosexuality
is never the dominant sexual mode for a society; it is always
a minor activity subsidiary to heterosexual behavior. Even
among the other mammals, homosexuality is only a variation
for some individuals. The key difference among societies
seems to be in the attitude towards those people who practice
this variation. As has been shown, some societies condemn
it, some condone it, and some simply tolerate it.

SOCIAL HEREDITY—

THE SIGNIFICANT DIFFERENCE

Many areas and types of sexual behavior have been dealt
with here.[17] From this diversity of belief and behavior, one
can see that learning is a dominant factor in a people's sexual
behavior. If an American baby were brought up among
the Todas, she would believe in polyandry and premarital
coitus, just as a Toda baby brought up here in America would

16. Ford and Beach, *op. cit.,* pp. 131-32.
17. Other types of behavior follow similar lines, e.g., masturbation is
also viewed more permissively in non-Western societies. However, even in
America, Kinsey found that in his sample, 93 per cent of the men and
62 per cent of the women had masturbated. The taboo in this area may
well be weakening.

likely believe in monogamy and oppose coitus outside of marriage.

The learned aspect in sexual behavior can be seen within one society also. For example, people with higher education are more likely to engage in premarital petting to orgasm, more likely to masturbate, prefer to have coitus with some sort of light in the room, engage in more oral-genital play and so forth. These are the findings of Kinsey's studies. Clearly, more highly educated people are not of a different species, so these differences must be learned.[18]

Physiological factors, hormones, inborn tendencies relating to sexual behavior are present in all animals, including man. But as one follows the scale of evolution toward man, one finds that the learned factors become more and more significant and the physiological factors more and more modified and augmented. Observers have frequently noticed that a male chimpanzee will evidence rather decisive preferences for one sex partner over another and that often this preference seems based on an emotional compatibility with the preferred partner. Female chimpanzees also show such preferences, although females in estrus are less discriminating than males. This seems to indicate the presence of learned behavior that is modifying the purely physiological sexual drives. When one leaves the class of mammals, especially the apes, and goes to the reptiles, fishes and others, there is much less, if any, of this sort of selection—this sort of learned behavior. Conversely, as one approaches man, there is more and more of it.[19]

Women who have had ovaridectomies (removal of ovaries) usually still maintain their sexual drives. Among other ani-

---

18. Kinsey, *Human Male,* chap. xvi.

19. Ford and Beach, *op. cit.,* chaps. xii and xiii. For a recent discussion of this issue, see Robert Bierstedt, *The Social Order* (New York: McGraw-Hill, 1957), chap. x. Bierstedt discusses the point of the relative importance of culture and physiology.

mals, an ovaridectomy most often stops all sexual responses. Men who have been castrated (removal of testicles), although they react somewhat more negatively than women do to such operations, still, in many cases, retain their sexual desires. All that seems to be altered is potency. Even this is not seriously altered for all men; many castrated males seem able to carry on a normal sex life.

Many women who have passed menopause (change of life) feel that their sexual desire is over because of this physiological change. There is no necessity for sexual activity to cease. A woman, after menopause, can enjoy sexual relations just as much as before. In fact, due to the absence of a pregnancy fear, sometimes the enjoyment is increased. The individual's psychological reaction to menopause and these other physiological changes seems to be the crucial factor.[20]

Much of the modern psychiatric theory concerning homosexuality also reflects the importance of learning.[21] Many, though not all, psychiatrists and psychologists today view the sexual drive at birth as a relatively neutral force. They conceive of it as a tension which will persist until some sort of relief is afforded, but they do not believe that the sexual

20. Ford and Beach, *op. cit.*, chap. xii. This chapter has a good account of the differential effect of such operations and changes on humans and other animals. See also A. M. Krich (ed.), *Women* (New York: Dell Publishing Company, 1953), chap. xii, "Menopause: The Change of Life" by Dr. E. Novak. For an interesting discussion of the controversial male "change of life," see A. M. Krich (ed.), *Men* (New York: Dell Publishing Company, 1953), chap. xii, by Dr. G. Maranon. Kinsey mentions an 88-year-old man and his 90-year-old wife who were having intercourse regularly. See Kinsey, *Human Male,* p. 237. Kinsey also discusses the effects of castration and menopause. Kinsey, *Human Female,* pp. 731-45.

21. For a summary of the major approaches used by psychiatrists and psychologists, see Patrick Mullahy (ed.), *A Study of Interpersonal Relations* (New York: Hermitage Press, 1949). See especially "Changing Concepts of Homosexuality" by Clara Thompson, pp. 211-23. See also J. McCary and D. Sheer (eds.), *Six Approaches to Psychotherapy* (New York: Dryden Press, 1955), and R. L. Monroe, *Schools of Psychoanalytic Thought* (New York: Dryden Press, 1955).

drive of the male infant is aimed at female satisfaction and that female sex drives are structured so that only males can satisfy them.[22] Heterosexuality would be accented in all societies for without it the society could not survive.

The homosexual individual in America is thought to be, in most cases, a person whose upbringing has not effectively channeled his drive in a heterosexual direction,[23] i.e., due to frustrations with the opposite sex, due to fixations of attitudes in the family, due to contact with other homosexuals, etc. In all these ways and numerous others, the sex drive of the homosexual is satisfied in a socially unaccepted fashion. Psychiatrists report numerous cases where homosexuals have become heterosexual; this is brought about by redirecting their sexual drives, by finding out what channeled the drive, and by getting the patient into situations which will channel it in a heterosexual direction.[24] The human infant takes proportionately longer than any other animal to grow up, thus allowing ample time for all sorts of learning situations.

What is true of the sexual drive seems true of other physiologically rooted drives such as hunger. The prevalent view is that we are born with a hunger drive, i.e., our stomach con-

---

22. The books of a generation ago began accepting this position in psychology. See Laurance F. Shaffer, *The Psychology of Adjustment* (New York: Houghton Mifflin Company, 1936). See chaps. ii, iv, and xiii especially. See also Alfred R. Lindesmith and Anselm L. Strauss, *Social Psychology* (New York: Dryden Press, 1950), chap. xv.

23. The most widely accepted explanation of personality development in sociological literature can be found in somewhat difficult form, but most worthwhile, in George H. Mead, *Mind, Self and Society* (Chicago: University of Chicago Press, 1934); see especially pp. 135-227. This approach is very much in line with the psychological position being discussed. For a good summary of psychological views, see Calvin S. Hall and Gardiner Lindzey, *Theories of Personality* (New York: John Wiley and Sons, 1957).

24. Albert Ellis, "The Effectiveness of Psychotherapy with Individuals Who Have Severe Homosexual Problems," *Journal of Consulting Psychology*, XX (1956), 191-95. Good references can be found in this article on the treatment of homosexuality. The biological factors cannot be ignored in homosexuality, but in most cases they do not appear to be as crucial as learning.

tracts and makes us feel pain if we do not eat for a long period of time. But whether we satisfy our hunger by eating steak or by having an Eskimo dessert of body lice and stuffed intestines is a matter of learning. One should also note that our social experiences can intensify our desire for foods. Thus, it is impossible to discern what our inborn hunger drive was, for it may be increased or decreased due to learning processes. The same seems to hold true for our sexual drive—the type of behavior that satisfies it is learned, and the intensity of it can easily be affected by our experiences.[25]

a) What Is Normal? Since all cultures have a learned mode of sexual behavior, no culture has the "truly physiological" or "natural" or "normal" way of acting sexually. The question of which way is right is a separate one with which I shall deal later. It might be well to say a few words here on the use of the term "normal." It was not so long ago that any behavior outside actual coitus was considered abnormal. In fact, even coitus which did not involve the "proper positions" was considered abnormal. The present psychological and medical view is quite different. All sexual behaviors which do not physically injure a person or reflect great internal conflict are most often considered normal.[26] Even

---

25. Our culture develops less "erotic imagery" in women than in men. Perhaps this accounts for the male's greater sensitivity to psychological stimuli and the female's greater dependence on tactile stimulation. See my discussion of this point in chap. x.

26. See Louis L. Berg, M. D. and Robert Street, *Sex: Methods and Manners* (New York: McBride Company, 1953). For an early statement of this view, see Havelock Ellis, *Psychology of Sex* (New York: Mentor Books, 1954). Not all social scientists agree with this definition of normal but it is increasingly being adopted. The November 7, 1959 meeting of the Society for the Scientific Study of Sex discussed this point of normality in a panel composed of Wardell B. Pomeroy, Leo P. Chall, Henry Guze, and Milton Levine. Although lacking in full agreement, the consensus was to avoid using the term "normal" to denote behavior one morally disapproves of and to define it instead in terms of its psychological pathology. See also: A. C. Kinsey, W. B. Pomeroy, C. E. Martin, and P. H. Gebhard, "Concepts of Normality and Abnormality in Sexual Behavior," in P. H. Hoch and

the injurious behaviors are considered abnormal only because they seem to be symptoms of mental illness. Thus mouth-genital contact, masturbation, and all positions in coitus are accepted as normal today. There seems to be great variety in our sexual practices today, e.g., about half of the married couples in the Kinsey study stated they both practiced mouth-genital erotic play.[27] Our more objective approach to all such behavior is an attempt to broaden our understanding and remove our personal biases from our observations. Thus, although one may not approve of certain actions, one can no longer call them abnormal. One must state his disapproval on other grounds. Where one finds internal mental conflict of a high degree or other such symptoms, one may call the act abnormal, but this can occur with any action and need not occur in those acts of which we disapprove. Mankind is finally learning to use the term abnormal for disease-reflecting actions and not to apply it indiscriminately to any behavior that is merely disliked.

b) Body vs. Soul. Another important point relevant to this discussion concerns the oft heard "body versus soul" conflict. Let us clear this up at the very beginning. The issue here is the point of view which states that man is constantly in a battle with his "animal" nature—that the opponents in this contest of strength are man's ideas, values, or what some call his soul versus his hereditary "animal" drives, instincts, or what have you. Now, in the light of what has been discussed in this chapter, such a conflict is hardly meaningful. For example, when a man states that his soul tells him sexual relations are wrong, but his "animal" nature desires it and thus he is in conflict—is he accurately portraying his situation? Is it not more accurate and useful to put the situation as a

---

J. Zubin (eds.), *Psychosexual Development in Health and Disease* (New York: Grune and Stratton, 1949).

27. Kinsey, *Human Male*, p. 268.

conflict between a learned desirable way of satiating his partly physiological and partly learned sexual desires, on the one hand, and his learned ideas concerning right and wrong, on the other hand? In short, are not the conflicts between two or more learned ways of behaving, rather than between an ideology and an "animal" drive? No adult human has a purely physical drive for sex, food, or anything else. Learning has always entered in, so that any resulting conflicts are not between that non-directed, neutral, physiological drive and our ideas of right and wrong, but between the way we have learned to satisfy and develop that drive and the ideas of right and wrong which we have learned. This is an important point, for many people say that they are fighting just their "animal" drives when they fight sexual impulses—this is not quite correct, for the particular way their sexual drive shows itself is learned.

Since the above connotation of animal instincts or drives is a derogatory one, it will lead to much clearer thinking if we drop such prejudged terminology. The use of the word animal in this derogatory sense leads to much confusion. Man is an animal; thus his ideas as well his so-called "desires" are part of him, *qua* animal. The confusion is due to the belief that there is something "bad" about anything we share with other animals, such as sex desires. Since, to some degree, we share many things with other animals, according to this way of thinking, all these aspects should be "bad" and not just a few sexual characteristics. It is scientifically much better to drop such biased terminology and to stop using other animals as the basis for invidious comparisons.

c) *Culture.* Man is the only animal who has developed abstract thought, the use of language symbols to represent the distant past and the distant future. Accordingly, man is the only animal who thinks in terms of moral "oughts," or right and wrong. The advantages man's brain gives him allow him to perform these seemingly miraculous feats of breaking the time barrier and contemplating a better state of things. Because of his superior communication and thought ability, man can pass on what he learns in his lifetime to the next generation. He can pass it on by word of mouth or by writing it down—and all of this is possible because of the precious ability to think abstractly. Other animals do seem to be able to communicate, but, almost exclusively, their communication concerns the present, i.e., a screech signifying danger, a howl signifying present hunger, and similar expressive forms of communication. They also seem to pass on some slight informaton to the next generation but, again, nowhere near the degree that man does.

This body of information, this collection concerning ways of doing, feeling, and believing that man passes down to the next generation is what we, in the social sciences, call culture.[28] The word is used here more broadly than its commonplace usage which includes only art, music, and literature. We use it to include all that man shares with other men and passes down to his offspring—in short, culture is an entire way of life. It is this body of information, this culture, that distinguishes man from other animals and that is the foundation of human society. Culture binds men and generations together. Culture is to man what hormones and physiological factors are to other animals—it is his source of behavior, his place of obtaining ways of doing, feeling, and believing; it is his "social heredity." Man, then, is an animal who, by contact with culture, through his social relationships with other people, builds up a way of life, a way of satisfying and shaping his biological, social, and cultural desires. Each man

---

28. Those who desire to investigate this culture concept further should read the delightful and fascinating book by Robert H. Lowie, *Are We Civilized?* (New York: Rinehart and Company, 1929). See also any recent anthropology text for briefer statements.

takes and gives to his culture during his lifetime and picks and chooses the parts of his culture he will accept. Man is much more than any collection of words can describe. But let us, in examining his sexual life in America, consider man as a social and cultural animal.

Chapter Two

America's Sexual Heritage

CULTURE THEN, THE WAY OF LIFE OF A
group, seems to be the key explanatory variable for sexual
standards. Before we can profitably examine our culture and
sexual standards of today, we must briefly turn to our past,
to see how the culture of the past concerning sexual standards
is relevant to an understanding of such standards today.

Much of our way of life today in America is derived
directly from the European settlers who came over here in the
last three and a half centuries. Many fundamental parts of
that European culture grew out of the old Hebraic, Greek,
and Roman civilizations. There have also been vast changes
in our culture in the last few centuries here in America, which
are relevant to our present-day premarital standards.

Obviously, I cannot cover the many centuries of written
history in any amount of detail in one chapter. I will choose
only some of the major parts of that history which bear upon
premarital sexual standards in America today. This chapter
is *not* a detailed historical accounting, but rather a selective
discussion of *some* major historical developments that are
directly relevant to understanding our premarital sexual
standards today.

Written history goes back about fifty centuries. From the perspective of human life, this seems to be a very long time, but in a larger perspective, it is insignificant. Our planet has been in existence several billion years; life, about two billion years; and even man, a very late arrival, has probably been on this planet several million years. Thus, five thousand years is proportionately not very much, but it is all we have in terms of written history. We can go back 1,000,000 years in terms of fossil evidence of human cultures, but the evidence is so scanty that it is most difficult to do more than try to re-create a few physical artifacts. We will probably never know just what customs these early men had, but we can glean some ideas by looking at the available evidence which becomes increasingly clear as we approach the beginning of written history 5,000 years ago.[1]

Approximately ten thousand years ago, horticulture and agriculture were invented near the Caspian Sea and quickly spread throughout the Middle East. Man finally discovered a way of feeding himself in addition to fishing, hunting, and gathering. The advent of agriculture meant that a more stable existence could be had, that more people could live together and be supported by an existing area. The entire pattern of man's life must have been radically changed by this invention of planting seeds with a primitive "digging stick." The agricultural surpluses afforded men the time to stop and think— to take stock of where they had come and where they were going.

Now we know a great deal about agricultural societies,

---

1. Many books on our prehistoric period are available—I mentioned several of them in the last chapter. For a more technical coverage, see W. E. LeGros Clark, *The Fossil Evidence for Human Evolution* (Chicago: University of Chicago Press, 1955), and W. E. LeGros Clark, *History of the Primates* (Chicago: University of Chicago Press, 1957). See also the excellent account in M. Boule and H. V. Vallois, *Fossil Men* (New York: Dryden Press, 1957).

for most of the world is still agricultural, and much of it only very recently has become industrialized. Therefore, the life of cultures going back about five or even ten thousand years is not too difficult to deal with.[2]

Let me clarify a few points about historical records. In many cases, the only useful sources are in sculpture and other surviving arts. Often these sources contain pictures of a husband, wife, and child walking together through an estate or inspecting cattle, and this forms the basis for our judgment of the family system. An added difficulty is that even where the customs are clearly delineated, one must use his best judgment in deciding whether these customs were practiced and believed by all the people in the particular society or whether they were just for the upper-class aristocrats. Furthermore, we have only our judgment to determine how well people lived up to these formal customs. Of course, if there are written records giving all the needed information, the situation is greatly alleviated, although one still must be on guard for forgeries and inaccurate historians. As we approach modern times, our written records become more accurate. It is wise to keep these qualifications in mind when reading this chapter's account of our sexual heritage.

THE ANCIENT HEBREWS

One of the oldest and most important sources of our present-day sexual standards is the Hebrew civilization. Most of our information on the early Hebrews comes from the Old Testament and the Talmud. Hebrew culture came into

---

2. Previous to this time, before the agricultural revolution, there likely was a good deal of variety in social forms just as there is today. See Harry L. Shapiro, *Man, Culture and Society* (New York: Oxford University Press, 1956), and V. Gordon Childe, *Man Makes Himself* (New York: Mentor Books, 1951).

existence about thirty-five or forty centuries ago. It was from this culture that ultimately the Christian religion was born and to which many of the basic ideas in the Western world can be traced. In the beginning, the Jews were one of the many Semitic tribes who wandered in the Middle East. Their real flourishing and entrance into agriculture occurred after their exodus from enslavement in Egypt somewhere between 1450 and 1200 B.C.[3]

Marriage was arranged by one's parents, in particular, one's father. The legal age for marriage was twelve for girls and thirteen for boys. The Hebrews, like the ancient Sumerians, paid the girl's family a certain amount of money, a "bride price," when she married. This was not actually a purchase of the girl but merely a custom symbolizing a bond between the two families and reimbursing the girl's family for the loss of her services. Jacob's fourteen years of labor for Leah and Rachel is the most famous incident of "bride price."

Marriage, in almost all of these ancient cultures, was more of a unity between two families than between two people. It was a social and economic agreement to bind two families together. Thus, parents did the choosing and love was not of primary concern. Our customs of choosing our own mates and marrying for love could hardly have fit into an agricultural society where large families and economic motives were so powerful.

The Hebrew religion favored early marriage and many

---

3. Two brief but informative sources on the Hebrews are: S. A. Queen and J. B. Adams, *The Family in Various Cultures* (New York: J. B. Lippincott, 1952), chap. vi, "The Ancient Hebrews," and Rollin Chambliss, *Social Thought from Hammurabi to Comte* (New York: Dryden Press, 1954), chap. vi, "The Hebrews of the Old Testament." For more detail, see B. J. Bamberger, *The Story of Judaism* (New York: Union of American Hebrew Congregations, 1957); also four Volumes by H. E. Goldin, *Universal History of Israel* (New York: Hebrew Publishing Company, 1935), especially Vol. I.

children. Polygyny and concubinage are mentioned in the Old Testament, but monogamy became the favored form of marriage. The woman's place, as in most of the Semitic tribes, was in the home. She fulfilled her role by caring for the house and bearing and rearing the children. Male children were especially valued. The position of the father was similar to that in other Semitic societies and thus quite powerful.[4]

The double standard was apparent in the divorce laws which seemed to allow only men to initiate divorce proceedings. It is probable, however, that women could ask their husbands to initiate such proceedings:

> When a man hath taken a wife and married her, and it comes to pass that she find no favour in his eyes, because he hath found some uncleanness in her; then let him write her a bill of divorcement, and give it in her hand, and send her out of his house.[5]

The double standard prevailed in sexual morality also. Abstinence was the formal standard, and thus both men and women were forbidden to have premarital or extramarital coitus, but informally, the written punishments and social censure was much greater for the female than for the male. For example, if a husband should think his bride to be nonvirginal, he could order her to prove her virginity and if:

> . . . the tokens of virginity be not found for the damsel: Then they shall bring out the damsel to the door of her father's house, and the men of her city shall stone her with stones that she die:[6]

No such test of virginity applied to men. It should be noted, however, that if the bride proved to be virginal, then the husband paid a fine of 100 shekels of silver and was never

---

4. Deuteronomy 21:18.
5. Deuteronomy 24:1.
6. Deuteronomy 22:20-22.

permitted to divorce his wife. Much of our own double standard here in America dates back to the influences of Hebrew culture. Women were considered to be unfit for independence; they were always dependent on some man—their father or husband most often. It should be noted that women were valued in other ways and were not without influence, as illustrated by the well-known stories of Sarah, Rebekah, and Jezebel, in the Old Testament.

GREEK AND ROMAN CIVILIZATIONS

Two other cultures besides the Hebrew can be selected as of vital importance to the understanding of how our present-day sexual standards developed. These are the Greek and Roman civilizations.

In the fourth and fifth centuries, B. C., Athens was the intellectual center of the world. Socrates was telling all men that he knew nothing, thereby evidencing their ignorance. Plato was soon to write the *Republic*,[7] and Aristotle, in the fourth century, B. C., would teach philosophy to Alexander of Macedon and then watch him go off to conquer the world. Aristotle probably clearly reflected the common attitudes of the wealthy class of Greeks toward women. In his *Politics,* he quite emphatically states that women are by nature inferior to men and, as such, should obey men and perform their family functions well.[8] Women were to marry at 18 and men at 37. (Aristotle himself was thirty-seven when he married.)[9]

---

7. A. D. Lindsay (trans.), *The Republic of Plato* (New York: E. P. Dutton, 1950). See Book V in particular for Plato's suggestions regarding family life.

8. Richard McKeon (trans.), *The Basic Works of Aristotle* (New York: Random House, 1941); see the *Politics,* p. 1132 (1254:10-15).

9. A good source, although somewhat partial, for some of the key

To the average Greek of some wealth, a wife had the major duties of managing the household and educating the the children. She usually had a few slaves under her to do the menial work around the house. She herself would supervise them and do the more intricate weaving and child-educating. Her husband was her master, and his word was law for, after all, he was more possessed of reason than she. A wife was carefully guarded and often not allowed to even meet other men. A part of the house was set aside as the "women's quarter," and she lived most of her life there. Greek women were mostly excluded from public life.

The Greek husband had many forms of sexual pleasure when he was away from home. For man's sexual pleasures, Greece had created a class of Hetaerae, in addition to the common prostitute. The Hetaerae in Greek society were the higher-class prostitutes or mistresses. A Hetaera was often an educated woman, a woman much more cultivated than were the wives of most men. She was a woman who knew how to make herself attractive and how to please men. In certain cases, these women were associated with religious sects, and their prostitution was a vital part of their religious beliefs. This seems to have been the case on Cyprus and in Corinth.[10] Religious prostitution is quite common in the history of other countries, such as Babylon in Mesopotamia. In other cases, the Hetaerae became famous: Pericles eventually married Aspasia; Thaïs was the mistress of Alexander the Great; and Phryne was a model for Praxiteles when he created his statue of Aphrodite, the Goddess of Love.

aspects of Greek life is H. Licht, *Sexual Life in Ancient Greece* (New York: Barnes and Noble, 1953). See also *Everyday Life in Ancient Times* (Washington: National Geographic Society, 1951); this book is also valuable for describing Roman and early Mesopotamian culture. See also Crane Brinton, John B. Christopher, and Robert L. Wolff, *A History of Civilization* (New York: Prentice-Hall, Inc., 1955).

10. Licht, *op. cit.,* Part I, chap. vi.

Thus, a woman had predominantly two choices. She could become a wife and manage a household and bear and rear children, or she could become a Hetaera and entertain the husbands of other women. Prostitutes were not considered of the highest prestige, but they were accepted with much more status than they had in other societies. They were considered an essential part of life. Extramarital sex was strictly forbidden for women, but for men, it was the expected thing. The double standard was most certainly in force here. Demosthenes described the marital situation quite clearly as follows: "Man has the Hetaerae for erotic enjoyments, concubines for daily use and wives of equal rank to bring up children and to be faithful housewives."[11]

Another aspect of Greek society was its homosexuality. Married men not only visited their Hetaerae, but also had their young men with whom anal and oral intercourse were commonly practiced. Just as in the Siwan culture in Africa today, homosexuality was accepted behavior for the men in Greek society. Many of the Greek philosophers had young male lovers. Such homosexual behavior was not allowed for women.

Marriage was arranged by one's parents, and one lived thereafter with the groom's parents. Thus, here too, marriage was a union of two families, rather than two individuals. Marriage was encouraged, and laws were passed punishing bachelors. The marriage ceremony included a bridesmaid and a best man, and the bride wore a veil. Just as with the Hebrews, a feast was held to celebrate the wedding and was begun with a kiss by the newlyweds.[12] Kisses then were similar to ours today except for the "handle kiss" in which one holds the ears of the other person. Another interesting difference is that the Greeks viewed the onion as an aphro-

---

11. Quoted in Licht, *op. cit.,* p. 399.
12. Licht, *op. cit.,* Part II, chap. i.

disiac and frequently ate it before kissing. Premarital coitus was forbidden for women but tolerated for men. The Greek ideal seems to have been the full development of all human functions without any unnecessary restraints. This ideal was much more applicable to men than women.

Let us turn from Athens to Rome. Roman culture is also a basic source of our present-day sexual standards. The legal status of the Roman wife was similar to that of her Grecian sister. For much of the history of Rome, man was the supreme power in his family and had the right to put his wife and his children to death if he so desired! This legal right does not mean that such actions occurred frequently, but it is indicative of relative status. The courtesan class existed in Rome as it had in Athens, but in Rome it lost much respect and its members were not as highly educated or trained. It should be added that female virginity was highly valued in Rome, as it is in all double-standard cultures. Many ancient myths about virginity were held by the Romans, e.g., the sanctity of female purity was thought to hold sway over all nature, and, therefore, a virgin could make even a wild lion become docile and meek. It was popularly believed that wild animals were actually captured in such a fashion, but the more sophisticated scoffed at these folk tales even at that time.[13]

The Roman wife had one advantage over her Greek counterpart—she was able to sit at banquets with her husband and go to public places with him, while a Greek wife was often forbidden such privileges.[14] The Romans, much more

---

13. A thorough but somewhat one sided account of Roman sexual customs can be found in Otto Keifer, *Sexual Life in Ancient Rome* (New York: Barnes and Noble, 1953). For a most entertaining and satirical account of Greek and Roman culture written in the second century A.D., see H. W. Fowler and F. G. Fowler (trans.), *The Works of Lucian of Samosota* (London: Oxford University Press, 1939), 4 volumes. See also Queen and Adams, *op. cit.*, chap. vii, "The Ancient Romans."

14. The Hebrew wife had more freedom than either the Roman or

than the Greeks, idealized their mothers and women in general. They were more clever than the Greeks in regard to insuring virginity. Instead of depending upon keeping their women locked up and restricted or clamped in chastity belts, they taught them from birth to think of chastity as the highest good and thus imprisoned women much more securely by the walls of their own consciences.

The Romans were "coarser" than the Greeks; actions that were basically similar brought consequences that were different. The Greeks made sexual pleasure a companion of the arts; the Romans joined it with brutal gladiatorial shows. The esthetic element that the Greeks preserved, at least partially, in their premarital and extramarital sex activity was forgotten and replaced by the Romans with more earthly factors. In their attitudes towards their wives, there was perhaps more similarity, e.g., the ancient Greek saying was also part of Roman culture:

> Marriage brings only two happy days—the day when the husband first claps his wife to his breast and the day when he lays her in the tomb.[15]

Roman culture underwent some radical changes at about the time of the Punic Wars (286-146 B.C.). These wars meant that numerous men were absent from Rome for long periods of time. They led to wealth from the conquered areas, encouraged growth of the city area, the rise of a leisure class, the importation of slaves, and many other changes. Finally, the relations among men and women began to change also.

Greek wife. The Hebrew wife participated more fully in her husband's life and in general social organization.

15. W. E. H. Lecky, *History of European Morals* (New York: George Braziller, 1955), Vol. II, p. 304. This book was originally published in 1869. It is most interesting to discern how a nineteenth-century Englishman views these ancient civilizations. To see how one famous Roman viewed his culture, see: Ovid, *The Art of Love,* (Trans.) Rolfe Humphries (Bloomington, Ind.: Indiana University Press, 1957).

Women began to gain in status and legal rights. A wife was now allowed to relax with her husband instead of sitting while he relaxed. The power of death was taken away from the husband; women were able to inherit property freely; common-law marriage, which is still with us today, was strengthened in this period of transition as one form of marriage. The divorce laws were equalized, allowing divorce by mutual consent in many cases. Upper-class women participated more and more in life outside the home. All of this made the woman somewhat less of a chattel. However, the double standard, though weakened, still prevailed. As Cato said: "If you take your wife in adultery, you may freely kill her without a trial. But if you commit adultery or if another commits adultery with you, she has no right to raise a finger against you."[16]

It may be of interest to note that the Roman marriage ceremonies had many points of similarity to our own, and thus the cultural influence is clear. For example, marriage was a civil ceremony. Engagement was announced by placing a ring on the girl's third finger, left hand. There was a wedding cake and the bride had a dowry. After the ceremony, the bride was carried over the threshold by the groom—another indication of our heavy debt to the past.

THE CHRISTIAN INFLUENCE

The influence of Christianity was not felt for several centuries. For the first three centuries, most Christians were poor people, despised by others, and frequently persecuted for their radical ideas.[17]

---

16. Quoted in Keifer, *op. cit.,* p. 32.
17. Here also Queen and Adams, *op. cit.,* is a good source. See chap. viii, "The Early Christians." Another insightful book is Donald Day, *The*

The Christians opposed from the beginning the new changes in the family and in female status that had occurred since the Punic Wars. They fought the emancipation of women and the easier divorce laws. They demanded a return to older and stricter Roman, Greek, and Hebrew ideas, and, beyond this, they instituted a very low regard for sexual relations and marriage. The basis for this negative feeling was the belief in the Second Coming of Christ. If Christ was soon to return to the earth, all men should spend their time contemplating God and cleansing their souls, rather than enjoying sexual pleasures or raising families. Ultimately, these early Christians of the first few centuries accorded marriage, family life, women, and sex the lowest status of any known culture in the world. To further show the extent of this depreciation of heterosexual relations, let me quote from St. Paul:

> It is good for man not to touch woman. Yet for fear of forni-cation, let each man have his own wife, and let each woman have her own husband. . . . But this I say by way of concession, not by way of commandment. But I say to the unmarried and to widows, it is good for them if they so remain, even as I. But if they do not have self-control, let them marry, for it is better to marry than to burn . . . the virgin thinks about the things of the Lord, that she may be holy in body and in spirit. Whereas she who is married thinks about the things of the world, how she may please her husband . . . he who gives his virgin in marriage does well, and he who does not give her does better.[18]

Thus the early Christians felt that marriage was a second-rate choice, but if one lacked self-control, he had to take such a choice. "It is better to marry than to burn." Such an

---

Evolution of Love (New York: Dial Press, 1954), especially Part V. This part is informative on early Christian culture. The book covers the entire historical period. It focuses heavily on literary works to illustrate the nature of various historical times.

18. Corinthians I, 7.

ascetic view of life was indeed a harsh change for many people at that time. It conflicted with Roman law which favored large families and levied a fine on bachelors. For the first four centuries of Christianity, priests were allowed to marry, if they found it necessary, but thereafter, the formal ruling of chastity was gradually imposed on the clergy.[19] This was inevitable in a sect that thought of sex as something unclean—something vile, to be avoided. Some of the early Church fathers castrated themselves to further show their attitude towards sexual pleasures. Origen was perhaps the most famous of such men. Women were the temptresses, the Eves carrying the forbidden fruit! Eve tempting Adam had led to all men being tainted with "original sin" and made Christ's coming to earth necessary to save men's souls. Thus, women were very much at the root of sinfulness. Tertullian most clearly expressed this view of women:

> You are the devil's gateway: You are the unsealer of that forbidden tree: You are the first deserter of the divine law: You are she who persuaded him whom the devil was not valiant enough to attack. You destroyed so easily God's image, man. On account of your desert—that is, death—even the Son of God had to die.[20]

For over four centuries, the Church's attitude towards divorce was uncertain, but in the early fifth century, the ancient privilege of divorce by mutual consent was erased and marriage became indissoluble. At the Council of Trent (1545-64), marriage finally officially became a sacrament of the Church. The early Christians would never have made marriage a sacrament of their Church—marriage was a concession to sin. Divorce was acceptable to some only be-

---

19. Henry C. Lea, *The History of Sacerdotal Celibacy in the Christian Church* (New York: Russell and Russell, 1957). This is the most complete source for information on chastity in Christianity.

20. Alexander Roberts and James Donaldson (eds.), *The Ante-Nicene Fathers* (Buffalo: The Christian Literature Company, 1886), Vol. IV, p. 14.

cause it allowed one to enter into that holy state of abstinence. Even the abolition of divorce in the fifth century was based somewhat on the view that men remarried only for lust.

Quite a few married people did live in chastity for long periods of time, indulging only when they desired another child. Abstinence for married people the night before a Church festival was a prerequisite for attendance. The churchmen often looked upon early marriage as a sign of an evil, uncontrollable temperament. Jerome best expressed the limited view of sex even in marriage when he said: "He who too ardently loves his own wife is an adulterer."[20a]

It is known that, in some respects, the status of women under Christianity reached depths never before approached. Women, as the source of sin, were, of course, not allowed to own or inherit property. The Christian woman was offered the alternative of a nunnery or marriage—a much different choice from the Hetaerae or marriage which the Greeks and Romans offered their women. "Non-sexual" females, however, were respected. The woman who was not a temptress could perform a respectable role in Christian society.[21]

The Christians' ascetic attitude increased the value of virginity in both men and women, but particularly women. The double standard of the Hebrews, Greeks, and Romans had always valued virginity in women, and Christianity stressed this to an extreme. The opposition came when the asceticism was also applied to men and to marriage. The Christians favored abstinence (no intercourse outside marriage for men as well as women)—in this sense, they gave women more equality.

A command that is given to men applies logically also to women. It cannot be that an adulterous wife should be put away and an

---

20a. Quoted in Morton M. Hunt, *The Natural History of Love* (New York: Alfred Knopf, 1959), p. 115.
21. Queen and Adams, *op. cit.,* chap. viii.

unfaithful husband retained. . . . Among the Romans men's unchastity goes unchecked; seduction and adultery are condemned, but free permission is given to lust to range the brothels and to have slave girls, as though it were a person's rank and not the sensual pleasure that constituted the offense. With us what is unlawful for women is equally unlawful for men, and as both sexes serve God they are bound by the same conditions.[22]

This the Greco-Roman world would not accept, and in time, the Church did *informally* modify its doctrines and tolerate a double standard of morality. Of course, *formally*, only abstinence is tolerated. But in practice, by church members themselves and often in the minds of churchmen, the old double standard is somewhat accepted, and it is mainly women who are strictly controlled and censured. Nevertheless, the Christian influence has given our culture an element of guilt associated with all sexual behavior outside of marriage. We still have this attribute to a considerable degree at the present time.

THE BIRTH OF ROMANTIC LOVE

One could not possibly understand sexual standards in America in the twentieth century unless he understood the roots of those notions of courtly love, or, as it is popularly called, romantic love, which the Normans brought to England,[23] and which are still with us today. By the eleventh century, the notion of romantic love was becoming well known among the aristocrats. This notion basically consisted of the idea that one could become obsessed with the beauty and character of another person, and that this love would

---

22. From a letter written by Jerome to Oceanus in 399 A.D. Quoted in Queen and Adams, *op. cit.,* p. 159.

23. For a view of Anglo-Saxon England, see B. Thorpe (ed.), *Ancient Laws and Institutes of England* (London: Commissioners on the Public Records of the Kingdom, 1840).

make one eternally happy as long as it were returned or eternally damned if one were spurned.

On the continent and in England, Christianity had spread its somber dogma concerning the sinfulness of sexual pleasure and the importance of duty and obedience in marriage. The adherents of courtly or romantic love may have been in revolt against such restricting doctrines. In fact, De Rougemont believes they were members of a heretical religious movement allied with Manichaeism and the Catharist Church.[24] Suffice it to say that there was much brutality and lawlessness in European feudal society, and there were many severe religious restrictions. This new concept of love was a reaction against that part of their culture. Out of the Christian degradation of sex rose the romantic idealization of it. Beliefs in romantic love were common only among the aristocratic ladies and among the knights and troubadours. The lower classes were not yet aware of this movement.

Here indeed was a strange contrast to the Christian conception of woman as a temptress—as the gate to hell. To the knight and the troubadour, his lady was an angel, a collection of perfection. The troubadour would come to serenade his lady; he would compose ballads to her beauty and his immortal love for her. Knights would engage in mortal combat in order to win honors for their chosen lover. Like our adolescents today, they would wear some object of their beloved into battle—a handkerchief, a swatch of cloth around their necks in honor of their lady.

---

24. Denis de Rougemont, *Love in the Western World* (New York: Harcourt, Brace and Company, 1940). This book is a most interesting account of love, but one which should be read with caution. For a brief account of the development of romantic love, see Hugo G. Beigel, "Romantic Love," *American Sociological Review*, June, 1951, pp. 326-34. Dr. Beigel will soon publish a book on romantic love, elaborating many of the ideas in the above article. For a recent well-written statement covering the entire history of Western society see Morton M. Hunt, *op. cit.*, esp. pp. 145-50, where Hunt discusses the possible reasons for romantic love.

This account of romantic love may sound familiar, but lest one deceive himself, he should realize that this love affair was almost always between a bachelor knight or troubadour and a married aristocratic woman. Most of these love affairs were encouraged by their setting—a castle filled with bachelor knights and troubadours and but one or a few aristocratic ladies. This is a perfect setting for idealizing the aristocratic female. There were many other reasons for bachelors and married women being involved in love affairs; one basic reason was that people in those days generally believed that love and marriage would not mix, so they did not think of love in connection with their mates. At many points in the romantic love movement, it was also thought that to consummate love with sexual intercourse was to destroy it. Love, to last, must remain free of marriage and sex. In the year of 1174, one of the many courts of love (which used to meet to discuss love questions just as many of our "advice to the lovelorn" columns do today) met at the house of the Countess of Champagne and stated officially that the "true" relation between love and marriage is as follows:

> We declare and affirm, by the tenor of these presents, that love cannot extend its rights over two married persons. For indeed lovers grant one another all things, mutually and freely, without being impelled by any motive of necessity, whereas husband and wife are held by their duty to submit their wills to each other and to refuse each other nothing.
>
> May this judgment, which we have delivered with extreme caution, and after consulting with a great number of other ladies, be for you a constant and unassailable truth. Delievered in this year 1174, on the third day before the Kalends of May, Proclamation VII.[25]

---

25. De Rougemont, *op. cit.,* p. 25. There are two first-hand accounts of romantic love which are especially rewarding: Andreas Capellanus, *The Art of Courtly Love,* trans. John J. Parry (New York: Ungar Co., 1959); Baldesar Castiglione, *The Book of the Courtier,* trans. Charles S. Single-ton (New York: Doubleday Anchor, 1959). There is evidence in these books

In the early phases of courtly love, there was often little sexual element involved. It consisted mainly of admiration from a distance, with perhaps a kiss on the forehead as a reward for a heroic deed or a newly-composed or well-sung ballad. The knights and troubadours, for a while at least, were content with the idealistic element of their love and even seemed to glory in their self-denial. Of course, in true double-standard fashion, these bachelors had other lower-class women with whom they could release their sexual restraints.

Love relationships introduced tenderness and affection into the relations among men and women in a way that contrasted with the male-dominated, low female-status society of the Middle Ages. It further strengthened the desires for love and affection that went unsatisfied due to the rigors of feudal life and Christianity.

By the sixteenth century, the lovers' deeds began to be regularly rewarded by carnal favors rather than with a kiss on the forehead. The transition was slow from the beginning of romantic love in about the eleventh century. Even in the early days of romantic love, however, the knight or troubadour was often allowed to fully undress his beloved and put her to bed—providing, of course, that he did not take any sexual liberties. On other occasions, he was rewarded by spending the night with his lover if he swore continence. In the course of a few centuries, the system broke down, and sexual intercourse became the reward which was *informally* taken; by the middle of the sixteenth century, extramarital coitus was *formally* given as the reward. In addition to this liberalization movement, there was a spread of romantic-love ideas to the new middle-class merchants who were quick to adopt them. But this formal acceptance of rewarding love

---

that some people may well have mixed love and marriage and also love and sex. However, Beigel and Hunt feel that in the early phases of romantic love, such factors were kept separate by most people.

with adultery bothered many of the aristocrats and, especially, the new conservative bourgeoisie. The new middle class had come to value love very highly—they wanted to be like the aristocrats, but they also valued faithfulness in marriage. How to obtain both was the problem.

The seventeenth century saw the working out of a solution. Romantic love had now spread to much of the populace and the love object was rapidly changing from a married woman to a single girl. In this way the adultery problem could be solved, but as we shall see, many more problems arose. This shifting of love to the single girl occurred almost exclusively among couples who were engaged. This is as it had to be for, if the reader recalls, the parents were still choosing mates— there was no such thing as casual dating with a woman of one's own class. A few formal dates with a parentally-approved girl were all the preliminaries needed for an engagement. After the engagement, one had a somewhat better opportunity to get to know his prospective mate. Thus, some people began to fall in love with each other and, thereby, challenged the ancient rulings of the courts of love that had decreed love and marriage incompatible. The next step was inevitable. If young people were falling in love and marrying, then young people would demand the right to pick and choose the person they could best fall in love with and marry that person. Parental right to choose a mate was seriously challenged. Young people wanted to marry for love and not only for money or status as was the custom. This was indeed a radical departure from the way things had been done for centuries. As has been pointed out, marriage formerly was more a union of two families than of two people. By the eighteenth century the revolt had secured many adherents and was increasingly successful, so that by the end of the nineteenth century, in many parts of Europe and especially in America, young people were choosing their own mates and love was a key basis for marriage. The revolution had been won! Many other movements such as feminism, urbanism, and the industrial revolution helped in this change.

Romantic love was not unknown before the middle ages. It was, however, not common to even a class of people previous to that time. Most cultures viewed romantic lovers as somewhat mad, and such lovers were probably relatively rare.[25a] It should be clear, though, that many husbands and wives in all cultures, in time, developed great fondness or love for each other, but such a "practical" brand of love was not the basis for marriage nor was it the same as romantic love. Outside of the Western world—among many other cultures—the notion of romantic love is today laughed at, scorned, and thought to be ludicrous and impractical. These peoples cannot conceive of picking a life-mate on the basis of an emotion. This is a clear example of the spread and integration of an idea to one part of the world, and its consequent appearance as a perfectly "natural" and right form of behavior, while another part of the world looks with amazement on such behavior.

From its beginning less than 1,000 years ago, romantic love changed from a non-sexual attachment, with a married woman, that was unrelated to marriage, to a sexual attraction, for a single woman, which was the basis for marriage. Of course, the meaning of love changed in these centuries also.[26] The original accent on a "one and only love" which would lead to "eternal happiness" has survived the ten centuries since its birth, but it also has been sharply altered. In America

---

25a. I am restricting the meaning of romantic love to heterosexual love. If we include homosexual love, then the Greeks did have a "romantic" form of such love. The "Ode to Atthis," by Sappho, describes the symptoms of love which are still present today in many romantic lovers. However, in this poem, the love spoken of is a homosexual love.

26. For an excellent collection of love stories, see John J. Maloney (ed.), *Great Love Stories* (New York: Bobbs-Merrill Company, 1952). These stories range from Da Porta's *Juliet* to Faulkner's *The Wild Palms*.

today, with such increased contact among young people and so many of them falling in love several times in their courtship period, and a one-in-four divorce rate, it is difficult to sustain the "one and only" notion. Our young person's concept of love today seems more "hardboiled," more realistic, but still with an emotional if not intellectual attachment to some of the older romantic ideas.[27]

It is most important to note here that the joining together of love and sexual behavior, by the romantic love movement, formed the groundwork for love to become the justification for sexual intimacies in a more liberal and equalitarian pre-marital sexual standard. Young people increasingly came to justify their sexual behavior by their love feelings. In this fashion, the romantic love movement encouraged the growth of new premarital sexual standards.[28]

THE FEMINIST REVOLT

Intimately related to the success of the romantic love movement was the feminist revolt. There had been protestors fighting for women's rights in the times of the Greeks and Romans, but in the last 300 years, this movement took on renewed and unprecedented vigor. During the seventeenth century, women began publicly to proclaim their objections to the low status and unfair treatment to which they were subjected. Mary Astell in England was one of the first pro-ponents of feminine rights, although she was not as violent as her followers. Ben Franklin, in our own country, fought

---

27. Burgess and Wallin found that two-thirds of their engaged couples refused to say that they were "head over heels" in love because it sounded too much like childish romanticism. See Ernest W. Burgess and Paul Wallin, *Engagement and Marriage* (New York: J. B. Lippincott Company, 1953), p. 170. See also chap. vii, "Love and Idealization."

28. See chap. x of this book.

moderately for a fairer treatment of women. The first modern, thoroughgoing feminist was Mary Wollstonecraft whose daughter married the romantic poet, Shelley. Mary Wollstonecraft's most famous work was her *Vindication of the Rights of Women,* in which she advanced arguments for the education of women in all matters and thus for the end of the double standard and its doctrine of female inferiority. She sums up her witty and satiric arguments as follows:

> Let woman share the rights, and she will emulate the virtues of man; for she must grow more perfect when emancipated, or justify the authority that chains such a weak being to her duty. If the latter, it will be expedient to open a fresh trade with Russia for whips; a present which a father should always make to his son-in-law on his wedding day, that a husband may keep his whole family in order by the same means; and without any violation of justice reign, wielding his sceptre, sole master of his house, because he is the only being in it who has reason; the divine indefeasible earthly sovereignty breathed into man by the Master of the Universe. Allowing this position, women have not any inherent rights to claim, and by the same rule their duties vanish, for rights and duties are inseparable.
>
> Be just then, O ye men of understanding. and mark not more severely what women do amiss than the vicious tricks of the horse or the ass for whom ye provide provender, and allow her the privileges of ignorance, to whom ye deny the rights of reason, or ye will be worse than Egyptian taskmasters, expecting virtue where nature has not given understanding.[29]

This was the "Age of Reason" when Voltaire in France was demanding sweeping reforms, Thomas Paine was denouncing the Judeo-Christian religious tradition and, together with many of the founders of our country, declaring himself a Deist.[30] Two revolutions had swept the world—one in

29. Mary Wollstonecraft, *Vindication of the Rights of Woman* (Philadelphia: Mathew Carey, 1794), pp. 334-35. This is a book well worth reading in order to obtain the spirit of the early feminists.

30. For a most critical but interesting statement of Paine's position, see Thomas Paine, *Age of Reason* (New York: Willey Book Company, 1942).

America and one in France, and the latter gave women greater rights than before. It was the time when many people felt the world was going to radically alter its way of living. But most of these people were wrong; for the next generation, the early nineteenth-century generation, reverted to a more conservative way of life.

Nevertheless, the feminist pressure was too powerful to be denied. It soon regained its lost momentum. In Seneca Falls, New York, in the year 1848, the first "Woman's Rights Convention" was held. The leaders at that time were Lucretia Mott and Elizabeth Cady Stanton. They opened the meeting with their famous *Declaration of Sentiments,* "We hold these truths to be self-evident; that all men *and women* are created equal."[31] These women were the true descendants of Mary Wollstonecraft.

Queen Victoria of England had set the pace for the nineteenth century, and it was indeed a conservative one. The good Queen felt that "Woman's place was in the home," just as the Old Testament Hebrews said three thousand years before Victoria. Many other women, both in England and the United States, felt that Queen Victoria had the proper notions about female behavior. But the feminists rose up in violent disagreement, and the latter half of the nineteenth century smelled the smoke from the vast battles the feminists were waging.

Elizabeth Cady Stanton was the orator for the movement, but she could have accomplished little without the organizing genius of Susan B. Anthony. They struck out at those who said women were intellectually inferior to men—the same enemy that Mary Wollstonecraft battled two generations earlier. Christianity, in the Bible and in the Pulpit, had

---

31. See Sidney Ditzion, *Marriage, Morals and Sex in America* (New York: Bookman Associates, 1953), pp. 257-60. This book contains the full text of the declaration.

preached the inferiority of women, and, thus, the feminists attacked organized religion. They did not just want to "honor and obey" the superior male nor did they want to eliminate religion. They wanted a reformation of existing beliefs and practices.

Although most men were indifferent or hostile to these new-type females, some men backed the feminists in their demands. John Stuart Mill in England wrote *The Subjection of Women,* and this pamphlet did much to help the cause of the feminists, one of whom was Mrs. J. S. Mill.[32] Mr. Mill, supported by Florence Nightingale, soon introduced the first suffrage bill to Parliament. In this country, Robert Dale Owen was aiding the feminists as well as other liberal movements. The feminists received the vote in Wyoming, in 1869, and might have won suffrage in many other states had they not made a serious political error—they added to their aims the prohibition of alcohol. This prohibition plank in their platform alienated most of the men who would have otherwise supported them. It was at this time that Carrie Nation and her famous axe paid nightly visits to the local bars and left them in ruins. She began her fanatical attacks on saloons after her first husband died of acute alcoholism.

The feminist movement itself was far from fully united. There were many splits, starting around the 1870's when Lucy Stone and Julia Ward Howe split from Stanton and Anthony and formed a conservative branch of feminism. Lucy Stone was one of the feminists who refused to give up her maiden name when she married. Her husband, Henry Blackwell was quite adjusted to such feminist activities; he had two sisters who were the first women doctors in America and a sister-in-law who was the first female minister.[33]

---

32. J. S. Mill, *The Subjection of Women* (Philadelphia: J. B. Lippincott, 1867).

33. For an interesting, though incomplete, pictorial account of femi-

The feminists ran into much opposition from the double standard. One incident which illustrates this best is the famous adultery trial of the Reverend Henry Ward Beecher. The result of this trial was the conviction of Reverend Beecher's "companion," Mrs. Tilton, of adultery, while the Reverend was acquitted of adultery by a hung jury![34]

Many changes occurred in the life of American women in the decades after 1848. Women began to go to college in larger and larger numbers. In 1910 there were 11,000 women graduated from college, and President Eliot of Harvard University stated publicly that women were too frail to stand the pace of college life. Today, one-third of the approximately three and one-half million college students are women.[35]

Another major change besides eductation came in the area of work. Women began to earn their own livings as secretaries, sewing machine operators, etc. Today one-third of our labor force is made up of women, over 20,000,000 women, and about one-half of them are married.[36] We are so dependent on women workers that our economy could not function if women ceased to work. This movement of women to industry in the last one hundred years is, of course,

---

nism, see Oliver Jensen, *The Revolt of American Women* (New York: Harcourt, Brace and Co., 1952). See also parts of Day, *op. cit.,* for entertaining accounts. For a worthwhile story of six feminists, see M. F. Thorp, *Female Persuasion* (New Haven: Yale University Press, 1950).

34. For an account of this trial see Gerald W. Johnson, "Dynamic Victoria Woodhull," *American Heritage,* June, 1956, pp. 44-47, 86-91. For a book-length account of this scandal see Robert Shaplen, *Free Love and Heavenly Sinners* (New York: Alfred Knopf, 1954).

35. *Statistical Bulletin of the Metropolitan Life Insurance Company,* XXXVIII (August, 1957), 6-8. Over 100,000 women have received a first degree every year since 1949. See: U. S. Department of Health, Education and Welfare, *Earned Degrees in 1954-55* (Washington, 1956).

36. For detailed information see the report of the Department of Labor, *Women as Workers* (Washington: Government Printing Office, 1955). See also National Manpower Council, *Womanpower* (New York: Columbia University Press, 1957), and Robert W. Smuts, *Women and Work in America* (New York: Columbia University Press, 1959).

closely related to the need for workers created by the industrial revolution.

By the turn of the century, the feminists were winning their battles on all fronts. Women were now wearing lipstick and rouge and were beginning to smoke. Silk stockings and shorter skirts were coming into style and were being displayed at the bars which women were attending. Bathing suits were shortened to expose the knees. There was opposition, to be sure. In 1904, a woman was arrested for smoking on the streets of New York, and, as late as 1922, women were arrested on the beaches for exposing too much of their arms! These changes may make one smile today, but the only women who wore make-up, smoked, drank, and earned their own livings back in the mid-nineteenth century were prostitutes! Now, most women were accepting such behavior as normal and, of course, this shocked most of the older generation in the early 1900's. But these people were not to make the most radical inroads. As I shall discuss later, the generation that really altered our way of life seems to be that born between 1900 and 1910. It was this generation which appears to have started the tremendous increase in premarital coitus and almost all other forms of sexual behavior.

On August 18, 1920, the suffragettes won their battle and women were given the vote. This was a long-awaited goal, one that had been put forth in Seneca Falls by Mrs. Stanton back in 1848. But the feminists had won much more than the vote; they had revolutionized the place of women. For the first time, women were independent economically. They no longer needed to depend upon men for their sustenance. Women were being educated along with men, entering professions with men, becoming freer sexually, and in many other ways equalizing the gap between the two sexes. The gap has not closed, and the double standard, in a much weakened form, is still with us in sex, industry, education, and many other aspects of our life; but more has changed in the last one hundred years than in the previous five thousand years.

THE INDUSTRIAL REVOLUTION

One final occurrence which I shall discuss very briefly and which was one of the most vital factors in making possible the feminist revolt and most of the other recent changes in our sexual standards, is the alteration in our economic way of life—the industrial revolution.[37] Movements like the industrial revolution have no specific point in time when they begin. However, the arbitrary date, when the effects of this change first became apparent, is the middle of the eighteenth century in England. The industrial revolution brought about changes comparable in scope to those effected by the invention of agriculture ten thousand years earlier. The textile industry was the first to be affected The change occurred very slowly; at first a few farmers took on a part-time task of making small amounts of cloth. Then eventually, because they were not sorely needed on the farm due to agricultural improvements, and because they were earning good money, some farmers left the farms and entered into cloth-making full-time in small factories employing about a dozen people. By the middle of the nineteenth century, thousands of people had left the farms, and large factories, employing many scores of workers, were established. Other industries were also developing, and trade and colonization increased tremendously, for the more one manufactures, the larger the market one needs.

What happens when farmers leave the farm? First of all,

---

37. For those who want to gain insight quickly, there is a very brief but well-written essay on the industrial revolution: Frederick Dietz, *The Industrial Revolution* (New York: Henry Holt and Company, 1927).

they congregate in specific areas near the factories, and this means the growth of cities, ever larger and larger. As of 1959, about 100,000,000 Americans, over half of our population, lived in or near cities of 50,000 or more people.[37a] A city means the lessening of the intimate, primary relationships that characterize the rural areas of the world. It means a change in the way of life of the family also. Space in the city, unlike the country, is extremely expensive. One cannot easily rent an apartment to house fifteen family members. Furthermore, most farmers who came to the city did not want to do that, because they were either bachelors or they came with their wives and children only. Thus the city breaks up the extended family which has been so common throughout history and replaces it with a nuclear family composed of the husband, wife, and children. Once more, one can see how customs eventually change as their integration in society becomes altered.

Children became less economically desirable, thus making the nuclear family even smaller; in fact, the modern city family is the smallest family the world has ever known. Were it not for people entering the city from rural areas, cities would constantly decrease in population, for the modern urban family does not usually reproduce itself. Children on the farms were an asset. This was particularly true of boys and they were therefore more highly valued than girls. This preference for male babies is still with us, even though over two-thirds of us are now urban dwellers. Customs often outlive their original supports and display a certain type of social inertia.[38] But in time such customs often die away, which seems to be the case for many of our older customs.

37a. U. S. Bureau of the Census, *Current Population Reports: Population Characteristics,* Series P-20 (Washington, January 25, 1960).

38. Compensatory customs often make it possible for conflict ridden or "outdated" customs to survive. See a paper by the author entitled: "Functional Narcotics: A Compensatory Mechanism for the Social System," delivered at the Eastern Sociological Society in April, 1958.

Another change in the family brought on by the industrial revolution was the authority of the husband. On the farm, if a wife did not obey her husband or the children their father, they were in great danger. Where could one go, how could one live, without staying on the farm? But with the industrial revolution, any child of ten years or more, male or female, could get a job in one of the textile mills. For the first time in history, great masses of women were afforded a good chance of leaving home and earning a living. By the mid-nineteenth century, there was a labor shortage, and female work was further encouraged. One of the main props of masculine authority was economic power. This prop was now on the way out, and, accordingly, there were many more opportunities for females and children to express their distaste for masculine authority and actually free themselves of that authority. This situation led to husbands and fathers becoming less tyrannical and less dominating and started a slow movement toward equalitarian marriage that is still in progress. More and more, double-standard areas became weakened, and the feminist cause was furthered.

Another consequence of city life was the lessening of social controls and resultant increases in divergent viewpoints. In short, the city did not have the intimacy, the control by reputation and gossip which the farm or the small town had. People hardly knew their neighbors and were not as strongly concerned with their opinions. Then, too, in the small town, there was usually general agreement on what was proper; in the city, this agreement was often lacking, so that if one group of people criticized a person, it would not be difficult to find another group supporting him in his position. Thus, individualization of behavior was encouraged. This situation, of course, helped destroy many of the older sexual standards and made possible the growth of newer, more liberal and equalitarian standards.

From the foregoing, it can be seen that our new type of urban-industrial society has sharply changed our courtship and marriage standards. By the time of World War I, dating without chaperons was common. The feminists had won out here also. No longer did a girl and boy meet at a church affair and, after their third or fourth meeting, announce a parentally-approved engagement. Girls and boys met in all sorts of unchaperoned places—schools, dances, drugstores— and they did not consider it necessary to become serious with each other. With the new accent on picking one's own mate on the basis of love, there came a responsibility to find the mate one could best love and live with. This search necessitated a courtship change, and dating as we know it today was the result. Of course, much dating is not aimed at discovering compatibility but is done merely for social pleasure. This, too, is a new event in American courtship. Dating is another example of a custom which developed to fit the needs of a changing society. Along with such unchaperoned dating came the growth of more liberal and equalitarian sexual standards.

SUMMARY

All of these modern movements have increasingly weakened the double standard and abstinence and made our sexual standards more liberal and equalitarian. All of these so-called revolutions are still going on. The number of mutual supports among them are endless. Together they have altered our older way of life tremendously. We still, however, have many traces of the past; we still retain much of our heritage from the Hebrews, Greeks, and Romans. We, in America, are in transition; we are somewhere between the old and the new, in a world not fully formed or structured.

This period of transition is not a period of disorganization only. It is also a period of construction and reorganization.[39] But there is much confusion, for we still are not clear on our relations to the past or the future. For the first time in several thousand years, some of our core sexual standards (abstinence and the double standard) have not only been temporarily questioned but seem to be increasingly challenged. The old way is decaying rapidly, but what is replacing it?

This historical account has been highly selective, but it should help in seeing how our customs fit together and why our sexual standards are changing. Our society is like a man whose past way of life has been challenged. He cannot ignore the challenge, for the challenge originates within himself. Yet he is so strongly tied to the past that he is not certain that he wants to or is able to change. This is a portrait of internal conflict—this is the setting in regard to our sexual standards in America today.

---

39. For a documentation of the presence of organization in the family and a statement of some new forms of family organization, see Talcott Parsons and Robert F. Bales, *Family* (Chicago, Ill.: The Free Press, 1955); see in particular chap. i.

Chapter Three

An Objective Approach to Our Sexual Standards

Now THAT THE NECESSARY FACTORS HAVE been clarified, we are ready to examine our present-day sexual standards more closely. Let me now quite briefly spell out what my basic approach will be.

Perhaps the best way to explain it is by showing what are believed to be drawbacks in the approaches taken by some others. Any newsstand display is convincing evidence that sex is constantly being written about. A closer look at the content of the vast majority of these articles reveals the level of understanding present. Most of these authors have little training in the social sciences; few of them are familiar with the studies which have been done.[1]

One should also note that contact with sexual activity does not necessarily give a person deep insight into such

---

1. See G. C. Schauffler, M.D., "It Could Be Your Daughter," *Reader's Digest,* April, 1958, pp. 55-58. This article is a good example of a doctor who is more moralistic than analytic. Similar articles by all types of people are not hard to find.

activity. Many prostitutes are quite ill-informed regarding the more profound aspects of sexual behavior. A recent book by a notorious madam indicated that even an intelligent human being, who for several decades was directly involved in supervising sexual activity, may not gain any special insight into such behavior.[2] Perhaps this discussion can be summed up by saying that observation or participation in an activity, whatever it may be, does not guarantee understanding of that activity. The entire history of science can be viewed as the discovery of insightful ways of looking at the world.[3] Man existed and so did the world for thousands of years before the sixteenth century, and yet very little in the way of science developed until scientists found a new way of looking at the world via Newton and his predecessors. In the twentieth century scientists have tried another approach via Field Relativity theory. All of these scientific viewpoints have paid off in increased understanding, in making us aware of many vital aspects of our world. So it seems to be in all scientific fields. Looking is not enough; one must know how to look, what to look for, and when and where to look. A good commonplace example of this is the person at his first sporting event. He "sees" as much as anyone, but because he does not know how to look, he understands very little. He does not

2. Polly Adler, *A House Is Not a Home* (New York: Popular Library Editions, 1954).

3. For insight into the nature of science, see James B. Conant, *On Understanding Science* (New Haven: Yale University Press, 1951). For more detail on the social sciences, see Robert M. MacIver, *Social Causation* (New York: Ginn and Company, 1942). For more technical insight into science, see M. R. Cohen and E. Nagel, *Logic and Scientific Method* (New York: Harcourt, Brace Co., 1934), and W. P. D. Wightman, *Growth of Scientific Ideas* (New Haven: Yale University Press, 1953); also see A. N. Whitehead, *Science and the Modern World* (New York: Mentor Books, 1948), E. A. Burtt, *The Metaphysical Foundations of Modern Science* (New York: Doubleday Anchor, 1954). The last two works are particularly good for gaining insight into the development of science in the last three centuries.

know the rules that regulate the game. An organized way of viewing is essential to all objective understanding.

The social sciences—in which I include the fields of sociology, anthropology, psychology, government, history, and economics—are trying to find better ways of looking at human behavior, better in terms of gaining increased objective understanding. Thus, it is here that one should expect to obtain the formal professional training for understanding sexual behavior in America, for gaining the approach needed to find out the "rules of the game."

COMMENTS ON TEXTBOOK TREATMENT OF SEXUAL BEHAVIOR

When one looks at the professionally trained social scientist or the person who has educated himself in the social science literature, he expects to find someone with a sound approach to the understanding of sex. This very often is the case as I shall later show by reference to several of the major researches. However, in one particular field concerned with sexual standards, the situation is not so satisfactory. This field is composed of the authors of the "Marriage and the Family" textbooks used in our colleges.[4]

I shall deal here only with one major criticism. Not all texts are "guilty" of this particular fault, and thus I have selected four as illustrative. Although representative of much of the writing in the "marriage and the family" field, the tone of these texts, in fairness, should not be generalized to all others.

---

4. For an elaboration of this point, see an article by the author entitled, "The Treatment of Premarital Coitus in 'Marriage and the Family Texts,'" *Social Problems,* IV (April, 1957), 334-38. See also the comments by the author in Edwin Diamond, "Young Wives," *Newsweek,* March 7, 1960, pp. 57-60. See especially p. 59.

Here are some quotations from these four selected textbooks:

> It is difficult to make a strong case for premarital sex relations, for most arguments seem to stem from the rationalization of one's desire to satisfy his sex urge whenever he wishes without regard to the social experience of previous generations.[5]

> Instead of its [premarital intercourse] being something through which love is expressed, something that is an essential part of a deep and growing oneness in marriage, it becomes only a means to satisfy an appetite.[6]

> We have been reared to expect tenderness and romance in our love life and are unprepared for sex relations without genuine intimacy [such as occurs in premarital intercourse].[7]

> The major if not the total emphasis of the premarital experience is self-centered sex gratification; physical techniques are developed which simply emphasize the one goal, satisfaction, or release from a physical pressure.[8]

The general conception of premarital coitus held by these social scientists shows clearly through their statements. They believe premarital sexual intercourse is an almost exclusively physical relationship, devoid of affection and tenderness, promiscuous and lustful. It is exactly at this point that they have taken up the popular emotions derived from our early Christian attitudes toward sex. It is here that their analysis is subject to criticism.

There is no doubt that much of premarital sexual intercourse is of a lustful and promiscuous nature. This no one

---

5. R. E. Baber, *Marriage and the Family* (New York: McGraw-Hill Book Company, 1953), p. 596.

6. H. A. Bowman, *Marriage for Moderns* (New York: McGraw-Hill Book Company, 1954), p. 184.

7. E. M. Duvall and R. Hill, *When You Marry* (New York: D. C. Heath and Co., 1953), pp. 134-35.

8. J. T. Landis and M. G. Landis, *Building A Successful Marriage* (New York: Prentice-Hall, Inc., 1953), p. 143. For similar statements, see pp. 222, 231, 304, in the 1958 edition.

can deny—most of the coitus under the double standard would probably fit this description. However, the important question to be answered is not whether such sexual behavior and standards exist; rather, it is how widespread this "body-centered" kind of behavior is and whether there are other, more "person-centered" kinds of sexual intercourse and sexual standards? The authors in question seem to accept abstinence as the only correct standard. This belief tends to prevent them from seeing any but the "worst" aspects of premarital sexual intercourse.[9]

There is ample evidence indicating that many people have premarital sexual intercourse in an unselfish, affectionate, and psychically enjoyable fashion. Many engaged couples indulge in sexual intercourse, and the likelihood is that these couples will not have a purely physical, lustful, and selfish relationship. Moreover, many people who are not engaged, but are in love or extremely fond of each other, also engage in premarital coitus. Again, one hesitates to think of such sexual relationships in terms of the kind of behavior referred to by these social scientists. Let us now look at the evidence on this point from other more objective, social scientific research.

Research in the area of premarital sexual behavior is only about thirty years old. Although there are dozens of studies, they all are of a limited scope and do not give information relevant to all Americans. All of these studies are much more applicable to the white, higher-educated groups in our urban areas than to other segments of society. Furthermore, the past studies focused on sexual *behavior* rather than sexual *standards,* so that we must infer what standards were involved.

---

9. For an interesting discussion by many of the authorities in the field, which shows clearly the confusion present, see Robert A. Harper (ed.), "Premarital Sex Relations: The Facts and the Counselor's Role in Relation to the Facts," *Marriage and Family Living,* XIV (August, 1952), pp. 229-38, and W. R. Stokes and D. R. Mace, "Premarital Sexual Behavior," *Marriage and Family Living,* XV (August, 1953), pp. 234-49.

Nevertheless, science is an ever-continuing process and, although our information is scanty, it is most probably better than the hunches of the man in the street and can be quite useful if used with proper qualifications.

There are several studies which are generally recognized professionally as being representative of the best work in this area, e.g., the Terman study, the Burgess and Wallin study, the Kinsey studies, and the Ehrmann study.[10]

In addition to the studies named above and many others, I will refer to my own researches in this area as supplementary evidence. My own research is composed of hundreds of informal, impressionistic interviews and discussions, over the last twelve years, with college students and others concerning their sexual standards; and a more precise questionnaire study of about 1,000 high school and college students.[11]

The Terman study was published in 1938 and dealt with 800 married couples in California; the Kinsey studies were published between 1948 and 1953 and were based on interviews with 12,000 people married and single, from all over the country, but concentrated mostly in the Northeast;

10. For a book with excellent articles about all these studies see: Albert Ellis and Albert Abarbanel (eds.), *Encyclopedia of Sexual Behavior* (New York: Hawthorn Press, 1960).

11. The more precise research on 1,000 students is only in the preliminary stages of analysis. However, it will be used here whenever possible. Most of the students were from Virginia and New York and were between 16 and 22 years old in 1959. Four of my students helped greatly in this particular research: Ron Dusek, Martha Fisher, Richard Shirey and John Stephenson. My more impressionistic research was done between 1948 and 1960 and was mainly of a "participant observer" type, i.e., it consisted of conversations held with acquaintances, mostly without their knowledge that I was investigating sexual standards. I spoke to a total of approximately 1,000 individuals born mostly in the Northeast between 1920 and 1940, about 60 per cent of whom had a college education. Both of these researches were exploratory in nature, aimed at finding out what standards exist in the area of sexual behavior. The four major standards discussed in this book, and some of what I say about them is derived from these researches. I have also undertaken some smaller researches into this area and will refer to them when relevant.

the Burgess and Wallin study was published in 1953 and consisted of 1,000 engaged couples from Chicago and a follow-through of those who later married. The Ehrmann study was published in 1959, and focused on 1,000 single college students from Florida.[12] The Terman study included people born mostly before 1910. Kinsey's studies contained mainly people born between 1900 and 1930; Burgess and Wallin focused on those born between 1910 and 1920; Ehrmann dealt mostly with people born between 1920-30.[13]

All of these studies are subject to many criticisms in terms of sampling, types of questions asked, and other sources of error. They include too many college graduates and urban people, for one thing. However, these studies, plus others to be mentioned are the best sources of information available today. Used together, they seem to give us an adequate indication of sexual *behavior* in some major segments of America,

---

12. L. M. Terman *et al., Psychological Factors in Marital Happiness* (New York: McGraw-Hill Book Company, 1938); A. C. Kinsey, W. B. Pomeroy, and C. E. Martin, *Sexual Behavior in the Human Male* (Philadelphia: W. B. Saunders Company, 1948); A. C. Kinsey, W. B. Pomeroy, C. E. Martin and P. H. Gebhard, *Sexual Behavior in the Human Female* (Philadelphia: W. B. Saunders Company, 1953; E. W. Burgess and P. Wallin, *Engagement and Marriage* (New York: J. B. Lippincott and Company, 1953); Winston W. Ehrmann, *Premarital Dating Behavior* (New York: Henry Holt and Co., 1959). Another volume which we will refer to frequently and which uses the data of the Kinsey studies is Paul H. Gebhard, Wardell B. Pomeroy, Clyde E. Martin, and Cornelia V. Christenson, *Pregnancy, Birth and Abortion* (New York: Harper and Brothers, 1958). Gebhard became the new director of the Institute for Sex Research when Kinsey died in 1956.

13. The Kinsey studies, despite their drawbacks, seem to be the most reliable and extensive of the studies done in this field. See p. 36 in *Human Female* for a list of groups to which his study least applies. For an analysis of its approach, see Cochran, Mosteller, and Tukey, "Statistical Problems of the Kinsey Report," *Journal of the American Statistical Association,* Vol. XLVIII (December, 1953), pp. 673-716. One of the best single sources for analysis of Kinsey and sexual studies in general is Himelhoch and Fava (eds.), *Sexual Behavior in American Society* (New York: W. W. Norton and Company, 1955). The above article is contained in this volume. See also: Donald P. Geddes and Enid Curie (eds.), *About the Kinsey Report* (New York: Signet Books, 1948).

such as the middle and upper classes. They are not primarily concerned with sexual *standards,* although such information can be deduced from them. As far as I know, this present work is the only book primarily concerned with sexual standards as well as sexual behavior. My own interviewing was concerned with sexual standards and will be used to supplement these other researches in this respect whenever feasible.[13a]

The Terman, Burgess and Wallin, and Kinsey studies cover couples from California, Chicago, and New York, and in many instances, the results are strikingly similar. All three of these major studies showed that, in their sample of the people born after 1900, about 50 per cent of the women entered marriage non-virginal. Considering the geographical and time spans that separate these studies and their respondents, such findings are indicative of high validity. Another relatively similar finding is that from half to two-thirds of the female subjects who had engaged in premarital coitus reported they indulged only with the man they later married.[14] Thus, it seems that the largest outlet for sexual intercourse for women was this affectionate, "person-centered" type of coitus. There is evidence from these studies that such behavior, although less frequent, is significant for men also. The vast majority of these people, engaging in this "person-centered" type of coitus, seemed to accept their behavior as correct, i.e., they believed in a sexual standard which allowed indulgence when in love. Therefore, one of the major standards of premarital coitus—one in which most non-virginal women seem to believe—is one which accepts

13a. Other studies have dealt with sexual standards but not in any thorough or complete fashion. For example, see: Ehrmann, *op. cit.,* chap. v; Dorothy D. Bromley and Florence Britten, *Youth and Sex* (New York: Harper and Brothers, 1938); Zemo D. Rockwood and Mary E. Ford, *Youth, Marriage and Parenthood* (New York: John Wiley and Sons, 1945).

14. Terman, *et al, op. cit.,* p. 321. Burgess and Wallin, *op. cit.,* p. 330. Kinsey, *et al., Human Female,* pp. 286, 292, 299. Since Ehrmann dealt only with single people his study cannot be compared here.

intercourse as right predominantly when strong affection, love, or engagement is present. It seems clear, then, that our popular writers and many of our textbook authors have biased the over-all picture of premarital intercourse by almost totally ignoring this standard and the behavior which goes with it.

Since our culture is predominantly double-standard, one can expect more women than men to fabricate about the extent of their sexual activity. Probably some women who stated they only engaged in sexual intercourse with their future spouse were fabricating; probably some women who stated they were virginal at marriage were fabricating.[15] But, in general, the skill of questionnaire construction and the interviewers' techniques is demonstrated by the fact that, in all three studies, about half of the women admitted indulgence in premarital coitus. This is a most difficult admission to obtain from half of all women. The guarantee of secrecy and anonymity and the professional training of the interviewer obviously were helpful in approaching the truth. Thus, it is felt that, although there are undoubtedly errors in these studies, they may not be as great as might be supposed at first. One often gives strangers information he would never think of giving his close friends or family. These studies indicate something of American sexual behavior. To gain more exactitude, it would be necessary to study several million Americans in all walks of life, and no agency has yet set aside sufficient funds to undertake such a study.[16]

---

15. Men, too, may fabricate their responses in the opposite direction and exaggerate their experience, since that is our social expectation for men.

16. For a list of researches on sex carried on between 1922-47 with help from the National Research Council Committee for Research in Problems of Sex, see Sophie D. Aberle and George W. Corner, *Twenty-Five Years of Sex Research* (Philadelphia: W. B. Saunders Company, 1953). This is the organization that helped support the Kinsey studies and many other well-known researches; but it, too, is limited in the amount of financial aid it can offer. For a list and in many cases a description of past studies on sex, see Kinsey, *Human Male,* pp. 23-34; Kinsey, *Human Female,* pp. 94-95; Ehrmann, *op. cit.,* pp. 33-34; Burgess and Wallin, *op. cit.,*

Since it appears to be established that many people engaged in person-centered coitus, what can be said about the characteristics of such sexual relations? Burgess and Wallin asked the engaged couples in their study who were indulging in coitus together whether they felt such sexual behavior had weakened or strengthened their relationship, why they felt as they did, and what feelings they had concerning their sexual relations in general. Over 90 per cent of both the men and women stated they felt sexual intercourse had strengthened their relationship; most felt that the reason it had was that because of the increased intimacy, their love for each other had increased. Ninety-six per cent of the men and 84 per cent of the women said they felt no guilt about their behavior. Many of them added that it afforded them great relief from physical tension.[17]

Keep in mind that these were engaged couples of mostly a college background from Chicago. Perhaps different groups of people would react differently; perhaps there was some rationalization and deception, but the evidence still clearly indicates that there are many people who have standards quite different from abstinence and who practice a type of intercourse which differs sharply from body-centered coitus. Thus, the presence of sexual behavior does not necessarily indicate that people are violating their standard of abstinence—it may well mean that people have a different standard which allows such behavior. Social patterns usually have cultural sources. One can be opposed or favorably inclined to premarital coitus of any kind, but one must recognize and fairly describe all the existing types and standards.

It is proposed that there are two basic types of sexual *behavior* which shade into one another on a continuum: (1)

chap. xi. The Kinsey studies are one of the few studies to be based on interviews exclusively, rather than on written questionnaires.

17. Burgess and Wallin, *op. cit.,* pp. 371-79.

body-centered and (2) person-centered. The first one accents the physical aspects of the act, and the second emphasizes the particular person with whom the act is being performed.[18] There are, in American culture, several sexual *standards;* some of these standards tend to accent and lead to body-centered and unaffectionate sexual behavior, and others of these standards tend to lead to person-centered and affectionate intercourse. Both kinds of sexual behavior and sexual standards must be considered in any significant analysis of sexual intercourse.

OUR APPROACH: STANDARDS IN PREMARITAL INTERCOURSE

It is essential to any inquiry into premarital coitus to begin by listing all of our major sexual standards. Behavior alone is not enough, if one desires to understand the standards which regulate sexual behavior and compare the standards in terms of their social consequences and integration in our society. Regardless of whether or not sexual behavior is body-centered or person-centered, one needs to know if it is accepted by the individual involved. It is important to distinguish between two people who behave in the same overt way, except that one of them is doing what he or she feels to be correct and the other is violating his or her standard. This crucial information concerning personal or group standards is necessary in order to examine the consequences of coitus and thereby see how such behavior fits in our culture.

---

18. It should be clear that person-centered coitus does not overlook the physical aspects of the act. In fact, at times in a love relationship, the act may be performed for almost pure physical reasons, but, and this is the key point, the act is still person-centered since the people involved know that this act is occurring in a context of a love relationship and the opposite person is still all-important.

Knowledge of standards is also essential if one is to understand trends in sexual behavior, for such trends are related to changing standards.[19] Standards help organize one's view of sexual behavior, as well as make a comparison of norms possible.

Past studies of sexual behavior have often stressed the psychological and biological determinants of such behavior. As a sociologist, my main interest is in the shared cultural standards underlying the patterns of sexual behavior which occur in society. By taking this approach, we do not deny the relevance of these other fields, we merely point out that our focus of interest is different. This is true of all sciences —the interest of a chemist in a human bone may be quite different than that of a social scientist, but what both have to say may be equally valid. The sociological approach has been neglected, and it is this book's major purpose to remedy, at least in part, this situation.

When we speak of standards, it should be clear that we are not proposing that people actually think to themselves, "My standard is such that I believe premarital petting and coitus are wrong under the following specific circumstances." People are not so neatly or rationally organized. Rather, it seems that we have a hierarchy of values in the area of sexual behavior, and the balancing of these values determines one's standards. The values involved are love, pleasure, security, respectability, independence, religion, safety, and so forth. The relative importance of each is what constitutes a hierarchy or structure of values which, depending on the particular hierarchy, will support certain behavior as valu-

---

19. See W. W. Ehrmann, "Some Knowns and Unknowns in Research into Human Sex Behavior," *Marriage and Family Living,* XIX (February, 1957), 16-22. See in particular p. 22 where Ehrmann says: "The most astonishing void of all, however, is the almost complete absence of any scientific concern with sexual behavior and sex codes of conduct (the single and double standards)."

able and other behavior as valueless. Our standards derive from such sources, and thus it is easy to see that people are not always fully conscious of all the value-balancing which goes into their standards. Formal declarations of standards often overlook these more subtle aspects. This is especially true for newer standards which may be largely unconscious and not yet overtly formulated. In future chapters, some of the major "negative" and "positive" values underlying sexual standards today will be examined in order to better understand the nature of our sexual standards.

Logically, there can be three major types of sexual standards: one stating that premarital intercourse is wrong for both people; one stating that premarital intercourse is right for both people; and one stating that premarital intercourse is right for one participant but wrong for the other participant. Empirically, America has sexual standards which fit all three of these logical possibilities. All Americans are not fully conscious of these standards, but the standards are clearly evidenced by people's behavior and by a knowledge of our culture. Some of these standards are, to a considerable degree, part of our informal or covert culture, rather than part of our formal or overt culture.[20]

Our major premarital sexual standards are as follows: First, there is a standard of abstinence for both sexes as

---

20. For a discussion of covert culture see: Arnold Rose, *Theory and Method in the Social Sciences* (Minneapolis: University of Minnesota Press, 1954), chap. xxi. There is ample evidence for such informal standards in the major researches on sexual behavior. The greater condemnation of women for sexual liberties indicates the existence of the double standard, while the presence of guilt-free intercourse among engaged couples supports the existence of a permissiveness-with-affection type of standard. Furthermore, historical study makes us aware of standards both new and old. My questionnaire study of 1,000 high school and college students bears out the presence of these standards in every respect. Finally, the direct questioning involved in my own informal research of the last 12 years was aimed at revealing the nature of our sexual standards, both overt and covert.

our formal or overt standard. This standard is closely tied in with our religion. It is a "single standard" since it forbids intercourse outside of marriage for *both* men and women. In sharp distinction to this standard are those single standards which accept intercourse as *right* for *both* men and women. The people who accept these permissive standards fall into two general groups: (a) those who accept intercourse only when there is a stable relationship with engagement, love, or strong affection present, and (b) those who accept intercourse when there is mutual physical attraction, regardless of the amount of stability or affection present. Both of these standards are *informal* standards which violate our *formal* code of abstinence, but are, nevertheless, acceptable to some groups of people. Finally, we in America fill in the last logically possible standard with the age-old double standard which states that men may indulge in premarital intercourse but women may not. The double standard is our most widespread informal standard. This conflict between our formal standard of abstinence and these other three informal standards leads to vast areas of confusion and conflict in our sexual customs.[21]

Even though many people may have tendencies toward more than one standard, most Americans can be classified as adhering predominantly to one or another of these four. Here they are in summary:

1) *Abstinence*—Premarital intercourse is wrong for both men and women, regardless of circumstances.

2) *Permissiveness with Affection*—Premarital intercourse is right for both men and women under certain conditions

---

21. Two books affording some insight into our conflicting attitudes of abstinence and the double standard are: Albert Ellis, *The Folklore of Sex* (New York: Charles Boni, 1951) and Albert Ellis, *The American Sexual Tragedy* (New York: Twayne Publishers, 1954).

when a stable relationship with engagement, love, or strong affection is present.

3) *Permissiveness without Affection*—Premarital intercourse is right for both men and women regardless of the amount of affection or stability present, providing there is physical attraction.

4) *Double Standard*—Premarital intercourse is acceptable for men, but it is wrong and unacceptable for women.

The second standard, permissiveness with affection, is seriously neglected by much of the present-day literature on sex. It is the person-centered behavior in accord with this standard which seems most at odds with the descriptions of premarital coitus given by our textbook writers today. Of the three informal standards, only permissiveness with affection is likely to lead to person-centered coitus. Permissiveness without affection and the double standard are most likely to involve a body-centered type of coitus. Permissiveness with affection is one of the more liberal and equalitarian standards which has developed in the last few generations.[22] *My approach, then, will be to compare all four standards as to their characteristics, consequences, and trends, in order to*

---

22. These four standards are put forth hypothetically. Future study may yield other standards or subtypes which may be applicable for certain segments of our society. A full discussion and elaboration of these standards follow in this book. It should be clear that I am interested only in heterosexual standards and not homosexual standards. As regards other cultures in the world, these four basic standards may well apply in general but have different subtypes and have different degrees of relative popularity, e.g., the double standard seems much stronger in South America than here, and permissiveness with affection much stronger in Sweden. For information on other cultures in the Western world, see: Ellis and Abarbanel, *Encyclopedia of Sexual Behavior,* chapter by Ira L. Reiss, "Changing Sexual Standards," and *passim.* Geoffrey Gorer, *Exploring English Character* (New York: Criterion Books, 1955); Eustace Chesser, *The Sexual, Marital, and Family Relationships of the English Women* (New York: Roy Publishers, 1957); Arnold Rose (ed.), *The Institutions of Advanced Societies* (Minneapolis, Minn.: University of Minnesota Press, 1958); Allen Edwardes, *The Jewel in the Lotus* (New York: Julian Press, 1959).

show their relative integration in our culture.[23] I shall first describe and analyze the characteristics of each of our three permissive standards and then compare their integration in terms of social and cultural consequences. Finally, abstinence will also be analyzed to complete the picture of premarital standards in America.

WHICH STANDARD IS RIGHT?

The social sciences constantly examine the values of different cultures, i.e., what each culture feels is desirable and what each feels is undesirable. This is probably one of the most important areas of the social sciences. In the first chapter, it was shown how cultures disagree as to what is acceptable and unacceptable. There is also, of course, disagreement concerning such questions of right and wrong within one culture.

Let it be quite clear that a final answer to questions of right and wrong, decisions whether this or that culture is right, whether this standard of sexual behavior is right or wrong, cannot be made by sociology or any other science. Sociology can give one information on the consequences of a particular form of behavior—it can tell one about the relation of this form of behavior to other forms; it can give one full accounts of all the variables involved in the situation; it can inform one of trends which are occurring. But the final decision—the final statement: "This is the correct way to

23. The accent on relating these standards to each other and to their integration in our over-all society makes this approach basically a functional one. For a clear specification of the functional approach, see Robert K. Merton, *Social Theory and Social Structure* (Glencoe, Ill.: The Free Press, 1957), pp. 46-60 especially; and Kingsley Davis, "The Myth of Functional Analysis as a Special Method in Sociology and Anthropology," *American Sociological Review*, XXIV (December, 1959), 757-72.

behave" cannot come from sociology.[24] Such a final evaluation must be based upon one's individual values. Whether
one's values are the best is a question on which sociology
may help but cannot resolve. The sociologist's role is not to
debate the pros and cons of an issue, but rather to examine
the structure of an entire situation.

It is one's own values, applied to his knowledge of the
situation which tells one whether he believes an action to
be right or wrong. These values "weigh" the various consequences or aspects of the situation and, thereby, a decision
is reached. Here is an example to show how several people
looking at the same set of consequences, or the same situation, can arrive at different final decisions because of the
different values they possess. Suppose, upon examining the
question of contraception, all agree that if more people use
contraception, the following will occur: lower abortion rates,
healthier mothers, a higher standard of living, fewer unwanted
children, and more violations of certain religious groups'
beliefs. One person may look at these, and, because his
particular religious beliefs are not opposed to contraception
and he places strong positive values on the other consequences, his balance may come out in favor of contraception.
Another person may agree with him, even though his religion
is opposed to contraception, because he feels that the other
consequences outweigh his religious objection. A third party
may be opposed to contraception because, although he values
the other consequences, he gives supreme "weight" to the
fact that his religion opposes such behavior. Here, then, are

24. For a rather strong statement of this scientific position, see G. A.
Lundberg, "Science, Scientists and Values," *Social Forces,* XXX (May,
1952), 373-79. See also the clear article by Frank Hartung, "Cultural
Relativity and Moral Judgments," *Philosophy of Science,* II (April, 1954),
118-26, and the classic statement in Gunnar Myrdal, *An American Dilemma* (New York: Harper and Brothers, 1955), App. 2, especially pp.
1059-64.

three people who agree on the consequences, the factual aspects of the situation, but disagree on their final evaluation, because each holds different values, and because a certain value may be more important to one person than to another.

Now, can one prove that the person who abided by his religion was wrong—that he should have valued the other consequences more highly? Or can one prove that the person who violated his religious code was wrong—that he should have valued his religious code more? How could such a statement be backed up if it were made? All one could say is "I think, on the basis of my values, that such and such is more important and is the right path of behavior." But this is exactly what the other people would say. A more objective approach to such disagreement would seem to be to recognize that here we have several people who, even though they have examined all the consequences, do not agree on the relative importance of certain values. An individual may believe one position to be right, but he cannot prove himself to be correct.

However, this does not mean that one must constantly doubt if he has found the right set of values or whether or not there is such a set. It merely means that one recognizes the fact that his particular set of values is based on a faith that these values are an approximation to what is right. The sociologist can neither assert nor deny the existence of universally valid values.[25] This is not an empirical question—

25. For a statement on universal values, see Clyde Kluckhohn, "Values and Value Orientation . . ." in Parsons and Shils's, *Towards a General Theory of Action* (Cambridge: Harvard University Press, 1951). For an elaboration of the position taken here, see the paper the author delivered in Atlanta, Georgia, in 1956, at the Southern Sociological Meetings, "Sociology and Values: A Case Study," and the paper he delivered at the 1959 meetings of the Society for the Scientific Study of Sex: "Personal Values and the Scientific Study of Sex." See also Abraham Edel, *Ethical Judgment* (Glencoe, Ill.: The Free Press, 1955), in particular, pp. 205-20.

it is a philosophical one which necessitates knowledge of what is good or bad.

Of course, we can examine our values for consistency with other values, and we can alter our values, and because of experience, place more weight on some values than we formerly did. People always believe that certain facts underlie their values. We can objectively examine the facts which we believe underlie a particular value. Then we can reject, or reinforce, our values depending on how the underlying facts turn out and how we evaluate them. But there is still no objective way to prove one set of value weights to be the best.

The situation is really not so different from that in science. Science, too, is based on faith, i.e., on assumptions concerning the nature of the world—assumptions such as those which hold that the world can be known through the senses and that it is orderly. These assumptions cannot be proven scientifically, for before science is possible these assumptions must be accepted. Even a specific scientific theory has an element of faith in its acceptance, for, as has often happened, there is always the possibility of a better theory being devised. Thus, all our knowledge in science, as well as in morality, is based on faith in certain assumptions about our world.

Chapter Four

The Ancient Double Standard

DESCRIPTION
OF THE DOUBLE STANDARD

THIS STANDARD IS KNOWN AS THE DOUBLE standard because it entails using one standard to evaluate male behavior and another standard to evaluate female behavior, making it possible for a man and a woman to be judged quite differently on the identical sort of behavior. It should be familiar to all Americans because it is our dominant, informal sexual standard. Most of the double-standard men to whom I spoke did not think of this standard as ideal and fully right. They rather viewed it as merely acceptable or permissable. Their ideal standard was very often abstinence. They justified their behavior by various rationalizations, such as "boys will be boys" and "that's the way the world is." Nevertheless, they did not seem to be too bothered by qualms or guilt feelings.[1]

---

1. It is relevant to add here that I examined numerous college textbooks on "marriage and the family" in order to see if they contained any information on the double standard. Not one of these texts contained more

The double standard is relevant for more than just sexual behavior. The double standard can be seen in action in almost all spheres where men and women meet—in education, in business, in politics, and in religion. There is a general tendency to pay men more for doing the same type of work and having the same qualifications. In 1958, the full-time salary for males was $4,927, and for females, $3,102. Also, when one compares men and women in the same area of work, men invariably earn more.[1a] There are cases where the explanation is given that women do not stay on the job as long as men because they marry and have babies, and thus they do not deserve as much. In some cases, these explanations may be the true reasons, but in many cases, they are just rationalizations for a person's feelings that women just do not deserve as much as men, that women somehow are, as Aristotle said, inferior by nature. The many middle-aged women who are not married, and not likely to give birth, and who still receive lower pay than similarly employed males are good examples of the frequent falsity of the "practical" explanation given above.

In the professional world, there is a similar situation. A woman doctor or lawyer often has a difficult time getting established.[1b] At least part of the explanation must be that many people, both men and women, feel that women would

than the briefest mention of this standard, and none of them gave the reader any understanding beyond an occasional statement that the double standard was weakening. Ira L. Reiss, "The Double Standard in Premarital Sexual Intercourse: A Neglected Concept," *Social Forces,* XXXIV (March, 1956), 224-30. See the above article for a listing of these textbooks.

1a. U. S. Bureau of the Census, *Current Population Reports: Consumer Income,* Series 1260 (Washington, D.C., January 15, 1960), pp. 19, 40-44. For full-time primary and secondary school teachers in 1958, males earned an average of $5,651, and females, $4,261. Of course, some of this is due to males having higher jobs. But then, why do they get the higher jobs?

1b. Josephine J. Williams, "Patients and Prejudice: Lay Attitudes Toward Women Physicians," *American Journal of Sociology,* LI (January, 1946), 283-87.

not be as good as men at something like medicine or law. Women are good at homemaking and child care but are not as competent at these other tasks—such is the reasoning of the double-standard believer. They are quite adamant, even though the scientific evidence is opposed to their views.[2] It should be emphasized that the double-standard adherents include women as well as men. Many women are convinced the double standard is correct—just as many women were convinced feminism was wrong.

In religion, too, ample evidence of the double standard can be found. The first woman preacher appeared in this country a little over a century ago, and she still is a rarity. Many Americans find it difficult to listen to a woman tell them about right and wrong and about God. This seems "out of place" to many, for men are supposed to be dominant and women submissive, and how can a minister in a pulpit look submissive? Here again, women frequently are not allowed the same rights as men. The old Hebrew conceptions of "woman's place is in the home" and "the man should be dominant" are relevant. This should make it apparent why there is a double standard in politics also.

Much of this double-standard aura of our culture is changing, and women are being accepted more and more on an equal basis; it should be kept in mind, however, that despite the vast changes wrought by the feminists and the industrial revolution in the last century, there still is a strong recognizable double standard in America.[3] The double stand-

---

2. Johnson E. Fairchild (ed.), *Women, Society and Sex* (New York: Sheridan House, 1952). This is a collection of thirteen articles on many phases of woman's place in American society today. Some of them are quite good in giving insight into the effect of the double standard on women today. For recent evidence on working women see the excellent source, Robert W. Smuts, *op. cit.*, especially pp. 104-9.

3. In a small research conducted in 1958 on students in Virginia by myself and R. W. Kernodle, it was found that the girls wanted to marry a man "they could look up to" but they did not want a man who would

ard in premarital sexual behavior is obvious in our norms which state that premarital coitus is wrong for all women, and thus women who indulge are bad women. Premarital coitus, however, is excusable, if not right, for all men, and thus men who indulge are not bad men.

SOME SOURCES

OF THE DOUBLE STANDARD

Why are there so many cultures that hold to the double standard in sexual behavior and in other spheres also? Why, in the examination of historical cultures in the second chapter, was there noted such a strong acceptance of the double standard? Is it just "natural"? Answers to such questions are not easy. Here is what seems the most plausible explanation, but bear in mind that this is only an educated conjecture.

The core of the double standard seems to involve the notion of female inferiority. The standard gives men more rights than women and assumes such distribution is proper. It is not just a question of different roles—anyone looking fairly at the division of roles will see that women's roles are given low status as compared to men's roles. The particular role does not matter; whatever a woman does is valued less and whatever a man does is valued more, e.g., if men

---

"help them in making decisions." Boys had only small desires for a "woman they could look up to" and were more likely to want a girl who would "understand their moods and stimulate their ambition." Thus, the double standard is still active, not in a radical "master-servant" form, but in a more equalitarian, but still unequal version; at least that is the implication of this research. Here, too, we find that the double standard is not something fully *imposed* on women, for women seem to "need" it and want it in some form. This, of course, has changed and will continue to change in time. It would be interesting to investigate whether women in certain groups are now more double standard than men.

herd then herding is highly valued—if women herd, it is not. This is the state of affairs in double-standard societies.[4]

In searching for the origins of the double standard, one should try to discover why men viewed the female of the species as inferior. First, it should be clear that not all cultures did or do define women as inferior. Many non-literate societies today view women as equals, and, historically, Egypt, for part of her history, gave females relative equality.[5] The vast majority of societies, however, did place women in a subordinate position.

Man's muscular strength, muscular co-ordination and bone structure may have made him a better hunter than woman; it may have made him more adept at the use of weapons. Couple this hunting skill with the fact that women would often be incapacitated due to pregnancy and child rearing, and we have the beginnings of male monopoly of power. Man would control the economic factors of life; thus, he would have a powerful hold on the female. A woman could also hunt and could certainly fish and gather berries or such, but she could probably not survive as well as the woman who had a male to help her. A man alone was at a disadvantage also. If he hunted and fished all day, he might not feel up to preparing his own food, making all his weapons, utensils, clothes, and shelter. He might also like to have someone who would supplement his food supply with some berries or lizards which had been caught near "home." It seems that there were good economic reasons for men and women to live together right from the beginning—economic

---

4. Some recent evidence on this was reported at the 1958 Southern Sociological Society meetings: George L. Maddox, "Occupational Prestige: Some Empirical Applications of the North-Hatt Rating Scale." Evidence showed women and men were ranked differently on the same jobs by most people and pay differed also.

5. For more information on Egypt, see *Everyday Life in Ancient Times;* Chambliss, *op. cit.,* chap. iii; and Brinton, *et al., op. cit.,* Vol. I, chap. i.

reasons which supplemented the sexual motives and aided in keeping men and women in more permanent relationships. The ever present reason for men and women living together seems to be that man is not self-sufficient. Even today when people are self-sufficient economically, it can be seen that they are not self-sufficient emotionally. One need have little fear for the marriage institution—it is well-founded on the insufficiency of the isolated individual.

This sort of economic relationship, which early men and women may have formed thousands of years ago, afforded man the opportunity, though not the necessity, of usurping control of the relationship. Even though both man and woman needed each other, man's position was somewhat more advantageous since he brought home the all-essential food. Also, if such a division of labor prevailed, it meant that men would become more "worldly-wise" in military and political affairs, thereby increasing their power.

This need not always be the case. It was possible that since both men and women had work to do, they would view each other as equals, essentially as coworkers and would share in political leadership. It was also possible that because woman brought life into the world she would be afforded even more prestige than man. But the situation more often turned out in favor of male dominance since man did have the controlling factor in the economic sphere. However, there is nothing "natural" about the double standard. The same physical differences are present today, but in an urban-industrial society, they do not tend as much toward a double standard.

As agriculture developed and great cities grew, the acquisition of power meant greater possibilities of profit, thus perhaps increasing the desirability of usurping power. In any case, by five thousand years ago, man had gained political control as well as economic control in the Western world, and customs had been set up by the ruling group of males which gave man the dominant hand in social life. These double-standard customs are still with us.

There were many factors which supported the sexual aspect of the double standard. Inheritance rules in all the ancient cultures, except Egypt, gave the dominant property rights to male heirs. This meant that the sons of one's wife or one's daughter would inherit one's property. This sort of situation would certainly make a husband or father desirous of keeping his wife or daughter virginal outside of a marital relation. Otherwise these men might have property disputes with some illegitimate male child conceived by a wife or daughter.

Further reasons for the double standard may be found in the notion of property. If man considered woman as his servant, almost as a piece of valuable property, then the same notion of private ownership would apply. No daughter or wife should betray her father's or husband's property rights by giving herself without permission to another man. The Tenth Commandment made the view of women as property explicit and clear:

> Neither shalt thou desire thy neighbour's wife, neither shalt thou covet thy neighbour's house, his field, or his man-servant, or his maid-servant, his ox, or his ass, or anything that is thy neighbour's.[6]

Men were free to act as they pleased for no one owned them, although even their behavior was somewhat restricted by parental authority as exercised (usually) through the oldest male.

Jealousy and pride must have often entered into the sexual restrictions placed on women. If women were similar

---

6. Deuteronomy 5:18. One's wife is clearly listed here along with the male's other possessions or property. For a comparison of the property view of women and Negroes, see Myrdal, *op. cit.,* pp. 1073-79.

to property, and one wished to control the legitimacy of his heirs, he had to restrict female sexual behavior. One would be a fool in the eyes of the community if he failed at that restriction. Much of the anger of a husband whose wife has been false to him is based on the social disgrace of such behavior and not only on his own feelings concerning his wife. Pride and jealousy made a good team throughout history to reinforce the double standard.

In sum it would appear that man's physical abilities afforded him economic, political, and military advantages and made it possible for him to define woman as inferior. His attitude toward her as property to be jealously guarded, so as to avoid loss of pride and inheritance, also seems directly relevant to the presence of the double standard to regulate male-female relationships. With man in power in other areas, it is easy to conceive of his usurping special sexual privileges in addition. The type of sexual behavior encouraged by the double standard is thus pleasure-centered and body-centered for the male and chastity for the female.

This situation is quite similar to that existing between many dominant and submissive groups. For example, look at Negro-white relations in our own country. Many centuries ago the white man assumed his superiority to the Negro, and most of the legal and social rules regulating white-Negro relations reflect this white-supremacy notion. The white man is privileged to do many things which the Negro cannot. Likewise, most men can engage in premarital intercourse with little social criticism, while the female, who is the male's partner, will be strongly condemned. When man defines a group of people as inferior, he buttresses his judgment by giving that group low prestige and few privileges.[7] Such

---

7. Robert K. Merton, *op. cit.*, chap. xi, "The Self-fulfilling Prophecy." This reading shows the mechanisms which lead a group defined as inferior to actually become inferior in many ways.

was the case with the male-female relationships and therein lies the root of the double standard.

SUBTYPES:
ORTHODOX AND TRANSITIONAL

It should be clear at the outset that there are two main subtypes of the double standard. One subtype I shall call the *orthodox*. The adherents of this subtype abide fully by the double standard and allow few, if any, exceptions from its dictates. The second subtype I shall call the *transitional*. This has become increasingly popular in the last century as shall be demonstrated in chapter ten. In this case, exceptions are made, and the woman who engages in premarital coitus because she is in love or engaged is not condemned. This is still the double standard, for men are allowed to engage in coitus for any reason—women only if in love or engaged. I have chosen to call this the transitional subtype, because it is a standard which is between the older orthodox double standard and the newer standard of permissiveness with affection which allows equal freedom to both men and women. In reading the discussion of the double standard, it would be well to keep in mind the differences between these two subtypes. The discussion will focus on the orthodox type of the double standard. However, the vast majority of the sexual behavior in both subtypes will be body-centered. The key difference is that the transitional subtype will also accept some person-centered coitus.

INITIAL DIFFICULTIES

The first characteristic of the double standard in pre-marital intercourse is that such a standard is self-contradictory. It supposedly allows sexual freedom to men but not to women. How is such opposed behavior possible? A man cannot have sexual freedom unless he has a woman with whom to exercise this freedom. But the double standard holds that no woman should engage in premarital coitus and thus no man is able to either! This is the sort of paradoxical situation brought about by the double standard.[8]

The men who favor a double standard must resolve this basic contradiction in some fashion. Historically, the situation was remedied by the gradual development of a class of prostitutes who would engage in sexual activity with men. This would still leave most of the females virginal and would afford a sexual outlet for men.[9] This was the solution which the Hebrews, Greeks, and Romans arrived at. Thus, it is clear why the double standard encourages prostitution. Of course, prostition exists for other reasons besides the double standard. It affords an outlet for any system of sexual regulation, i.e., regardless of the sexual customs, some people will be unable to satisfy themselves thereby and may resort to prostitution.[10]

---

8. A classic example of the effects of the double standard, written in the nineteenth century, but still containing much of merit for us today is: Guy de Maupassant, *A Woman's Life* (New York: Lion Books, 1954).

9. The double standard thus is an "evasion," i.e., it is a social custom which evades the rulings of another social custom; in this case the "evaded" custom is abstinence. By means of this evasion, abstinence tends to increasingly become a matter of "lip service" for many people and pressures toward more permissive changes are temporarily channeled into the double standard evasion. See Robin M. Williams, Jr., *American Society* (New York: Knopf, 1956), chap. x. Speak-easies during Prohibition were a similar type of evasion which temporarily relieved the pressures toward repeal. The double standard is for more conservative groups a "compensatory custom" rather than an "evasion." In these groups, the double standard does not really evade abstinence, for many of these people still accept abstinence and feel guilty—in these cases it just "compensates" for the strain between abstinence and sexual desires.

10. For a statement concerning the "reasons" for prostitution but one which does not deal explicitly with the double standard, see Kingsley Davis, "The Sociology of Prostitution," *American Sociological Review,* II (December, 1938), 744-55.

The connection between prostitution and the double standard is helpful in understanding the ambivalent attitudes prevailing toward prostitutes—how, on the one hand, they are thought of as bad and worthless women because they violate the code of chastity; yet, on the other hand, they are thought to be performing a necessary function for the double standard and thus are not without some prestige. After all, it is the violation of the double standard by women which enables men to abide by it.[11]

Up until the late nineteenth century, prostitution was one of the major answers to the double standard dilemma. It probably accounted for a good portion of the male's sexual outlet before marriage. But even in the nineteenth century, and increasingly as time passed, other women more and more supplemented the prostitutes as sources of body-centered sexual behavior for double-standard males.[12] With the increased freedom women were obtaining in the twentieth century, came a change in sexual behavior. Many more women began engaging in premarital coitus of both the body-centered and person-centered types. Some men reacted to these women in an equalitarian fashion and did not question their right to equal sexual privileges, but most men probably felt that only "bad" women would indulge. Men began to look more and more for these women as sexual partners.

Traditionally, the double standard stated that a man should not try to seduce a "nice" girl. Many men copulated solely with prostitutes in order not to corrupt "nice" girls. But now the double-standard male was becoming more and more intimate with single women who were not prostitutes. Of course, this was not strictly a new event. But the frequency of such permissive female behavior was new, as were the

---

11. For lower educational- and occupational-class males, prostitution is still an important sexual source. See Kinsey, *Human Male,* p. 376.

12. *Ibid.,* pp. 599-603 and chart on p. 410.

opportunities a large city offered for taking advantage of such behavior. It should be noted here also that many double-standard men began to feel more compassion for the woman, since she was at times a neighborhood girl. It is probably here that the transitional subtype grew, and more men began to accept coitus for women if they were in love.

The single criterion of loss of virginity as "proof" of who was a "bad" woman is clearly not sufficient as a means of obtaining new "bad" women. All women are virginal at one time, and there must be a way to label women "bad" while they are still virginal so as to justify engaging in intercourse with them and making them "bad" non-virginal women. Double-standard males in the past, and today, pick some of their "recruits" from those women who display some desire to go astray through their action or dress—thus indicating that they are potentially "bad." Other women are obtained from groups which are thought of as inferior or as "different." This includes girls from lower-income classes, or different racial groups, or members of a different religion. These are some of the social criteria for finding potentially "bad" girls.[13] Some double-standard men do not limit themselves to certain types and may try to have coitus with all the women they see socially in order to discover which girls are "bad." Virginity is still valued highly, and many men prefer

---

13. William F. Whyte, "A Slum Sex Code," *American Journal of Sociology,* XLIX (July, 1943), 24-31. This account applies to most double-standard areas and not just slum areas, although lower-income groups may be more double standard. Much of this article gives empirical support to many of our assertions. Kinsey found that the lower educational and occupational groups had more premarital coitus—for men whose education stopped at eighth grade, 98 per cent had premarital coitus; for college men, the rate was only 67 per cent. Ehrmann cites strong evidence of high percentages of dates with lower-class females and of several times higher rates of intercourse with these lower-class females. See Winston W. Ehrmann, "Influence of Comparative Social Class of Companion Upon Premarital Heterosexual Behavior," *Marriage and Family Living,* XVIII (February, 1955), 48-53. See also Ehrmann, *Premarital Dating Behavior,* chap. iv.

non-virgins, but at young ages and in times of scarcity, "bad" virgins of the above types are substituted.

One can glean something of the old Christian attitude towards sex in the present-day double standard in America. The view that sex is evil and women who indulge are especially evil contains, for many, almost a religious fervor of conviction of the "badness" of non-virginal women. The non-virginal female is disliked and disrespected. She portrays the temptations the male feels. Accordingly, the virginal female is placed on a sort of pedestal by the double-standard male. She is pure and angelic and far removed from such lusty and somewhat dirty behavior as premarital sexual intercourse—so go the thoughts of the male. There are differences here among men—some of them feel very little animosity towards a non-virgin. But the worse the man thinks of the non-virgin, the better he thinks of the virgin. The male, in many cases, views himself as a likeable "devil" and the female as a lovable "angel." The two notions reinforce each other. The more devil he is, the more angelic he wants his love to be so as to purify him. There may well be here in this aspect of the double standard the roots of the idealization of women in romantic love.

I recall a pertinent incident during my employment in a clothing factory before I went to graduate school. One of the employees told me that he was now sure he was going to marry the girl to whom he was engaged. I asked him what had made him certain, and he said that he had checked quite carefully with his fiancée's past boyfriends and was now convinced that she was a virgin. I asked him if he would have broken off his engagement if he had found his fiancée to be non-virginal, and he emphatically replied yes. Even though he loved this girl and knew her as she was now, this past activity would have been enough to break off the relationship for, as he said, he felt a non-virgin must be a bad woman.[14]

Males who accept the transitional type may not think ill of a woman who engages in premarital coitus if she is engaged or in love. Otherwise, however, they too will not hesitate to remove the woman from their list of "nice girls."

WANDERLUST

Since this standard declares almost all female sex partners to be "bad," it would be expected that men would seek these partners away from their home neighborhoods or at least avoid incorporating these females into their close-friendship groups. This seems to be the reasoning of the double-standard males, in particular orthodox ones, in America today.[15] Furthermore, women in the same neighborhood would avoid sexual activity with these men in order to save their reputations. Double-standard men switch partners rapidly; their lack of respect for the girl with whom they indulge often makes them feel disgusted with her. There is little attempt to get to know the girl in terms of personality traits—such girls are valued mainly for sexual pleasures.

The double standard seems also to increase the likelihood of some groups of women dating outside of their own neighborhoods. Many women reject the double standard re-

14. Three plays which illustrate this aspect of our double standard are: Tennessee Williams, *Streetcar Named Desire* (New York: New Directions, 1940); Sidney Kingsley, "Detective Story," in *Best Plays of 1948-49* (New York: Dodd, Mead and Company, 1949); Eugene O'Neill, *Anna Christie* (New York: Boni and Liveright, 1923).

15. Besides my own interviewing, there is the evidence, previously quoted, of Whyte's, Ehrmann's, and Kinsey's studies on men. See Kinsey, *Human Male,* p. 561 for additional evidence. For an interesting view of such behavior in Spain, see G. Brenan, "Courtship in Granada," *Atlantic,* August, 1957, pp. 33-38.

strictions placed upon them. They feel they can engage in sexual activity and still be "good" girls in their own eyes. These are the women who accept permissiveness with affection or permissiveness without affection. These females often date out-of-town men who do not know the double-standard males in their home neighborhoods. In this way, they can act as they like with these "out-of-town" men and have no fears about their reputations being ruined at home. Some of the girls who go outside for sexual partners are full double-standard adherents who believe coitus to be wrong for women, but they indulge for other reasons, e.g., to gain special economic gifts or go to places they ordinarily could not afford to attend—or to date men who usually would not go out with them.

Many country resorts serve similar mobility purposes for some of the more promiscuous girls and boys. They are well known for attracting a young crowd from many different cities. Girls and boys both vacation at such resorts often with the idea in mind that the anonymity of the resort, the chance of meeting a stranger, will afford them the proper setting for obtaining sexual intimacies without any word getting back to their home neighborhoods—these resorts provide a setting in which inhibitions can be abandoned. It seems that "distance makes the heart grow fonder."[16] It should be clearly stated here that many millions of American women do not fit this description for they do not desire an escape from double-standard restrictions. Such females would be believers in female chastity or in the single standard of abstinence.

Double-standard men often find their "bad" women in those girls who are fleeing other double-standard males. This aspect of the double standard is encouraged by our urban-industrial development which allows a much wider range

---

16. Such resorts are "compensatory customs" of the sort I spoke of in chap. iii, and earlier in this chapter.

of acquaintances and encourages more liberal and permissive sexual attitudes on the part of females.

The mobility aspect leads to a definite confusion in the moral evaluation of women. For example, let us look at a girl who engages in light petting with her home-town double-standard boyfriend. This same girl may have engaged in sexual intercourse with two out-of-town boys, one of whom was double standard and the other single standard. This sort of situation would mean that her home-town double-standard boyfriend will think of her as a "good" girl; the double-standard out-of-town boyfriend will think of her as a "bad" girl, and the out-of-town single-standard boyfriend will not think ill of her because of her sexual behavior. This is an excellent example of the confusion present in the type of moral evaluation which the double standard contains. Such a confusing situation can lead to much conflict on the girl's part—she may find it difficult to have a clear conception of herself since so many people seem to judge her differently. We base a great deal of our self-evaluation on other people's feelings about us, and, in such cases as above, other people's feelings differ greatly. Additional conflict can occur when and if a double-standard male finds out that other men are classifying his "good" girl as a "bad" girl. This is probably a frequent occurrence, for these men take pride in telling others of their "conquests" and thus word travels quickly over double-standard communications.

VIRGINITY: LOST AND FOUND

This characteristic is connected with the "mobility effect." The contradiction here is derived from the fact that double-standard men believe non-virginal women to be "bad" and therefore desire to marry virgins. At the same time, however, their sexual standard makes them constantly strive to render as many women non-virginal as possible. This means that they are lowering their own chances of marrying a virgin. The more successful these men are in their search for sexual partners, the less are their chances of marrying a virgin. Even those transitional subtype males who accept non-virginal females when love or engagement is involved are participating in self-defeating behavior, because most of their sexual behavior is not so discriminate; they, therefore, do decrease the number of women whom they would want to marry.

Most of the double-standard men to whom I have spoken denied this as a real contradiction, for they hold they are lowering the number of virgins in groups outside of their home neighborhoods or groups to which their future mate does not belong. Since they will marry a girl from these other groups which they have not successfully "attacked," they feel they are not behaving in a contradictory fashion. The rationalization in this explanation is obvious as soon as one takes an over-all view. It is clear that, although certain groups of women may have been by-passed, it still is possible that other men were successful where one failed. Thus other men may be indulging in sexual relations with those women from whom one is planning to choose a wife. The former discussion showed that there is evidence that some women will give out-of-town dates more sexual privileges than home-town men. Therefore, the double standard insures that practically all groups of females will be under "attack" by some groups of men.

The "virginity paradox" can lead to the conflict mentioned before when a man discovers his girlfriend indulged with someone else. It may also lead to conflict when a husband discovers his bride is not virginal, or even to internal conflict when he discovers he is acting in a contradictory fashion. Such a situation certainly increases the amount of distrust and suspiciousness between men and women and opens up many new possibilities of conflict. The double standard seems to snare many individuals into a net of contradictory and unfulfilled desires, especially in an urban-industrial society such as ours.

Many women very strongly resent this contradictory virginity-attitude on the part of men. These women feel it most unfair for a man to date a girl, try to seduce her, and then if he succeeds, condemn her and cross her off his marriage-possibility list. Many girls find themselves upset when they become fond of a particular boy and would like to be more sexually intimate with him, but must keep restricting their advances for fear of losing his respect. Such restrictive behavior, such fear of disapproval for sexual behavior, may well make later sexual adjustment more difficult.[17]

Many girls who tease are merely playing the man's game. If men are so interested in sex, but dislike girls who "go too far," the logical thing to do, these girls feel, is to play up their sexual attributes to attract men and then restrict sexual behavior. The double-standard male creates his own "enemies"—he makes women use sex as a weapon instead of an expression of affection; in this case, the weapon is in the form of the tease. This sort of situation leads to the anomalous case of a female who, on the surface, seems highly-sexed but who internally may be quite frigid—a sweet "sexy" virgin whose dual nature may well cause her much internal conflict. Such a virgin is similar to wax fruit—in both cases the appearance may be appetizing but the object is incapable of fulfilling its promise. This situation also leads to an accent

17. For support on this from a recent research, see Eugene A. Kanin and David H. Howard, "Postmarital Consequences of Premarital Sex Adjustments," *American Sociological Review*, XXIII (October, 1958), 556-62. See chap. ix of my book for a fuller discussion of this point. Kanin and Howard found that, although the restrictive background was a hindrance, it often was overcome in marriage.

on a sensual type of sex which may constantly frustrate both persons in their attempt to maintain this sensual sort of attraction. In short, this sort of behavior makes people accent the surface aspects of sexual relations.

In previous times, in more rural societies, "virginity paradoxes" would not be as common.[18] In those days, a woman was very much under the social controls of the small town and would not be able to easily escape these controls by meeting a different group of men in a different city. Public opinion would tell one who the "good" girls were. The growth of urban centers in the last hundred years then was quite disruptive of the double standard. It gave women a freedom of activity which they never had before. Feminism and other movements helped to further free women from the tight social restraints to which they formerly were subjected. Dating, too, has equalitarian tendencies which conflict with the double standard. Accordingly, the contradictions inherent in the double standard have become enlarged and much more widespread in the last one hundred years. Both the "mobility effect" and the "virginity paradox" are consequences of this change.

THE DOUBLE STANDARD AND JUSTICE

Our notion of justice appears to hold that where two individuals co-operate in the performance of an activity, they should *both* be praised or blamed. It would seem that premarital sexual intercourse is such an instance and allows no mitigating circumstances.

In premarital coitus the male is most often the aggressor

18. For a most entertaining novel about a rock which was a foolproof test of virginity, a novel which reveals much of the confusion and humor contained in the search for virginity and non-virginity, see Margaret Sharp, *The Stone of Chastity* (New York: Avon Publishing Co., 1955).

or at least he is quite willing to engage in such behavior. It is, thus, necessary to devise special reasons to allow the male to condemn the female for such action and still not condemn himself for being her partner. The major reason for such completely different judging of men and women would be some relevant difference between the sexes. In former times, the inferiority of women and their innate deficiencies were listed as reasons. There is an old Russian saying that best portrays this point of view: "A hen is no bird, a woman no human."[18a] Psychologists are in agreement that general intellectual capacity, as far as can be told, is equal in men and women. Training accounts for existent differences. Furthermore, genetics is clear in its stand on inheritance of physiological characteristics only. Ideas and morality are not inherited. Today these old reasons cannot be accepted. Because of this, new rationalizations have developed to support the old double standard. In my interviews of double-standard men, I found two main arguments which are often held. These arguments are put forth by transitional as well as orthodox adherents:

a) The female sex drive and sex desire is not as great as the male's, and thus the woman has less compulsion to such behavior.

b) The female takes a greater risk because she can become pregnant and she is more easily condemned. Thus she has more reason to abstain.

a) Differences in Sex Drive and Sex Desire. There is much scientific evidence which indicates the female sex drive (that which is inborn) is not by nature significantly less than the male's sex drive.[19] In the first chapter, I mentioned several cultures in which men and women are equal in their initiation

---

18a. Quoted by Alexander Goldenweiser in Freda Kirchwey (ed.), *Our Changing Morality* (New York: A. and C. Boni, 1924), p. 129.

19. Ford and Beach, *op. cit.*; this is probably the best single source for such references. Some studies do report differences such as periodicity in

of sexual activity and also cultures where women initiated more sexual activity than men. It seems clear that, if so trained, women would have as much desire for sexual intercourse as men do, and that whatever innate differences exist are quite capable of modification. Even with the present unequal training, there are many women highly desirous of sexual activity.[20]

Picture how men would behave sexually if they were brought up as women are. Boys would be told quite young they would one day marry and raise a family and this state of affairs was very desirable. When they reached puberty, instruction would be given about the dangers of sexual intercourse outside of marriage. They would be told if they did allow themselves to step out of line sexually, their lives would be ruined—that no girl would marry a boy who had lost his virginity. Moreover, even on a dating basis, girls would not

female sex drive and greater susceptibility to psychological stimulants in male sex drive. Ford and Beach's view is that such differences do not make the male sex drive innately stronger than the female's, and, further, that much of such differences are due to learned variables and not inborn factors. For a similar conception, see Margaret Mead, *Sex and Temperament in Three Primitive Societies* (New York: Mentor Books, 1950), especially Part IV. The psychological differences between men and women, such as men thinking more aggressively of holding an attractive woman and women thinking more submissively of being held, may be due largely to differential cultural training and not to any biological differences nor to "female modesty." Kinsey's findings that man's sex outlet is highest in the late teens and woman's is highest in the late twenties and early thirties is not conclusive evidence of sex-drive differences. Sex outlet is not necessarily a reflection of sex drive. One's sexual outlet frequently increases due to frustrations in non-sexual areas. Learned inhibitions prevent many people from giving vent to a sex drive which is stronger than that of some other people who engage in sexual activity quite frequently. It would seem quite possible that women have higher frequencies of sex much later than men because of the inhibition barriers which have to be broken down. Men are freed quite early and after an initial "fling" may settle down to a more regular rate of indulgence. This may be the explanation of such differences. Learned factors again seem of most import. In any case the differences which may exist do not seem to be in terms of inborn strength of sexual drives.

20. Kinsey, *Human Female*, p. 688. Kinsey found that about one-third of the women equalled the men in their sensitivity to psychological stimuli.

respect non-virginal boys. In addition, these boys would be taught it was a "girl's world" and girls were allowed more freedom than boys and one must accept this. The boy's role would be to marry, care for his family, and not be too upset when girls had special sexual privileges for, after all, girls will be girls. Suffice it to say that if boys were brought up in this fashion, which, in large measure, is the way many girls are brought up today, the male's sex drive would also be in-hibited—so inhibited he could not give vent to his sexual desires as easily as he does today.

Today the difference in sexual desires (desire is a com-bination of inborn drive and learning experience) is not as great as one might suppose. A century ago when many more women entered matrimony with no sexual experience, beyond perhaps a few kisses, there must have been a much wider disparity between male and female sexual desires. Today, however, it seems that many women (over half, according to recent studies) enter marriage non-virginal, and the majority of the virginal group has considerable experience in sexual behavior. An indication of this can be obtained from Kinsey's findings. For those virgins in his sample who had been kissed and who were born after 1910 the following percentages apply:

    100 per cent—kissing
     74 "   " —deep kissing
     72 "   " —breast manipulation
     32 "   " —oral stimulation of breast
     36 "   " —received masturbation
     24 "   " —performed masturbation
     17 "   " —contacted bare male genitals with own
      3 "   " —received oral-genital contact
      2 "   " —performed oral-genital contact.[21]

---

21. Kinsey, *Human Female*, pp. 254-55.

The evidence from studies seems to show that petting of a fairly heavy nature is common among virgins. Today's virginal female, thus, is much different from her counterpart of 100 years ago. She is probably, in many cases, a woman who has strong sexual desires but who is striving to keep them within bounds. Kinsey stated that about 20 per cent of the virginal females in his sample stated they wanted to lose their virginity but had not yet had the proper opportunity.[22] Exact figures are impossible to obtain, but from the available evidence, it is guessed that at least half of the virgins today are sexually "awakened" women. It seems, therefore, that the experience many of today's females have guarantees development of strong sexual desires. One key difference may be that the female has built up, via training, more controls and thus does not yield to her desires as much as the male does.

The folklore about a male "needing" coitus more than a female has little basis in fact. No male has yet died from lack of coitus. As for speed of arousal, the female can be quite quickly aroused—witness evidence from other cultures. Further, the female climax can be brought on in a matter of minutes with proper clitoral stimulation.[23]

Finally, it should be added that even the present-day differences which do exist between men and women are not necessarily a "reasonable" basis for condemning female indulgence and allowing male indulgence. From a strictly logical and "reasonable" point of view, if some men desire sexual activity more than some women, this does not mean such

22. *Ibid.*, p. 314. Ehrmann, *Premarital Dating Behavior*, p. 46. Ehrmann found that about half of his virginal women had engaged in breast or genital petting.

23. Kinsey, *Human Female*, p. 163. Most females reached orgasm by masturbation in less than four minutes. The greater time required in coitus may be due to difficulty in contacting the clitoris and inhibitions. This speed of orgasm indicates similarity between men and women.

desires are right and good or should be gratified. Even if it is assumed that desires should be satisfied, these particular men should be allowed to have more sexual activity than those particular women who are less desirous of such relations. Thus, lessened desire, even when present, may be an argument for less indulgence but not for complete abstinence— if it is an argument at all. Thin men may desire less food than fat men; this does not mean that thin men should starve and fat men should eat—it rather could imply that thin men should eat less than fat men, or fat men should diet or thin men should fatten up! In short, a difference is not necessarily an argument for continuing such a state of affairs. It rather may be an argument for equalizing the situation. Thus, the double-standard arguments concerning sex drives and desires are not objective supports of their position. What difference there is between men and women can be used just as easily as an argument for changing such differences as for maintaining them. This belief, then, is a social rationalization.

b) Differences in Risks Involved. The second common rationalization double-standard men put forth as a justification for their position is that women risk more than men because they can become pregnant and are more easily condemned, and thus women have more reason to abstain.

For simplicity's sake, I shall focus on the risk of pregnancy. How great is the risk of pregnancy? In chapter seven this issue will be dealt with at length. Suffice it to say here that authorities on birth control state that the male condom or the female diaphragm with jelly, when properly used, affords security.[24] Therefore, if such care is taken, pregnancy has only a minute chance of occurring. Therefore, this consequence is not nearly as significant as it was before the devel-

---

24. Robert L. Dickinson, M.D., *Techniques of Conception Control* (Baltimore: Williams and Wilkins, 1950), p. 24, and *passim*.

opment of rational means of contraception. The difference, of course, still exists.

One can point up the rationalization quality of the double-standard position without going further into this argument concerning pregnancy or other consequences such as social condemnation. One basic part of our notion of justice states that one should not entice another person to perform an action which would endanger this other person's well-being. If one believes the risk of pregnancy and other consequences to be significantly different between men and women, then it follows that men should abstain so as to avoid bringing these undesirable consequences to women. If it is believed the risk of pregnancy and other consequences are not significantly different, then there is no reason to judge women differently. From a strictly logical approach, woman's chance of becoming pregnant may merely mean that she should be cautious or that men should not tempt her.

The explanations given by double-standard people today are thus often rationalizations after the fact, i.e., the origin of the double standard probably is somewhat close to that given earlier in this chapter; today, after thousands of years, people are calling this code into question and adherents are searching for reasons to support their position. One reason for adherence to the belief in the double standard seems quite simply to be that these people were brought up in a society which accepted it; most of them unthinkingly did likewise and became emotionally attached to this belief. This is true of most beliefs. As I pointed out in Chapter Three, one is hard put to fully support their beliefs rationally, and ultimately must resort to a value judgment or emotional appeal. However, beliefs do differ in terms of their inner consistency —in terms of their degree of conflict with other beliefs.

Most customs come into existence gradually and in an unplanned fashion. The justifications for their existence come later.[25] It seems clear that the double standard, in both its orthodox and transitional forms, conflicts with our present-day equalitarian notion of fairness and justice, although in other ways it may be well integrated in our society.

c) Other Conflicts. Many other facets of American culture conflict with the double standard—for example, our notions concerning proper treatment and choice of associates. The separation of sex and affection in the double standard leads to behavior which, in one sense, is not socially acceptable. In general, our culture holds that one should associate with people who are respected and avoid people not respected or thought of as "bad." The double standard, however, demands that one associate with women who are not respected. The vast majority of double-standard interviewees said they felt disgusted with their female partner and themselves after the sexual act was over. Part of the reason for this disgust is the desire to get out of a situation which involves association with someone not respected, thereby entailing behavior believed to be wrong. Once the sexual forces are satiated, the other aspects of the situation come to the fore and lead to these disgust feelings.

Our culture holds that people should be treated as worthwhile, valuable individuals. In treating these particular women in a contrary fashion, the double-standard male often feels disgust for the entire relationship. But men are taught that coitus for them is acceptable and these women are "bad" anyway. They thus continue this behavior and derive what physical pleasure they can from it, despite these drawbacks.[26]

25. Many times these shared rationalizations are acting as "compensatory beliefs," i.e., they help maintain the double standard despite the fact that it conflicts with other parts of our culture by somewhat compensating for the strain of such a clash via their compensatory rationalizations.

26. Another reason for "disgust" feelings is the fact that many double-standard men feel that abstinence is, in one sense, "really" right, and thus they feel they are doing something wrong. Such conflict may well be stronger among middle-class males who are more indoctrinated with abstinence.

GENERAL INTEGRATION
OF THE DOUBLE STANDARD

It has been shown how the double standard today is very much involved in conflicts and contradictions. It is an ancient sex code in a modern society. It is evident that the feminist movement, with its platform of equality, greatly weakened the double standard. Furthermore, the development of contraception meant that the fear of illegitimate offspring and venereal disease was no longer so applicable as a support for female virginity. Romantic love also favored, in its later stages, an equalitarian attitude towards women. Women were to be loved psychically as well as physically. Love and sex could be joined according to the later romanticists; this was opposed to the double standard. Finally, the industrial revolution and urbanism gave women greater opportunities to exercise their new-found rights, without the restrictions of small-town gossip and social controls. In sum, then, most of the recent changes in social organization and culture are opposed to the double standard and accentuate its conflicts and contradictions. The transitional subtype developed in response to these changing conditions, as an attempt to reduce conflict. It is believed that this standard has grown considerably in the last few generations. By and large, however, it is involved in the same basic conflicts as the orthodox subtype, even though it eases the tension by its more equalitarian aspects. Let it be clear—one can accept this standard in spite of all its conflicts. All standards have some conflicts; this one happens to have more than most. This standard, however, still has the buttress of being informally widely accepted and is a means of easy sexual pleasure for the male. Many people are able to abide by this standard and not feel excessive conflict. It is likely that the orthodox double standard is strongest at the lower social levels while the upper social levels would be more likely to modify their double-standard beliefs and accept the transitional double standard.[27]

Furthermore, it should be mentioned that the double standard helps maintain other aspects of our culture. The most obvious aspect of American culture that is strengthened is the notion of male dominance. The double standard gives men an excess of privileges over women in the sexual sphere, which helps buttress the notion of male dominance in many other areas. The man as the "head" of the family, as the protector of women, as the "breadwinner," as the leader, are all notions supported by the double standard. There are still many people who favor such notions of male dominance and accordingly, there are many people who favor the double standard. If the double standard in sexual behavior disappears, such notions will be seriously affected. A culture or a society is an integrated system, and if one part is altered, it will most often affect many other parts. The events of last century illustrate the direction and types of changes involved in the weakening of the double standard. Many Americans today are caught in a dilemma, for they approve of many of the changes which have caused the weakening of the double standard, and yet they are still emotionally attached to parts of the double standard.[28]

---

27. See Whyte, *op. cit.* This is a somewhat debatable point, and one we shall return to later in the text.

28. There is a wide variety of evidence concerning the strength of the double standard today. For example, Kinsey found that the average male born after 1910 had a total of 1,523 orgasms before marriage, from all sources. The comparable figure for females was 223. There were also large differences in the number of partners in coitus. Only 6 per cent of the women had more than 10 partners, while 23 per cent of the men had more than 10 partners. Kinsey, *Human Female,* pp. 519-20, 683. Burgess and Wallin also found such significant differences. Twenty-two per cent of the men had more than 24 partners in all their sexual activity (kissing, petting, etc.), whereas only 5 per cent of the women had this many partners. Ehrmann and Terman report similar findings. All of this indicates that, although weakened, the double standard in many ways is still very much with us.

Chapter Five

Permissiveness
Without Affection

ALL SOCIETIES HAVE RULES AND REGULATIONS
governing premarital sexual behavior, but, in many cases,
requirements of affection are not among these rules. Usually
there are requirements concerning the age of the participants;
also, there are most often requirements restricting coitus to
single individuals. Finally, there are minimal rules set up to
take care of single pregnant women. Remarkably few women
in such permissive societies seem to become pregnant.[1] Since
these societies do not have our cultural heritage, our notions of
love and its connection with marriage, this situation is quite
understandable. In American culture, such an affectionless
standard runs into many difficulties. This standard is probably lowest in number of adherents of any of our four major
standards,[2] even though the recent equalitarian and rational

---

1. Low pregnancy rates may be due to the lowered fertility abilities of
teenagers; see Paul H. Gebhard *et al., op. cit.,* pp. 32-33.
2. In a pilot study of over one hundred students which I undertook in
1956, I found only one full-fledged adherent of this standard. There were,

117

trends in our culture have probably somewhat encouraged its growth. Americans have not been able to free themselves from their Puritan past enough to accept such body-centered coitus. This standard has most likely existed in Western culture for many millenniums as a minor "radical" custom.[3]

The adherents of permissiveness without affection in our culture place a very high value on physical pleasure. Their standard dictates that if a man and woman are physically attracted to each other, then they should be allowed to indulge and gain the physical pleasure involved. Some of these adherents add other qualifications. They require that both people fully accept such behavior and that precautions be carefully taken against such consequences as pregnancy and venereal disease.

There are two main kinds of believers in this standard: (a) orgiastic—those who seek highly promiscuous coitus with precautionary measures of secondary importance, and (b) sophisticated—those who seek physical pleasure in a more controlled and careful way.

ORGIASTIC

These people aim at pleasure in a more open and all-consuming fashion, and they relegate most other behavior to an inferior status. The extreme example of such an orientation would be the "high school sex clubs" mentioned so frequently in our newspapers in the early 1950's. Many of

however, a few other sympathizers. This study was done in Virginia. In my other interviews, the percentage of such adherents was also quite low. Bromley and Britten, *op. cit.,* p. 104, found 4 per cent of the females accepted this sort of standard.

3. Such radical "pleasure philosophies" are quite common from the time of Epicurus to Jeremy Bentham. See Bertrand Russell, *A History of Western Philosophy* (New York: Simon and Schuster, 1945). This work contains a good discussion of such philosophies.

these accounts were fallacious, but some appear to be valid.[4]

For these "clubs" to be taken as representative of this subtype, there must be more than just impulsive, erotic behavior. If there is no shared set of values underlying the behavior of these teen-agers—if their behavior is compulsive —then it is a subject for a psychological, not sociological, study.[5]

My own research evidence and other evidence previously cited indicate that many people have taken a few sensational incidents of sexual promiscuity and exaggerated them out of all proportion. This is not to say that sexual behavior of a body-centered sort is a rarity—it is, in fact, quite common. But such behavior most often takes place in a double-standard setting wherein only the male's behavior is viewed as acceptable. It is relatively rare to find such behavior occurring, *and* being accepted, as right for *both* the male and female, as is the case in permissiveness without affection. However, this may be truer of the middle and upper classes than of the lower classes. For if Kinsey is right, then the lower classes have a larger number of people who accept the orgiastic standard. My own interviews among lower education- and occupation-class males does not fully support this. Most of my lower-class males were orthodox double-standard adherents. However, my questionnaire study of 1,000 high school and college students, does show good evidence of permissiveness without affection among the Negro students. More research

4. The following book must be read with a critical eye. I mention it only as a reference to be carefully and selectively read. S. U. Lawton, M.D. and J. Archer, *Sexual Conduct of the Teenager* (New York: Derby Press, 1951). Such clubs held regular orgiastic meetings, some of which are described in the above book.

5. For a most interesting and revealing set of case studies on the psychological side of sexual behavior, see Benjamin Karpmann, M.D., *The Sexual Offender and His Offenses* (New York: The Julian Press, 1954). Dr. Karpman's explanations are not sociological. He emphasizes instincts, incest, and other Freudian notions and injects his own value judgments. The cases are interesting, nonetheless.

is needed here to clarify the sexual standards of our lower classes.[6] Permissiveness without affection may be strong among certain lower-class groups and quite weak among other lower-class groups. For example, as cited above, there is evidence indicating that Negroes have significantly higher rates of premarital coitus. This is particularly true for the lower-class Negro. Perhaps the very lowest-class groups have the most adherents to this subtype. Such groups lack permanent employment and have much less marital stability, which may encourage fewer restrictions on coitus before marriage. From a sociological point of view, it would likely be most rewarding to examine some of the above groups more closely.

SOPHISTICATED

The other major subtype of this standard involves a more "balanced" approach. In many of our cities today, there are people who accept sexual relations without affection as right and proper behavior because they feel it is "natural." These people do take precautions to avoid venereal disease and pregnancy. They are better classified as "pleasure lovers" than "revolutionaries." In my interviews, the sophisticated adherent was usually a well-educated bohemian iconoclast. My interviewees were mostly middle-class—perhaps in a lower-

---

6. For Kinsey's discussion on this point see Kinsey, *Human Male,* chap. x, especially pp. 382-83. Gebhard reports data on Negro women showing higher rates of premarital coitus: see Gebhard, *op. cit.,* chap. vi, "The Negro Woman." If looser, informal norms are found at the lower levels, they may result from the fact that the social structure does not allow for easy achievement of formal norms, and thus these people devise other ways of getting what they want. This reasoning would apply to many other aspects of lower-class social behavior. See also Allison Davis, "Class Differences in Sexual and Aggressive Behavior Among Adolescents," in R. F. Winch and R. McGinnis, *Selected Studies in Marriage and the Family* (New York: Henry Holt and Co., 1953), pp. 264-67.

class sample a different kind of person might espouse the same hedonistic philosophy.

The sophisticated adherent feels that since men and women desire sexual intercourse, there is no reason why they should not have it. Sexual intercourse is viewed as natural and neces- sary, as akin to eating and breathing. It is further held that physical pleasure is justification enough for the act. Many such people would probably agree that their standard is opposed to our conception of love, but they do not par- ticularly care. Some of them do not believe in love at all; those who do, feel they can have love in addition to their standard. They believe that some of their affairs will de- velop into love. Most of these adherents, however, seem more interested in transient pleasures with many people than in a serious love affair with one person. Sexual intercourse without affection is considered to be as good as sexual inter- course with affection. Many of these people insist that body- centered coitus is actually better than person-centered coitus, because it lacks personal obligations and is thus a "purer" form of pleasure. Here is the way Rene Guyon puts his position:

> How many painful disillusions would be saved if, instead of thinking themselves obliged to say "I love you," men would con- tent themselves with saying "I desire you." . . . In the light of this analysis, individualized love scarcely differs from ordinary sexual love. All that distinguishes it from the love of two partners who deliberately embark on a purely temporary union is its slightly longer duration—weeks or months, as the case may be.[7]

---

7. One of the best elaborations of the sophisticated type of permissive- ness without affection can be found in the source of this quote: Rene Guyon, *The Ethics of Sexual Acts* (New York: Blue Ribbon Books, 1941), pp. 372-73. For a brief summary of Guyon's views, see Rene Guyon, "The Doctrine of Legitimacy and Liberty of Sexual Acts," chap. lxv, in A. P. Pillay and Albert Ellis (eds.), *Sex, Society and the Individual* (Bombay, India: International Journal of Sexology, 1953), pp. 429-37. For a defense of body-centered behavior of more recent date, see Albert Ellis, *Sex With- out Guilt* (New York: Lyle Stuart, 1958), chap. v.

The sophisticated adherent differs from the orgiastic in that, since he has other interests, he does not give as much emphasis to sexual pleasures. Since sexual intercourse is natural and like good wine, one should be careful not to "drink" too frequently, lest he become controlled by the act and unable to truly enjoy the pleasures involved. Precautions to avoid disease or pregnancy are perhaps more frequent, for these people are pleasure lovers and such occurrences bring pain.[8]

It is believed by many that all prostitutes accept permissiveness without affection as their sexual standard. Many prostitutes, however, do not accept intercourse as being right for men and women. They often find their own professional intercourse distasteful. The desire to escape an unpleasant situation—very often low-income living—seems to be the major motive for girls entering prostitution. There are, of course, other motivations. Some enter because they are lesbians and want to live with other females; others are nymphomaniacs and become prostitutes to have sexual intercourse as often as possible. Emotional poverty is another important reason for girls entering prostitution. Some prostitutes marry later and often seem to adjust to marriage quite well.[9] The men who visit prostitutes are probably not predominantly permissiveness-without-affection. They most likely are double-standard males who lack respect for the prostitute and believe her behavior is immoral. Thus, although such sexual

8. A fictional account of a future society that accepts permissiveness without affection can be found in Aldous Huxley, *Brave New World* (New York: Harper and Brothers, 1950)—a most entertaining book. In current society, the Greenwich Village Bohemian is frequently a sophisticated adherent.

9. Adler, *op. cit.;* see especially chap. iv. Miss Adler operated one of New York's most famous prostitution houses from 1920 to 1945. Her revelations about prostitution are quite interesting and informative. Her over-all grasp of sexual behavior is limited, but she does know prostitution. Chap. iv gives her answer to why girls become prostitutes.

behavior is lacking in affection, one must know the manner in which the participants view this behavior, in order to determine if their standard is permissiveness without affection. A major purpose of the "four standards" approach is to enable one to distinguish among people who behave alike but who may differ sharply in the acceptance of their own behavior. Exact percentages are hard to obtain, but all four of our sexual standards would have adherents among prostitutes—even abstinence, although this should be the least supported, since it would lead to the most psychological strain. It should be kept in mind that prostitutes, too, are brought up in American culture, and our culture is strongly opposed to body-centered coitus for women. We would expect there to be many people, even in this group, who could not accept such behavior. These females still hold to their beliefs in other standards and feel disgust for the males who help place them in this situation.[10]

GENERAL INTEGRATION OF
PERMISSIVENESS WITHOUT AFFECTION

In our own culture, permissiveness without affection has never been a widespread standard. The entire history of Western culture is one of female subordination and restriction. A standard which allowed women and men equal sexual privileges never took hold. A single permissive standard violates the part of our culture which stresses the value of sexual intercourse and virginity. Our stricter religious tradition has always been opposed to such "free" sexual expression. Some religious groups still oppose all intercourse which is not aimed

---

10. For an intimate view of the prostitute, see Judge John M. Murtagh, and Sara Harris, *Cast the First Stone* (New York: McGraw-Hill Book Company, 1957).

at reproduction and view sexual pleasure, even in marriage, as a sin. Permissiveness without affection is also not well knit with our marriage institution, since it encourages casual, temporary, body-centered relationships. It is probable that such relationships will usually not lead to marriage.

The notion of romantic love, as it has grown in American culture, is diametrically opposed to such a casual view of sexual intercourse or of one's sexual partner. Romantic love stresses the importance of the individual and places great value on individual personality traits. It is reasoned that if love is valuable, then so must be the love objects, and if people are so highly valued, one cannot treat them as casual sex objects. Sexual intercourse is associated with love both in marriage and before marriage. Our more tolerant attitude towards sexual intercourse between two people in love is a reflection of the associations we make between love and sexual behavior. Love justifies sexual intercourse to many people—to some only in marriage, to others at all times. But love is strongly associated with sex, and permissiveness without affection violates this connection.

Many Americans will accept body-centered coitus for men and prostitutes, but they will not accept it as a standard for all women and men. To do this would be to give formal approval to sexual relations lacking in affection. We want to have our cake and be able to eat it too. Body-centered coitus is allowed for double-standard males as a "behind the scenes" activity, but other standards are insisted upon in serious courtship. It is paradoxical, but it is the inconsistency of the double standard—its granting of freedom only to men —that makes it more acceptable to most Americans. The double standard can be informally accepted, for it is not in complete opposition to our formal code. But to openly accept body-centered coitus for both men and women would require giving up completely our formal code of abstinence.

Societies, as well as individuals, can be inconsistent, and for analogous reasons.

It should be noted that there are parts of the permissiveness-without-affection standard which are at least logically, integrated with our culture. For example, this standard avoids many of the conflicts which the double standard entails. It does not conflict with our notion of justice because it treats men and women alike; it does not lead to a "virginity paradox" for it does not value virginity; sexual partners do not have to be sought away from home neighborhoods because coitus is acceptable for all; and it does not make one feel sexual behavior and sexual partners are "bad." In all of these respects, permissiveness without affection is generally considered better integrated with some of our basic values than is the double standard.

Chapter Six

Permissiveness With Affection

THIS IS THE THIRD AND LAST OF THE PERMIS-
sive standards in America. It is a much more popular standard
than permissiveness without affection, but less popular than
the double standard. It is a single standard since it accepts
coitus as right for *both* men and women when a stable affectionate relationship is involved. Strong evidence of this standard can be found in other parts of Western society. In particular, one can point to Sweden as the modern country which has
most strongly accepted permissiveness with affection as its
standard. Young people are frequently taught that when they
are in love, premarital coitus is acceptable.[1] The studies
in Sweden indicate that a large percentage of premarital
sexual intercourse takes place between people engaged or
going steady. In short, Swedish behavior seems to closely

1. One of the very few good popular accounts of this aspect of Swedish
culture may be found in Lester David, "The Controversy Over Swedish
Morals," *Coronet,* December, 1956, pp. 126-32. For more detailed information, see Anna-Lisa Kalvesten, *The Social Structure of Sweden*
(Sweden: University of Stockholm, 1953); see especially pp. 30-31 and
67-68. See also Nelson N. Foote, "Sex as Play," *Social Problems,* I (April,
1954), 159-63.

approximate a person-centered standard like permissiveness with affection. Sweden has a long history of a kind of "bundling" custom among the peasants, that was more liberal than our bundling in that it allowed coitus. When and if the girl became pregnant, the couple would marry. Such a custom has been reported for other European peasants. This custom lasted until the nineteenth century and was the basis for the liberal customs which developed during the urban-industrial revolution in Sweden. Thus, there are special circumstances in Sweden which have encouraged the growth of permissiveness with affection.[2] Nevertheless, the evidence from Sweden does indicate that men have more sexual experience than women. Thus, at least *some* of the person-centered affairs are probably instances of a transitional double standard, which allows men more freedom than women.

A few years back I asked a male Swedish student of mine about the sexual standards in his country as compared to our own. This student told me what many Swedish people have said—the American female is much freer with her sexual favors in all respects except intercourse. The Swedish female will not usually indulge in "heavy petting" unless she is seriously affectionately involved and therefore intends to have intercourse; otherwise, she feels, such behavior is far too intimate. The American female pets with much more freedom, and yet she stops short of actual coitus. To this Swedish

---

2. For insight into the eighteenth-century bundling custom in the New England and Middle Atlantic States, see Samuel Peters, *General History of Connecticut* (London: J. Bew, 1781). This is the only book published on bundling during its popular time. See also Dana Doten, *The Art of Bundling* (New York: Farrar and Rinehart, 1938). Doten does a fine job of showing how bundling was well integrated with our eighteenth-century society and how it disappeared when that society changed and became urbanized. The courting scene then shifted to the parlor and finally to the automobile. More sexual liberties seem to be taken in the twentieth-century automobile than were taken in the eighteenth-century bundling bed.

student, sex in America is too much of a "tease"—too much apart from the rest of life. To the Swede sexual behavior is accepted as a natural part of life, but it is more restricted for people who are seriously involved with one another. In this sense, one might say that although American women are more virginal than the Swedish women, they are still more promiscuous sexually!

FREE LOVE AND TRIAL MARRIAGE

At the outset, this standard should be distinguished from that called "free love." Free love is a doctrine which holds that if two people are in love, they should be allowed to indulge in sexual intercourse. Up to this point, free love is similar to permissiveness with affection, but free love adds something more. Free-love adherents further believe there is no need for the marriage institution; people in love will live with each other, and if they fall out of love or become incompatible, they can leave each other. In the early years of communism, Russia tried free love and later abandoned it. Also, some of the more radical feminists favored free love.[3] This is *not* a part of the permissiveness-with-affection standard. This standard states that two people who have built up a stable affectionate relationship may engage in full sexual relations. Marriage is to continue as is, and no such changes are part of this standard. It is hoped this explanation will prevent the confusion between free love and permissiveness with affection. Almost all believers in permissiveness with affection, to whom I spoke, accept our traditional marriage institution and reject free love.[4]

---

3. See Ditzion, *op. cit.*, for a detailed account of the nineteenth-century debates on free love.

4. It should be added that this is true for the believers of the other

Another misconception that should be dispelled immediately is that which connects permissiveness with affection and trial marriage. There is no necessary connection between the two. Trial marriage dictates that two people should live together for a few months before marriage, so as to discern if they are compatible. After the trial period, both people are given an opportunity to refuse to marry. Such a custom is common among some non-literate cultures. However, it should be clear that this is not the same as permissiveness with affection.[5] People who accept permissiveness with affection do not usually intend their behavior to be a trial marriage—in many cases, the people concerned are not definitely interested in marriage. Sexual intercourse is viewed as an expression of their feelings for each other and not usually as a test of compatibility.[6]

THE PLACE OF AFFECTION

Permissiveness with affection is perhaps most clearly distinguished from permissiveness without affection and the double standard by its incorporation of affection as a pre-

standards also. These are *pre*marital standards and are not intended to displace the marriage institution. On all of these standards (since, as was mentioned, other researches have not focused on standards as well as behavior), I must rely heavily on my own interviews to elaborate the standards' specific meanings.

5. See Judge Ben B. Lindsey and W. Evans, *The Companionate Marriage* (New York: Boni and Liveright, 1927). Judge Lindsey's book is often referred to as a manuscript on trial marriage. It really is a treatise pleading for divorce by mutual consent, an end to alimony, a waiting period before having children, and the use of birth control. It is, thus, an attempt to reform the marriage institution, not to alter it by instituting trial marriage. Ellen Key, *Love and Marriage* (New York: E. P. Putnam and Sons, 1911) is a more radical dissertation, stating that the ideal union of people is a completely free union of a man and a woman who are in love. The distinction between these views and those presented in this chapter should be clear.

6. Burgess and Wallin, *op. cit.,* pp. 381-82. Only one couple in this

requisite for sexual intercourse. This standard emphasizes affection. It states that without affection—and not only some affection but strong affection or love—sexual intercourse is incomplete and usually unacceptable. The intimacy of sexual activity varies according to the amount of affection involved, and is not determined solely by one's desire for a particular sexual act.

a) Relation to Permissiveness without Affection. As between any two related standards, there is an area that is difficult to identify. Does one reject all sexual intercourse, other than that which includes strong affection, in order to be classified as an adherent of permissiveness with affection? The answer depends upon which subgroup one belongs to. Some adherents accept intercourse, at times, without affection being present. These people feel that body-centered coitus should be viewed as acceptable but of very small value in comparison with person-centered coitus. They believe in the acceptance of body-centered sexual behavior but only rarely and under special circumstances. To practice such sexual behavior frequently would leave one less time to devote to developing stable, affectionate relations; it would mean sacrificing a greater good for a lesser one.

This group of adherents feels that to rule out body-centered behavior altogether might encourage the very thing opposed, by making it forbidden fruit. Such a stand might well lead to exaggerated importance being placed on body-centered coitus, which in turn might lead to many kinds of psychological guilt and compulsions. Thus, these people prefer to accept such coitus, but stress its relatively small value in comparison with person-centered coitus. Under special conditions, it is believed, there may be very strong reasons for body-centered behavior, e.g., my respondents often men-

---

study said they were engaging in intercourse to test their sexual compatibility.

tioned the instance of an unmarried person whose occupation requires constant travel. Such a person is hardly in any town long enough to establish a stable affectionate relationship, and his or her choice is between accepting body-centered coitus or remaining chaste for as long as the job lasts. Body-centered coitus would be acceptable to this subgroup under conditions such as this.[7]

It should be noted here that a great many of the adherents of permissiveness with affection will not accept body-centered coitus regardless of the relative frequency of such behavior. It is felt that sexual intercourse is too valuable an act to ever, under almost any circumstance, be had in such a casual manner. *Both* subtypes agree, however, that sexual behavior involving affection is most valuable; therefore, one should focus his sexual relations accordingly. Thus, even the most liberal adherent of permissiveness with affection can be distinguished from the adherent of permissiveness without affection. The adherent of permissiveness without affection minimizes any significant difference, or prefers body-centered coitus and will not focus on person-centered coitus. A few borderline cases may be difficult to discern, but most others will be fairly easy to classify.

b) Other Related Characteristics of This Standard. Other factors besides affection are of importance in this standard. As in permissiveness without affection, cautions against pregnancy and venereal disease are supposed to be taken, and each is supposed to have concern for the reputation and psychological state of the other. Affection alone is not considered justification for a relationship between a man and a woman, if, for example, the woman would have strong guilt feelings or the male refused to use contraception. Unless the couple feel that the total balance of consequences is favorable, the

---

7. For a defense of such "exceptions," see Ellis, *Sex Without Guilt,* chap. v.

action would not be considered acceptable, regardless of affection. Affection only helps to insure the occurrence of many "favorable" consequences. Although a necessary prerequisite, in and of itself, it is not considered sufficient.

American culture has always been somewhat tolerant of this standard. At least, for people in love, Americans regard coitus with much less disapproval than in other cases. This seems particularly true of the middle and upper classes. Everything else equal, condemnation varies with the amount of affection present. There is evidence to indicate that, in the eighteenth century, premarital intercourse among engaged couples in America was not too uncommon, and the general censor even in those puritanical days was not too harsh.[8] Many Americans feel that affection gives a relationship a better chance of yielding desirable consequences.[9] Furthermore, such a love relationship does not fully overthrow our older attitudes which held that all sex is bad—it only modifies this belief to read, "most sexual behavior is bad, but some is good."

It should be noted that most of the research evidence for permissiveness with affection comes from the college-educated

---

8. The eighteenth-century engaged couple was different from the engaged couple today, because they were much more likely to marry. Our engagement breakage rate is high—of the 1,000 couples in the Burgess and Wallin study, 15 per cent broke their engagements and many of these 1,000 couples had broken previous engagements. Also, the permissiveness-with-affection standard often allows coitus for people in stable affectionate relations even if they are not engaged.

It may be of interest here to note that some of the evidence for eighteenth-century premarital intercourse among engaged couples comes from Groton Church in Groton, Massachusetts, where 66 of 200 couples confessed to their minister that they committed fornication. Up until recently, some people were quite proud of their ancestors for having two distinctive initials, C. F., following their names in the Church records. This changed when people discovered that C.F. stood for Confessed Fornication! For a description of Puritan behavior based on church records see: Emil Oberholzer, Jr., *Delinquent Saints* (New York: Columbia University Press, 1956), chap. vii in particular.

9. See chaps. vii and viii for the evidence on this point.

segments of our culture. The college-educated group also is noted for its small number of permissiveness-without-affection adherents. Thus, it seems that permissiveness with affection is likely stronger at the middle- and/or upper-class levels, while permissiveness without affection is stronger in other parts of our society. Such education levels, at least among males, seem much more strongly predictive of sexual behavior and attitudes than other factors such as religion.[10]

Person-centered intercourse is entered into because it adds meaning to an existant relationship, and the affectionate bonds between the couple seem to demand such a sexual union. Such people are concerned with each other in a personal-individual sense that is usually not part of the other permissive standards. Of course, they also feel strong physical attraction to one another which forms the initial motivation for sexual intercourse. The physical factor, however, is not overly dominant; if it were, there would be no reason to restrict coitus to stable affectionate relations.[11]

Some adherents require that an affair be at least aimed at marriage, while others only require it to be a stable, affectionate relationship. In many cases, regardless of intent, the kind of love or the strength of feelings may not be sufficient for a marriage. In other cases, the two people, for financial,

---

10. Kinsey, *Human Male,* chap. x. College males had much less coitus with prostitutes and proportionately more with companions. Education and occupation levels in this study were the best predictors of sexual behavior. A college-educated Catholic, Protestant, or Jew would be quite different from a grade-school-educated Catholic, Protestant, or Jew. It is an important task of future researchers to spell out what cultural factors go along with educational and occupational levels and make them so important as predictors of behavior. It should be clear that in females Kinsey found religion was a better predictor than class. The upper class may be more conservative because of the greater possible economic loss and gain involved in marriage. This, however, may be modified by other factors such as better contraceptive knowledge.

11. Burgess and Wallin, *op. cit.,* chaps. xi and xii. These chapters contain the views of the engaged couples having coitus.

age, occupational, esthetic, religious, or other reasons may prefer to remain single. Frequently, it is felt to be better that a particular affair does not end in marriage. It is believed, however, by almost all adherents, that these affectionate relations are good preparation for stable affectionate living in marriage.[12]

TWO SUBTYPES:
LOVE AND STRONG AFFECTION

This standard may be divided into two main subtypes: (1) love—adhered to by those who require love and/or engagement as the affectionate prerequisite for intercourse; (2) strong affection—adhered to by those who accept strong affection as the prerequisite. In terms of subjective feelings, these two types may be very close and may, in some cases, even overlap. In most all cases, however, love will be a more intense feeling than strong affection. A category for medium or weak affection is not included since such degrees of affection characterize relations that are closer to the permissiveness-without-affection standard.

I will very shortly define in detail what is meant by the terms "love" and "strong affection." For now I am using these terms to refer to stable and well-founded emotional feelings. Persons who, because of youth or lack of emotional maturity, cannot experience these feelings should not, according to this standard, indulge in sexual intercourse. Feelings, such as it was "love at first sight" and "we just met but I know he's wonderful," are not generally accepted bases for a

---

12. A book which expresses the type of sexual relation often involved in this standard is Walter Benton, *This Is My Beloved* (New York: Alfred Knopf, 1945). The over-all "tone" of some of these relations can be obtained from this book.

sexual affair under the permissiveness-with-affection standard.

The adherent of the strong-affection subtype is most likely to accept occasional acts of body-centered coitus and place less stress on the need for premarital affairs to be marriage oriented. The adherent of the love subtype is most often opposed to all body-centered coitus and desires person-centered coitus to be aimed at marriage. In my interviews, most of the love subtype adherents were females, and most of the strong-affection adherents were males.

These findings fit in with our cultural background. We expect women to be more strict in their prerequisites for coitus, since they are brought up to be more abstinent than men.[12a] Furthermore, body-centered coitus is in direct opposition to our older Christian and Puritan views of sex, and it lacks any saving grace such as the presence of love; it is to be expected that such coitus will be most strongly condemned. Thus the permissiveness-with-affection standard, to the extent that it rules out body-centered coitus, is descendent from our past culture and is not really as radical as one might at first think.

Many strong-affection adherents argue that, according to their definition, strong affection is very close to love—labeling one state of feeling "love" implies a sizable difference. They believe that, even though it may be good to require love so as to further demonstrate the value of the sexual relationship, such a requirement may encounter difficulty. First, they contend that people rarely fall in love in a fully mature way. This means that, for example, in the ten years one is dating, he or she will fall in love perhaps two or three times. Such love affairs might last on the average of a year each. This still leaves over seven of the ten years of courtship during

----

12a. Ehrmann, *Premarital Dating Behavior*, p. 269 and chap. v. One of Ehrmann's major findings is the very high association between love and sexual behavior in the female and less so in the male.

which one will not be in love, and, therefore, no sexual intercourse can take place.

These adherents believe such abstinence would be difficult
for many people. Men in our culture, because of their upbringing, would find restricting their sexual behavior to love
quite difficult. Such a strict situation might encourage many
people to deceive themselves about the intensity and maturity
of their feelings, so as to justify coitus. Needless to say, the love
subtype rejects this reasoning and states that premarital
coitus is too important to be had without love, regardless of
these reasons.

THE WHEEL THEORY OF LOVE

I do not want to remove any of the awe and respect and
great value we hold for love—I do want to remove some of
the aura of mystery about this concept. Since love is of such
intimate relation to sexual behavior in our culture and is particularly relevant to permissiveness with affection, it is most
important that an objective description be given.[13]

There are a multitude of forms of love—there is love for
one's parents, for one's God, for one's country, for one's
brothers and sisters, for one's friends, and for one's marriage
partner. All of these cases are instances of love, but the love
object differs sharply. Every culture defines fairly clearly how,
and if, one should love these different love objects. In some
cultures, the love of a child for a parent must be non-demon-
strative and filled with respect; in our own culture, such love
is often supposed to be expressed in a demonstrative fashion

---

13. The following view of love can be found in somewhat more
elaborate and documented form in Ira L. Reiss, "Toward a Sociology of the
Heterosexual Love Relationship," *Marriage and Family Living*, XXII (May,
1960), 139-45.

and mixed with companionship. Love of God is shown in some cultures by prostrating one's body on the ground, in other cultures by looking up towards the sky. In some cultures, all these kinds of love are encouraged; in others, they are discouraged. Love seems to be a universal fact—an essential part of man's existence, but the exact nature of expressing it seems to vary considerably. I will focus on one type of love in our culture—heterosexual love—and try to reveal the processes involved in its development.

In our own society, two people usually meet at a party, a dance, in school, or in any other informal fashion and are ready to try to communicate freely with each other. They may talk to each other about inconsequentials and feel ill at ease, or they may feel very much at ease and somehow be able to discuss fairly personal topics quite soon. The key to the development of love lies in this communication process. With some people, we feel at ease and desirous of communicating; with others, we watch the clock until the evening ends. What are the characteristics which enable some people to put others at ease?

The process that goes on when two people communicate freely has variously been termed "role-taking," *Verstehen*, empathy, mutual understanding, or rapport.[14] Let us call it rapport. People vary greatly in the ability for rapport that they possess. When we talk to each other, we constantly try to put ourselves in the other person's shoes so as to understand him. We consciously or unconsciously ask ourselves what the other person is thinking and feeling and then react to this thought with pride, shame, joy, sadness, anger, or indifference, depending on what we believe the other person's feelings and thoughts to be. In short, we try to gain rapport, to understand the people we meet. Of course, when we act

---

14. For a more technical description of role-taking and other phases of human interaction, see Mead, *Mind, Self and Society*.

in anger or on impulse, we do not seek nor achieve such rapport.

Now, two people whose emotional make-up is such that they can understand each other's thoughts and feelings more easily than usual will often be at ease and relaxed with each other. Part of this reaction may be simply a matter of similar cultural backgrounds which help produce similar emotional needs and thus mutual understanding. But often the cultural backgrounds can be quite different, if they have produced two individuals who, although different, have complementary emotional make-ups.[15] Some of the initial attraction may be purely physical, but beyond this, there must be other bases for rapport if the relation is to last.

This occurrence of rapport often puts us at ease and leads to an even more vital event in the development of love, i.e., soul-baring or revelation. "Soul-baring" means sharing with a person one's wishes, fears, hopes, plans, problems, and so forth. Such confidences are most likely to develop with two people who are able to achieve that feeling of ease and naturalness which accompanies increasing rapport. Here too, culture enters in to define how much and what types of revelations are proper.

This sort of self-revelation is vital to the love process, for it is through it that mutual dependencies develop. As two people continue to confide in one another and engage in shared activity such as dancing, conversation, and sexual

15. The entire question of whether homogamy (similar background) or complementary needs leads to love will not be dealt with here. The most recent defense of the complementary need position is Robert Winch, *Mate Selection* (New York: Harper and Brothers, 1958). The evidence of some degree of homogamy is universally accepted, as is the evidence for some amount of complementariness. The dispute revolves about which of these two factors is more important in mate choice. For an explanation of homogamy, see Burgess and Wallin, *op. cit.,* and Ernest Burgess and Harvey Locke, *The Family* (New York: American Book Company, 1953). For a comment on this dispute see: Reiss, "Toward a Sociology of the Heterosexual Love Relationship."

behavior, they develop what may be called an interdependent habit system, i.e., one person's habits become dependent
upon another person's habits for completion. This accounts
for that feeling of loneliness and frustration when habitual
expectations are not fulfilled. It explains why one feels strange
when he enters a favorite dating spot with someone new.
The old interdependent habits or dependencies are the explanation.

A fourth process accompanies this growth of mutual dependencies. It is the fulfillment of personality needs via this
development of dependencies, revelations, and rapport. All
of us have personality needs such as affection, reassurance,
and companionship. Such deep relationships help fulfill these
needs.[16]

This brings us full circle to the emotional compatibility
which led in the first place to the initial rapport. It is because of our various personality needs that certain people
who can fulfill these needs blend with us emotionally and put
us at ease. These needs are related closely to our cultural
background, for it is out of our social experience that our
personality and its particular needs develop.[17] The circular
processes of rapport-revelation-dependence-need fulfillment
are continuous.

So far all that has been said is pretty much universal.
It takes place in every culture in the world. It is the description of a close primary relation, and is a typical se-

16. This approach to interpersonal relations is in line with recent de-
velopments. See William J. Goode, "The Theoretical Importance of Love,"
American Sociological Review, XXIV (February, 1959), 38-47; see also
Anselm Strauss, "Personality Needs and Marital Choice," *Social Forces,*
XXV (March, 1947), 332-35.

17. The relation of personality needs to cultural background was
clearly seen in the study on college students which I mentioned in chap.
iv, e.g., the girls' need for "someone to look up to" seems to be easily
derived from our culture's definition of what the proper male-female roles
are. More careful analysis can distinguish various sub-cultures by the type
of personality needs they create.

quence of events for the Fiji Islander or the New Yorker. This sequence of events seems an inevitable result of the universal make-up of human beings and human societies. Man seems to require nourishment from such primary relations in order to feel secure and to be socialized. The conditions under which societies encourage or discourage such close relationships vary tremendously. Our own society stresses these close relationships between a single boy and girl, when a certain culturally defined pitch or intensity is reached. Thus, love in our culture may be defined as the intense emotional feeling, which de-

The Wheel Process
In the Development of Intimate Relations

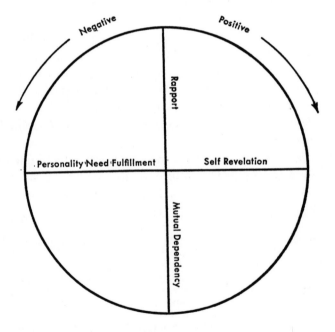

Figure 1.

velops via the above processes, involved in close heterosexual primary relations.

This conception of the development of love I will call the "Wheel Theory" because all the aspects are interdependent like the spokes of a wheel. All the processes must keep occurring if the "wheel" is to keep turning. In a real sense, all of these processes are going on at the same time, and they all reinforce one another. Should anger or a new attraction remove one's desire to feel rapport, then the "wheel" ceases to rotate and may start to "unwind" in the opposite direction.

A visual representation of this theory concerning the development of love is presented in Figure 1.

There are fashions and fads in the field of love which tell how intense the "wheel processes" must become before they can be labeled love. As time and experience pass, our definitions are altered accordingly, but basically our standards are shared with other Americans. Some people set standards so high that they never experience a relationship which fits their definition of love. Others set their standards so low that they are always falling in and out of love. The vast majority fall in between these extremes.

The sexual element plays an important role in the love process. It is often the initial stimulus which creates the interest. In our frustrated and inhibited culture, it is a key area of need-fulfillment and revelation.[18] Sexual compatibility can be a strong and significant part of self-revelation, adding to

---

18. It is proper to call our culture "sexually frustrated" even though there is a great deal of sexual behavior occurring. By making premarital coitus forbidden, via our formal norm of abstinence, and sending men to seek this pleasurable forbidden fruit, it is very difficult for people to be sexually satisfied. If one is seeking forbidden pleasures, the accent on both the forbidden and pleasurable aspects makes it difficult to ever be more than temporarily satiated. Frustration is relative to the distance between what one desires and what one has. Therefore, even if a great deal of sexual pleasure is gained, if the forbidden and pleasure-seeking aspects make full satisfaction unlikely, frustration can still take place. It is believed this type of "well-fed" frustration is typical of many Americans.

the sharing and closeness of the couple, but it cannot, for long, support a relationship by itself. If other compatible factors are not present, the relationship will most often not last.[19]

Basically, our present-day love notions are derived from ancient conceptions of romantic love. It was ten centuries ago that western Europe learned to define a particular type of heterosexual relationship as love. As previously pointed out, many young Americans, especially college students, refuse to dress their love relationships only in romantic cloth. Love to these people today is a more rational and realistic thing. They reject the Hollywood version of love as something which makes one walk into doors, stop eating, etc.—something which "hits" one immediately.[20] There is a more "rational" definition which is popular among the permissiveness-with-affection adherents. There is more understanding as to how love feelings are generated. Many know that rapport, self-revelation, mutual dependencies, and personality needs are crucial to the growth and continued life of such a relationship, and they feel that such love relationships are of utmost importance. Despite their rationality, these people still recognize that love is basically an emotional experience, and they do have emotional attachments to some of the romantic love notions.[21]

When the word "love" is used as a subdivision of permissiveness with affection, it will be used as most adherents would use it—to refer to a "rational" love which may be defined as a love feeling developed through full use of the wheel processes of rapport, revelation, dependency, and fulfillment.[22]

---

19. Americans have for generations stressed the all-important nature of sexual behavior. Recent evidence suggests that perhaps our "tease" type culture has exaggerated the importance of sexual relations. See Burgess and Wallin, *op. cit.*, chap. xx. This evidence will be discussed in detail in the next few chapters.

20. For a study of the romantic-love notions in America today, see Ellis, *The American Sexual Tragedy*, chap. v.

21. Burgess and Wallin, *op. cit.*, p. 170 and chap. v *passim*.

22. Burgess and Wallin's conception of the development of love, al-

This kind of love should go through this developmental process of rather constant interaction for at least a month or more, and it should involve considerable understanding and sharing of many different experiences, sexual attraction being only one of them.[23] The important aspect of this love is not whether it will lead to marriage but whether it is a sound basis for a relatively stable and affectionate relationship. Some rational loves are strong enough for marriage; some are not. Other, nonrational, types of love, such as romantic love or love in which the sexual aspect is emphasized, can also be fit to the Wheel Theory. I am not ruling them out; rather, I am stating that rational love is the only type acceptable to the permissiveness-with-affection adherents. These other kinds of love do not involve as full a usage of all the wheel processes, i.e., romantic love often occurs quickly with but a few "turns" of the wheel; sexual love involves mainly a sexual level of rapport, rather than the many levels involved in rational love.

Strong affection is also developed through the wheel processes, but it does not become intense enough to meet the cultural and individual definition of love. In every other way this feeling would resemble what has been called here rational love, since it also requires many weeks of becoming acquainted under many different conditions, before the feeling can be verified. Thus, these two terms refer to feelings that are neither identical nor too far apart. It is hoped that the Wheel Theory has made it easier to more specifically define these subtypes. Affectionate states which are not developed over many weeks and which do not involve numerous

---

though stated differently, is quite compatible with my Wheel Theory. See chap. vi where personality-need fulfillment is listed as the most crucial factor in love.

23. Further research is needed badly in this area. This definition of rational love seems to be about the same as most textbook's definition of "real" love. However, I am merely using the term to refer to one type of love relationship, whereas many textbooks ignore other love-types.

levels of rapport are not "strong affection," as this term is used by permissiveness-with-affection adherents.

Once the spokes of the wheel are known, one has something to check. By reflection, it can be seen just how much rapport, revelation, dependency, and need-fulfillment has taken place. A predominantly sexual relationship, even if the people feel they are in love, cannot, by this definition, be rational love. Such mistakes or deliberate misrepresentations cannot be made if the definition of rational love is abided by. Without a restricting definition such as this, many difficulties could arise over just what love or strong affection means. Some persons fear that men could easily take advantage of women by professing love. This is not true of the type of love defined by permissiveness-with-affection adherents.[23a] With this objective definition of rational love, many confusions about the concept of love can be avoided and the subtypes of this standard more clearly understood.

GENERAL INTEGRATION OF
PERMISSIVENESS WITH AFFECTION

Permissiveness with affection is an equalitarian standard, allowing premarital coitus for both men and women. It is not in conflict with our notion of justice, nor does it lead to any virginity paradoxes. It avoids creating associations with people not respected. In all of these ways, it is a less conflicting and more consistent standard than the double standard. It also has more cultural acceptance than permissiveness without affection, because it does retain affection as a dominant value. In other respects, however, it has

---

23a. There is evidence that lovers know each other for many weeks or months before coitus occurs. Bromley and Britten, *op. cit.*, p. 93; Burgess and Wallin, p. 161.

similar conflicts, e. g., it conflicts with the notion of female subordination since it offers equal sexual rights.

Another major area of American culture with which this standard conflicts is that of orthodox religion. Formally, orthodox religion supports a single standard of abstinence. In practice, religion tolerates the double standard, but it seems less willing to tolerate a single permissive standard. Related to religion is our traditional value of female virginity —this, too, is strongly opposed to permissiveness with affection.

Thus, this single standard also comes into conflict with parts of our culture. Nevertheless, this is one of the standards which has grown greatly in the last century. This is so mainly because the parts of our society in conflict with this standard are largely old and themselves changing. One should not, however, underestimate the power of some of these conflicting elements. Permissiveness with affection has been able to grow against such opposition only because the events of the last one hundred years were favorable to this development.[24] Furthermore, permissiveness with affection is still a "conservative" standard in its almost complete ruling-out of body-centered coitus. Such "conservatism" may well have aided in its growth among the middle and upper classes.

---

24. See chaps. ii and x for evidence here. For additional evidence on the popularity of this standard see Ehrmann, *Premarital Dating Behavior,* p. 179 and chap. v.

Permissive Standards and Negative-Value Consequences

NOW THAT WE HAVE DISCUSSED THE GENERAL characteristics of our three permissive standards, we turn to see in what ways these three standards are integrated with five "negative" consequences of premarital intercourse— "negative," that is, on the basis of general American cultural evaluation. These five consequences are believed to be the major negative socio-cultural consequences of premarital intercourse. The existing literature usually does not examine all these consequences together—a more piecemeal approach is most often taken. An over-all examination will be undertaken here in order to more systematically show the degrees of integration of our three permissive standards with these five major consequences.[1]

There are many erroneous conceptions in this area; thus,

1. The consequences in this and the next chapter are similar to the list of pro and con arguments contained in Kinsey, *Human Female*, pp. 307-10. However, these consequences are examined here for descriptive and analytic purposes, not for argumentative purposes.

although full evidence is not always available, it is worthwhile to undertake an objective analysis of the relation of consequences and standards. One of the main reasons for distinguishing so carefully among these three permissive standards of premarital intercourse is that it is believed that the social consequences of these conflicting standards are quite different. One cannot speak of consequences of premarital intercourse *per se;* to be clear, one must speak of the particular consequences of a particular standard of premarital coitus. This is the basic hypothesis which this chapter shall examine.

PREGNANCY

One of the age-old reasons for restricting female sexual activity has been the risk of pregnancy. The negative value of this consequence is a relevant part of our culture and well worth examining to see the relation of our three permissive standards to it. For centuries in Western double-standard society, people have desired to avoid illegitimate offspring because of the disruption such events could cause. Mothers have continually taught their daughters about the dangers of pregnancy. Some cases of frigidity seem to be aggravated by this fear.[2] In most cases, however, the fear is not so extreme, but acts chiefly to create guilt feelings or as a deterrent to premarital intercourse.

First, it should be clear that pregnancy can take place only when the female egg comes in contact with the male sperm.[3] Assuming two people have reproductive systems

2. Lena Levine, M.D., and Mildred Gilman, *Frigidity* (New York: Planned Parenthood Federation of America, 1951). Fear of pregnancy is one of the important causes of frigidity discussed in this pamphlet.

3. A good source for the person who desires general understanding of pregnancy and contraception, plus the opportunity to follow through on most topics of interest with many valuable illustrations is Robert L.

capable of producting offspring, the crucial factor is to ascertain the time period when the female egg and male sperm have the best chance of combining. This depends greatly on when the egg will be available for fertilizaton. Most all doctors agree pregnancy can take place in only three or four days of a twenty-eight-day cycle.[4] Both the egg and sperm are believed to live about one or two days. Ovulation, or the formation and descent of the egg, usually occurs about the midpoint of the female's cycle. However, due to irregularity or other factors, one is never positive as to the exact time of ovulation. Nevertheless, the length of the fertile period at the outside, would be two days before ovulation and the day or two the egg may live.

Kinsey gathered information on 460,000 instances of sexual intercourse, both with and without contraception, and found that about 18 per cent of the females became pregnant and conception occurred once in every thousand times of coitus.[5] If contraceptive measures had been more widely used, this rate would assuredly have been much lower. College-educated girls had a significantly lower rate of pregnancy, due in large part to their greater usage of contraception.[6]

Dickinson, M.D., *Atlas of Human Sex Anatomy* (Baltimore: Williams and Wilkins Company, 1949). See his *Techniques of Conception Control* which is also useful in informing one about pregnancy and its prevention. Dr. Dickinson was a world-famous gynecologist. He died at the age of 90 in 1950. He was a former president of the American Gynecological Society. The most recent source of information on pregnancy, birth, and abortion is the third volume from the Institute for Sex Research at Indiana University: Gebhard, *op. cit.* Gebhard's study uses the interview data which the other Kinsey volumes also drew upon.

4. For a brief account of these processes, see Becker and Hill, *op. cit.,* chap. x, "Taking Physical Factors into Account," by Edgar S. Gordon, M.D., pp. 305-40. See also Berg and Street, *op. cit.,* chap. xiv, "Theory of the Safe Days"; also Dickinson, *Techniques of Conception Control,* pp. 37-40. For more detailed information on fertility and sterility, see John Rock, M.D. and David Loth, M.D., *Voluntary Parenthood* (New York: Random House, 1949).

5. Kinsey, *Human Female,* p. 327. See also Gebhard, *op. cit.,* p. 39; chap. iii contains a breakdown of pregnancy rates for single women.

6. Gebhard, *op. cit.,* pp. 45-47.

What is the danger if contraception is used? The goal of contraceptive devices is to prevent the male sperm from meeting the female egg. Two of the most effective ways are the diaphragm-jelly or condom. Here is what Dr. Robert L. Dickinson has to say on their effectiveness: "The condom has in all studies demonstrated protection as efficient as any method, including diaphragm and jelly and, skillfully used, it *furnishes security*."[7] In actual clinical tests, such contraceptive measures have prevented about 95 per cent of the possible pregnancies. Many more pregnancies could have been prevented if these measures were properly used.

For pregnancy to occur, the sexual act must take place during the few days of feminine fertility, the condom must usually tear at or near the point of ejaculation, and/or remedial measures must be ignored or ineffective. The likelihood of all these consequences occurring together is extremely small. Most pregnancies seem to occur because contraceptive measures are not used or are used improperly. Carelessness, desire for a change, or over-confidence are factors conducive to pregnancy. As Dr. Dickinson states: "Actual reports show

7. Dickinson, *Techniques of Conception Control*, p. 24. An excellent source for a historical account of the development of contraception is Norman E. Himes, *Medical History of Contraception* (Baltimore: Williams and Wilkins Co., 1936). Himes covers thoroughly the famous handbill of Francis Place, in 1823, wherein Place recommended using the douche and a sponge on the cervix to control the rising birth rate of England. Attempts to suppress this and other contraceptive information only led to more publicity and interest. By 1880, after the famous Bradlaugh-Besant trial, most industrial countries began to use contraception to control their population, e.g., England's birth rate was cut in half between 1876-1936. See Warren S. Thompson, *Population Problems* (New York: McGraw-Hill Book Co., 1953), p. 162. The diaphragm and rubber condom came into use about the same time this birth-control movement took hold. Other interesting literature on this topic can be obtained from the Planned Parenthood Federation, 501 Madison Avenue, New York City. Probably the most remarkable usage of birth control is found in Japan, where the birth rate was cut in half in the ten years from 1947 to 1957! See *Statistical Bulletin, Metropolitan Life Insurance Company,* XL (September, 1959), 6.

that almost all unwanted pregnancies result from some omission of some detail or technique."[8]

There is now in process of perfection a pill contraceptive. In September, 1951, Dr. James B. Conant, then President of Harvard University, predicted such a pill would be perfected within ten years. His prediction seems to have almost come true. In 1957, oral contraceptives' research reported remarkable successes. The pill contraceptive, though far from perfected, is a reality.[9] The entire process of fertilization is a delicate one; many chemical reactions must take place and many other events must occur for an egg to become fertilized. It is in these delicate areas that a pill can throw off the balance and prevent pregnancy.

Some of the American Indians in the Southwest may have developed one of the first oral contraceptives. For centuries, the Shoshoni Indans have made a tea of the leaves of the desert plant, "lithosperum ruderale." This tea is used to prevent pregnancy. Recent tests on animals demonstrate this "tea" is an effective preventive of pregnancy. The ancient Hebrews developed the contraceptive methods which Francis Place recommended in the nineteenth century—perhaps the ancient Indians will be our source for the twentieth century's pill contraceptive. With this contraceptive pill, the chances of pregnancy are practically reduced to zero. The dangers of

---

8. *Ibid.,* p. 6.

9. A popular account of birth control by pills appeared in the October 7, 1952, issue of *Look Magazine.* A scientific account can be found in Paul S. Henshaw, "Physiologic Control of Fertility," *Science,* CXVII (May 29, 1953), 572-82. The more recent statements come from Dr. Rock, Dr. Garcia, and Dr. Pincus, of the Worcester Foundation for Experimental Biology, and from Dr. A. Q. Maisel's work in Puerto Rico. See A. Q. Maisel, M.D., "New Hope for Childless Women," *Ladies' Home Journal,* August, 1957, and Gregory Pincus, M.D., C. R. Garcia, M.D., and J. Rock, M.D., "Effects of Three 19-nor Steroids on Human Ovulation and Menstruation," *American Journal of Obstetrics and Gynecology,* LXXV (January, 1958), 82-97.

pregnancy seem more and more a thing of the past as man gains control over this phase of life.

Why it occurs. I think it can fairly be said that any two people who desire to avoid pregnancy and are willing to use the best existent methods can almost always succeed. Thus, theoretically, it may be said that there is little reason for pregnancy to occur under any of the standards which have been discussed. However, tens of thousands of women become pregnant out of wedlock each year.[9a] Let us now examine how the three permissive standards are related to, and help explain, these pregnancy rates.

I shall begin with the orthodox double standard. Were it not for fear of venereal disease, this standard might entail a great deal more pregnancy. Many of my double-standard male respondents stated they used condoms solely to protect themselves from venereal diseases they feared their female partners may have had. Orthodox double-standard males have no particular concern for their sexual partners. Such men switch partners quite frequently and probably feel they can act as they like and that it is the "bad" girl's responsibility to protect herself from pregnancy. Some of these double-standard males know that the law states that marriage is a voluntary contract, and thus no man can be legally forced to marry a woman for any reason whatsoever. Furthermore, the law holds that if paternity is proved, which is not always easy, the man need but pay for the support of the child. The exact amount of money and time of payment varies. In some states, the total minimum over the years is a little more than

---

9a. In 1957, there were 201,700 reported births out of wedlock. Since most premarital pregnancies end in abortion and many such births are not reported, this figure only gives one a vague idea of the number of premarital pregnancies. Almost two-thirds of the 201,700 births were to nonwhites. Such groups abort less often and may therefore have these higher rates. See mimeographed publication of U. S. Dept. of Health, Education and Welfare, May 1, 1959 and Gebhard, *op. cit.,* chaps. iii and vi.

$80.00; in other states it goes as high as $8,000. The minimum range would be between $1.00 and $40.00 per month for the care of the baby—a rather meager allowance but an expected one in a double-standard society.[10]

It seems that many of the females who indulge in sexual activity with orthodox double-standard males would most likely be permissiveness-without-affection adherents. An abstinent believer or a permissiveness-with-affection female may be involved, but these women would not be as likely to indulge in the type of casual sex affair which double-standard males desire. The permissiveness-without-affection females usually shift partners quite frequently, thus increasing their chances of running into a double-standard male who is careless and inconsiderate. Two factors, then, indicate that the double standard may lead to pregnancy: the lack of affection and concern between the sexual partners and the rapid change of partners.[11]

The situation in the permissiveness-without-affection standard is more difficult to ascertain. There is the same lack of affection and rapid change of partners. In actuality, however, it may yield different results. It is a more extreme social standard; it is less accepted and thus is more likely to attract radical groups. The over-all rate, however, may actually be less because of the effect of sophisticated adherents. These people seem to be quite rational about their sexual behavior, and because pleasure means so much to them, they want to avoid any possible pain such as pregnancy might entail. Furthermore, since sexual intercourse is accepted for

10. Summary tables on the laws concerning sexual behavior in each state can be found in Robert V. Sherwin, *Sex and the Statutory Law* (New York: Oceana Press, 1949). It is interesting to note that of the 48 states examined, 14 states do not classify fornication as a crime, and 5 do not classify adultery as a crime. In several other states the fines for such offense are minor, e.g., ten or twenty dollars.

11. See Kinsey, *Human Male,* pp. 561-62 and Kinsey, *Human Female,* p. 332, for support of this contention.

both men and women, there is respect for each other; thus they may not be as likely to take chances which may lead to pregnancy. However, there is the possibility of higher rates in the permissiveness-without-affection standard due to a lesser stigma on premarital pregnancy.[12] Only future research can test whether this is the case.

Couples who accept the single standard of permissiveness with affection would differ considerably from the couples in these other two standards. Since such people have strong affection or love for each other, changing partners would not be likely. There is much concern about the well-being of one another; each is unlikely to consciously bring harm to the other. Probably many precautions against pregnancy would be taken. Nevertheless, here, as in the other standards, there seem to be reasons and evidence to expect pregnancy to occur. Two people who are engaged in a long sexual relationship may, after a while, desire something new. They may become too confident of their ability to avoid pregnancy, or they may be engaged and feel they will be married soon. The security of the relationship may fool them into taking extra chances. Thus pregnancies do occur among this group of people also—although perhaps not as frequently as in the other two standards.[13]

---

12. This pregnancy rate, of course, applies only when one is speaking of two permissiveness-without-affection people engaging in coitus together. Pregnancy rates would possibly go up, as previously noted, if a permissiveness-without-affection female engaged in intercourse with a double-standard male.

13. There is some evidence from Kinsey and Gebhard to support this view. Gebhard states lower pregnancy rates for college girls and more acceptance of person-centered coitus by the college group. This, of course, is not proof of my contention, but is rather merely suggestive. See Gebhard, *op. cit.*, pp. 45-48; Kinsey, *Human Male*, pp. 561-62 and Kinsey, *Human Female*, p. 332. Also, Gebhard reports 89 per cent of white premarital pregnancies ended in abortion. This may be evidence that most pregnancies do not come from permissiveness with affection—those relations often lead to marriage rather than abortion.

Additional research is needed in this area to fill out our knowledge of how pregnancy varies by these three standards. For example, more information is needed on abortion and on the psychological reaction to pregnancy. One would expect the psychological strain and abortion rate to be least in the permissiveness-with-affection relationship since there is an affectionate bond and a possibility of marriage. However, one cannot be certain.[14]

VENEREAL DISEASE

This is an area heavily populated with "old wives' tales" inherited from our distant past. Just as we still frighten our women with tales about the dangers of pregnancy, so do we frighten them and our men with equally horrifying stories concerning the effects of venereal disease. The case is very similar to that of pregnancy, because in both instances, previous to the development of modern contraception and

---

14. Some women have several illegitimate offspring and do not seem to express regret. See Maud Morlock and Hilary Campbell, "Maternity Homes for Unwed Mothers" (Children's Bureau Publications, No. 309, 1946); Ruth Reed, *The Illegitimate Family in New York City* (New York: Columbia University Press, 1934). Reed found 15 per cent of her sample had previous illegitimate offspring. Gebhard, *op. cit.,* p. 40, found 19 per cent had previous illegitimate children. Kinsey, *Human Female,* p. 318, reports numerous women lacking regret over pregnancy. An excellent bibliography can be found in: U. S. Department of Health, Education and Welfare, *Selected References on Services for Unmarried Mothers* (U. S. Dept. of Health, Education and Welfare, 1959).

In regard to abortion, all we know now is that most illegal abortions are performed on married, not single, women and that the total number is up in the hundreds of thousands per year. See: Mary S. Calderone, M.D. (ed.), *Abortion in the United States* (New York: Harpers, 1958), p. 180, who estimates between 200,000 and 1,200,000 abortions per year. See also H. C. Taylor, Jr., M.D. (ed.), *The Abortion Problem* (Baltimore: Williams and Wilkins Company, 1944). Taylor estimates that up to 90 per cent of abortions are performed on married women. There is also evidence that Negro women have more premarital pregnancies but proportionately less abortion than white women, thus indicating a lesser stigma on such pregnancy. See Gebhard, *op. cit.,* pp. 155-62.

modern drugs, many of the warnings about pregnancy and venereal diseases were much more valid. Venereal disease could lead to death, and in many cases it did. If syphilis goes undetected for about ten or fifteen years, it will often attack one of the vital organs, e.g., the brain, the kidneys or the heart. Any of these organs can lead to death if the disease spreads far enough. In many cases in the not-too-distant past, even if the disease was detected by the chancre or the rash which usually occurs within a few months of contraction, there was little that could be done. Syphilis was most deceptive, for the symptoms would disappear in a few months, and the unsuspecting victim would think he was cured, only to be destroyed years later when the germs attacked one of his vital organs. Gonorrhea was dangerous also, for it could lead to sterility and at times could also lead to a form of crippling if left unchecked.

By the turn of the century, some scientific cures for syphilis were devised. In 1907, Wassermann devised a blood test to detect syphilis. This was just two years after the syphilis germ or spirochete was identified under the microscope by two German scientists, Schaudinn and Hoffmann. Then, in 1910, Ehrlich and Hata developed an arsenic compound, salvarsan, that could cure syphilis. Later on, arsenic began to be combined with bismuth and mercury, but even then, it took eighteen months of painful treatment to cure most cases and damaging side effects were common. Progress in containing this disease was hampered by the general "hush-hush" attitude people took towards it. In the 1930's, when Surgeon General Thomas Parran of the U.S. Public Health Service wanted to broadcast a discussion of syphilis, one of our major networks cancelled his broadcast![14a]

14a. Harvey Locke, "Changing Attitudes Toward Venereal Diseases," *American Sociological Review*, IV (December, 1939), 836-43. This article is a good historical review.

In 1943, the final break-through occurred. Dr. John F. Mahoney of the U.S. Public Health Service, in Staten Island, New York, announced that he had effectively eliminated syphilis in about eight days of treatment with a new wonder drug called penicillin! There was new hope for the millions of people in America who had syphilis. Like so many of our "new" drugs, penicillin was used in the form of molds by non-literate societies ages ago.

The figures tell the story of vast reductions in third-stage syphilis, in death rates and in number of people afflicted. Although penicillin could not restore destroyed tissues, it could cure syphilis in almost any patient and in almost any stage![15] Here is what the Public Health Service has to say about the effectiveness of penicillin treatment in an extensive test study: ". . . 99% of the patients with primary syphilis and 98% of the patients with secondary syphilis were successfully treated with penicillin."[16] There still are, however, over 100,000 cases of syphilis reported to our health department every year. As of January 1, 1955, there were an estimated 1,921,000 persons in the United States who required treatment for syphilis.[17] So, although we have come a long way, we still have much to do if we are to fully control this disease.

How the Odds Run. The situation with venereal disease,

---

15. There are many lengthy accounts of this disease but few good brief ones. One of the best short essays on syphilis can be found in E. Barnouw and E. G. Clark, M.D., *Syphilis: The Invader* (Public Affairs Pamphlet No. 24A, 1955). See also *VD Fact Sheet* (U.S. Department of Health, Education, and Welfare), No. 12, December, 1955, p. 10. The rate of syphilis was cut from 447 per 100,000 in 1943 to 76 per 100,000 in 1955! A good reference list of literature on venereal disease can be found in, *Milestones in VD Control* (U.S. Department of Health, Education, and Welfare, 1959).

16. J. K. Shafer, ScD., L. J. Usilton, Sc.D., E. V. Price, *Long-Term Studies of Results of Penicillin Therapy in Early Syphilis,* Bulletin of World Health Organization, X (1954), 574.

17. *VD Fact Sheet,* p. 2.

then, appears to be similar to that of pregnancy. There are good methods of prevention and cure that make it possible for a person operating under any sexual standard to avoid such consequences. The consequences, however, do occur. Let us look now to see which standard seems most closely associated with venereal disease.

It would seem reasonable to expect the body-centered co-itus associated with double-standard behavior to be more likely to lead to venereal disease. In this case, since the male does not care about his sexual partner, he is unconcerned whether or not she contracts venereal disease. He may have become infected himself from one of his "bad" girls and thus feel justified in giving the germ to another of his "bad" girls. The male's chances of becoming infected are high, because of his frequent changing of partners—the more partners, the higher the odds are that one will pick a female who has venereal disease.[18] By not using a condom throughout the act of intercourse, a male may contract and transmit venereal disease. Of all the double-standard adherents, the female who accepts the transitional subtype seems to run the lowest risk of VD. However, even here, her double-standard lover may inadvertently transmit to her a disease picked up from his body-centered coitus.

Permissiveness without affection should also lead to a high risk of disease because of the constant change of part-ners. The orgiastic type runs an especially high risk of vene-real disease, but the sophisticated type probably would be

18. Available evidence indicates that about half of the approximately 400,000 annual VD cases are teenagers. The rate for this group in recent years has gone up. This age group is least likely to know proper precautions. In our culture, permissive teenagers are most likely to be promiscuous and adherents of the double standard or permissiveness without affection. See E. G. Clark, M.D., "A Warning to America," *This Week*, September 2, 1956. The evidence from Kinsey seems to be in agreement with my reason-ing. However, he reports only 2-3 per cent of his female sample contracted VD. See Kinsey, *Human Female*, p. 332.

better informed on such matters. Males accepting this standard do not think ill of the female for indulging and may not be as carefree as double-standard men in exposing her to venereal disease when they can avoid it. This may put the incidence of venereal disease somewhat lower in this group.

The adherents of permissiveness with affection, because of their feeling for each other, would be especially concerned to avoid infecting each other. Because they stay with one person for a long period of time, their over-all chance of contracting such disease seems much less than either of the two other standards.[19] All these relationships are, of course, only hypothetical and must be further tested and refined, but they do indicate that this consequence also varies considerably by the standards of the adherents.

SOCIAL CONDEMNATION

Probably one of the major reasons many young people hesitate to engage in sexual intercourse is the fear of being condemned by other people.[20] Our *formal* standard in America is abstinence; one would suppose that both men and women would fear social condemnation equally. But because our *informal* standard is the double standard, women are in general much more severely condemned than men.

The social condemnation which is directed mainly toward women varies a great deal according to the type of sexual

---

19. Kinsey found much higher rates of venereal disease and pregnancy for lower income groups. These groups seem to be much more double-standard and permissiveness-without-affection than college groups are. *Human Male,* pp. 561-62. This lends some further support to our reasoning.

20. Kinsey, *Human Female,* pp. 315-22. Between 20-44 per cent of the women in Kinsey's sample said that social condemnation was one of the factors restricting their sexual activity. Only 14-23 per cent of the men had similar fears.

act occurring. As a rule, the more permanent a relationship, the more a relationship involves deep affection, the weaker the social condemnation. Where the relationship is between a double-standard man and a girl he has just met, the girl is usually strongly condemned and the man is more or less tolerated. Many of these women would be permissiveness-without-affection believers. The very women who make it possible for a double standard to exist are thus condemned. Without "bad" girls, all orthodox double-standard men would be virginal.

Permissiveness without affection will, by definition, involve no social condemnation from its own believers. However, as we have shown, such a standard has never met with wiespread acceptance. The females who accept this ultra-liberal standard will most likely, therefore, be sharply condemned by the people who reject such a standard.

Finally, permissiveness with affection, which also involves no internal condemnaton, should involve much less condemnation of the female from society at large because of its permanency and its incorporation of affection.

There are additional reasons which tend to alter the likelihood of condemnation of certain behaviors. Before an act can be condemned, it must be discovered. Under permissiveness with affection, because the two people are extremely fond of each other, they will not deliberately tell others of their relationship so as to invite condemnation. According to Kinsey's study, the odds are extremely high against being discovered while copulating; thus, someone must always talk before social condemnation can occur.[21] Since this standard does not involve rapid change of sex partners, it entails less people who may tell others of the relationship.

On the other hand, in the typical orthodox or transitional

---

21. *Ibid.*, p. 326. Kinsey's data showed that only six out of every 100,000 copulations were discovered while in process.

double-standard relationships, since the male has no concern for the female, he may feel quite free to talk about her. In fact, most of my double-standard interviewees spent considerable time telling their friends the details of their sexual relationships. The more such relationships, the higher the male's prestige is within his own group. Many girls find their reputations ruined as a result of this bragging process. Thus the double standard may lead to condemnation of girls of other standards. Some men go so far as to lie about their sexual exploits, so as to build up their status in their friendship cliques. This fabrication may be taken as the truth, and a girl's reputation is marred. Boys often apply this "smear" to girls who "tease." It is their way of getting revenge. Sexual intercourse to these males, is often a way of proving to themselves that they are virile and desirous and also a way of bringing their female partners "down" to their level. There is a sadistic element in this kind of sexual intercourse. Perhaps this is so because our culture forbids sexual coitus; yet, in the movies, on the stage, in books and in many other ways, it teases and tempts. This sadistic relationship can be further seen in the use of old, Anglo-Saxon slang words for sexual intercourse which also mean hurting or cheating someone.

Even if the double-standard male did not so willingly circulate the news of his sexual behavior, such news would be difficult to keep entirely secret due to the promiscuity of this standard. The situation is altered for that *part* of the transitional relations which involve love, but this is only a minor part of this subtype.

The rapid change of partners also endangers the secrecy of the sexual relationship between people who accept permissiveness without affection. Some of these people may be defiant enough to deliberately reveal their relationships to other people. Those who want privacy would find it difficult, for so many people are involved that it is probable that one of them would reveal the relationship. In this and other standards, it should be kept in mind that if one is living in a neighborhood where his behavior is accepted, then condemnation from outside groups may not be as disruptive as when one is a deviant in his neighborhood.

a) What's My Line? What about the condemnation which occurs because the two people believe in different standards? This is certainly an important part of social condemnation today. In a society as complex as ours, it is inevitable that people who do not think alike will come in contact. One can be sure that men and women will date people who hold different sexual standards. Such mixing of standards can lead to many complications.

A single-standard girl desiring to keep her reputation must be certain her sexual partner is not double standard, for if he is, he may likely condemn her for indulging and tell others of her behavior. This is particularly true for the orthodox double-standard male. A single-standard female accepting permissiveness without affection would be running the risk of condemnation if she indulged with a male who accepted only permissiveness with affection. Thus, avoidance of condemnation most often requires indulgence with a partner who thinks alike about premarital sexual activity. The problem here is in discovering the other person's attitude regarding premarital coitus. When the fact that some people deliberately try to deceive others about their beliefs is taken into consideration, the magnitude of the possible confusion is clear.

Young people today often discuss sex in their conversations, and this may be one method of finding out attitudes. Many men, however, may profess to accept a single standard of permissiveness in order to convince a girl to engage in sexual activity. Such attempted deceptions are not infrequent. It is felt, however, that the American girl today is quite sophisticated—she is not often victimized by a "line" unless she wants to be. It is altogether possible that the American male becomes a victim of his own line, i.e., a female may act as though she believes a man who says "I love you" in order to make him think she would not have indulged unless she thought he loved her. As long as we are in a period of change, we shall experience these types of deception. If most people accepted one standard, there would be no need for so much deception, but without this, attempted deception is inevitable.

Since permissiveness with affection involves a relationship in which the "wheel processes" have been in action for a month or more before any sexual intimacies take place, this standard should enable one to be fairly sure of the other person's feelings. The other two standards do not necessarily involve such previous interaction between two people and thus have an over-all greater chance of developing a case of "mistaken standards."

Unlike permissiveness without affection, the person-centered behavior of permissiveness with affection is considered acceptable by all permissive individuals except an orthodox double-standard male. Accordingly, permissiveness with affection not only makes it more likely that the man and woman can detect each other's feelings about sex, but it further insures that, even if one should be mistaken, the chances of condemnation are smaller.

b) Religious Rejection. The relation of our religious institutions in America to our three permissive standards deserves some mention in this discussion of social condemnation. All of our major Protestant, Catholic, and Jewish groups condemn premarital copulation. Let it be clear, though, that premarital coitus is not adultery and thus is not part of the Ten Commandments of these religions. Adultery must involve unfaithfulness on the part of a married person and, as part of the Ten Commandments, it is usually viewed as more important than premarital coitus. Premarital coitus need not involve, and usually does not involve, a married person.

Our formal Judeo-Christian custom is abstinence by both sexes. It can be recalled that the early Christian attitude viewed sexual behavior as something sinful, something to be avoided. This was gradually modified to acceptance of sexual intercourse, but only in marriage. As stated earlier, the more fundamentalist religious groups today hold that even marital coitus should be solely for the purpose of procreation and that sexual intercourse for pleasure is sinful. The more liberal groups allow married couples the privilege of sexual indulgence for mutual enjoyment. But since no organized religious group in America permits coitus outside of marriage, all three of our permissive standards are at odds with our organized religions' formal code of abstinence. Religious beliefs do seem to affect our sexual standards and behavior. The more devout individuals are usually more conservative sexually. However, there are signs of a liberalization of religious attitudes regarding sex.[22]

The clash between religion and our permissive standards is not as harsh as one might at first think. Formally, Christian-

---

22. An interesting discussion of the liberalization of American ministers' attitudes on sex can be found in *Look Magazine,* November 25, 1958, "What Ministers Are Learning about Sex," by Dr. Gelolo McHugh and J. Robert Moskin, pp. 79-86. One should not underestimate the potency of religious beliefs. Kinsey found such beliefs to be very important in altering rates of premarital coitus. See *Human Female,* pp. 304-7. To illustrate, by age 30, about 60 per cent of the "inactive" Protestant women had premarital coitus, whereas by age 30, only about 30 per cent of the "devout" Protestant women had premarital coitus. Of course, for a full causal explanation, one would have to check further to see if religion was the cause of these changes or just correlated to these rates. Also, for men, religion, though important, was nowhere near as highly related as was educational and occupational class. A low-educated active Protestant male would still have more coitus than an inactive, highly educated Protestant male. For additional evidence of the effect of religious beliefs see: Ehrmann, *Premarital Dating Behavior,* p. 94; Burgess and Wallin, *op. cit.,* p. 339.

ity opposes all premarital intercourse, but in practice the condemnation of women is much stronger than that of men.
Abstinence for men has most often been paid only lip service.
Judaism, too, has always had a double-standard orientation,
although it formally forbids intercourse for both sexes. Look
around at your fellow Christians and Jews and see how many
fully accept a single standard of abstinence. Read carefully
the passages in the Bible and you will find further evidence
of the close place the double standard has in our religious
institution.[23]

When one examines permissiveness without affection, it
becomes apparent that such a standard is most poorly integrated with our religious institution. Such a standard is too
openly pleasure-seeking to fit with our religion. Despite our
more liberal attitudes toward sexual behavior, the pull of the
past is most clearly seen in the still strong negative feeling
toward body-centered coitus. We are still part Puritan.

Permissiveness with affection presents an anomalous situation. Here is a standard which stresses deep affection amongst
human beings—a standard which disapproves of promiscuous sexual behavior, a standard which incorporates our notions
of the value of love and monogamy, and one which treats
both men and women as equals. Is the double standard better
integrated with our religion than this standard? The double
standard stresses promiscuous affairs and treats people as a
means for satisfying one's desires; it violates our notions of
justice in its treatment of women; it opposes our norms of
love and monogamy by stressing body-centered coitus and
rapid changes of partners. Is this standard more compatible
with the Judeo-Christian religion than permissiveness with
affection? In fairness, one must say that the double standard

23. For support on this point see the following study of ministerial
students: Austin L. Porterfield and H. E. Salley, "Current Folkways of
Sexual Behavior," *American Journal of Sociology*, LII (November 1946),
209-16.

is much less compatible with many vital aspects of our organized religion. Then why is it more accepted by Church members?

There are many reasons why so many people find the double standard more acceptable, despite its incompatibility. For one thing, it has the strength of age and general acceptance behind it. As in business, there is nothing that succeeds like success—so in society, there is nothing that gains acceptance like acceptance. However, just as important is the fact that the double standard can be hushed up—it can be acknowledged by knowing glances and winks, but it need not be written in the formal religious code. The double standard can be accepted because it can be hidden and kept out of sight on Sunday mornings. This could never be the case for permissiveness with affection. This standard could not be hushed up or swept "under the carpet." It is directly opposed to the single standard of abstinence. To accept it would mean that the double-standard positions to which many people adhere today would have to be revealed and altered. We would formally and openly have to reject abstinence and the double standard and formally accept permissiveness with affection. Most people would rather keep their precarious position than reveal it. People are accustomed to such "evasions." Thus, our religions, although in many ways closer to permissiveness with affection than to the double standard, are still opposed to any change in this direction.[24]

GUILT FEELINGS

a) Society—The Magic Mirror. The popular and textbook literature on sexual behavior contains statements concerning

---

24. For an informative elaboration of religious views towards sexual behavior, with special reference to the Kinsey reports, see Seward Hiltner, *Sex, Ethics and the Kinsey Reports* (New York: Association Press, 1953).

the strength of guilt feelings and the terrible toll such psychological reactions take from our young people. Such broad statements about shrouds of disaster are more the echoes of nineteenth-century Victorianism than the sound of twentieth-century science. What must be discovered now is how Americans *do* feel about premarital intercourse. Do people who engage in such behavior suffer from guilt feelings? Basically, the question is, how do our permissive standards relate to this negative value of guilt feelings?

The first deducible point is that men as a group would probably suffer less from guilt feelings than women.[25] Since our culture is predominantly double standard, this should be the case. Guilt feelings are to a large extent the individual's reaction to social condemnation which he accepts. In short, one feels guilty because he is looking at himself through the "eyes" or attitudes of those people in our culture who would condemn him. As a rule, the more an act is socially condemned, the more people will feel guilty when performing it. This, of course, has exceptions—some people may not be concerned with the opinion of many other groups, and, therefore, may not look at themselves through these people's eyes; such people may have other reference groups through which to evaluate their own behavior. Innovators, deviants, and martyrs are people who do not judge themselves by the general opinions but refer their behavior to other standards.[26]

None of our three permissive standards seem likely to lead to excessive guilt feelings for their adherents. The double standard, however, may lead to some qualms, since it is often

25. Kinsey notes such a difference on p. 332 of *Human Female,* and Burgess and Wallin, *op. cit.,* p. 375, found the same sort of difference. Exact figures are quoted later in this chapter.

26. This entire question of reference groups is now of central concern in sociology. Of particular pertinence here would be the effects of both membership and non-membership reference groups on one's feelings. See Merton, *op. cit.,* chap. ix.

viewed by its adherents as an evasion of abstinence. Logically, no full believer in permissiveness with or without affection should experience guilt feelings; by definition, one must believe such action to be right before he is classified as a believer. Nevertheless, the fact that society reacts more strongly against permissiveness without affection means that it will be more difficult for people to accept such a standard fully without serious qualms—more difficult than it would be to accept permissiveness with affection which is not so strongly condemned. A person may indulge in coitus with his or her fiance or lover and may find that neither feels too guilty about such behavior. Such a reaction could in time alter the person's intellectual and emotional belief. In our society, this change to acceptance is probably more likely to occur in person-centered coitus.

    b) *Choose Your Mirror.* Research evidence indicates that most young people who engage in premarital coitus do not act strongly against their notions of right and wrong. This seems to support our above analysis. Kinsey found that of the thousands of women he interviewed who had engaged in premarital coitus, over two-thirds expressed no regret at all about their premarital sexual behavior and almost 90 per cent said they had no major regret. In the case of men, the lack of guilt feelings was even higher. Furthermore, Kinsey found that the greater the number of years one engaged in premarital coitus, the less regrets felt. Women who had at least some of their coitus with their fiances had the least regret.[27] In addition to this evidence, 84 per cent of the engaged women and 96 per cent of the engaged men in the Burgess and Wallin study did not express any guilt feelings about

---

27. Kinsey, *Human Female*, pp. 316-21; Kinsey, *Human Male*, p. 562. See Table 92, p. 345, *Human Female*. Eighty-one per cent of those having coitus only with fiance had no regret. Only 9 per cent of this group expressed "definite regret," whereas 28 per cent of the girls who had coitus "with other men but not with their fiances," expressed definite regret.

their sexual intercourse with each other.[28] All these findings seem to support the contention that the people least likely to be bothered by coitus are most likely to indulge (self-selection). It also supports the notion that the longer one engages in coitus, the more likely one's qualms are to disappear. Finally, it seems to indicate that the person-centered coitus which accompanies permissiveness with affection or the transitional subtype of the double standard are the easiest standards for women to accept without guilt feelings. In conclusion, these figures indicate that, for the above reasons, strong feelings of guilt may not be as widespread as some writers would have us believe.

There is no doubt that some people suffer quite serious consequences from guilt feelings. I do not wish to minimize this consequence. If one tries to alter his beliefs too rapidly, he may indeed suffer strong qualms. Strong abstinence believers are likely to suffer from very disturbing guilt feelings. Furthermore, I do not want to deny that there may be other psychological consequences not covered by the terms "regret" or "guilt."[29] A person, for example, may have felt quite despondent about engaging in premarital copulation but may feel that there is no point in regretting it. Another person may have suppressed all guilt feelings about premarital intercourse from consciousness. A girl may feel bothered by the necessity to hide her non-virginity from people who would disapprove. There is serious need for a detailed analysis of the personality consequences of premarital intercourse of all types.[30]

---

28. Burgess and Wallin, *op. cit.*, p. 375. These percentages are based on responses from 74 men and 69 women. Of course, some deliberate deception may be present. But it is believed that deception will account for but a part of these high percentages.

29. For elaboration of this, see Lester A. Kirkendall, "Premarital Sex Relations," *Pastoral Psychology*, VII (April, 1956), 46-53. Mr. Kirkendall is now studying two hundred college males and their sexual activities. Here, too, however, sexual standards are not being focused on.

30. It may be noted here that Kinsey's findings on religion also support

WEAKENING OF MARRIAGE

a) Tendency toward Adultery. It is believed by many that one major way in which premarital coitus weakens the marriage institution is by leading to extramarital coitus (adultery). Let us now see if we can ascertain how our three permissive standards relate to this consequence. It is known that a higher percentage of people who engage in premarital coitus seem to engage in extramarital coitus. In the Kinsey study, 29 per cent of the women who engaged in premarital coitus had also engaged in extramarital coitus; 13 per cent of the women who had entered marriage virginally had extramarital coitus.[31] It is not known whether all or one type of premarital coitus is so conducive to extramarital coitus, or whether none of these is causally related and other factors explain this connection. Kinsey found that by the age of forty, about one out of every four wives and one out of every two husbands in his sample had engaged in extramarital coitus.[32]

The evidence indicates that extramarital coitus occurs for a multitude of reasons, and the fact that one had experienced premarital intercourse, in and of itself, may not be the most significant of these reasons. Correlations must be carefully interpreted to be able to grasp their full causal implications.

---

the self-selection notion. As noted above, he found many more "devout" people refrained and many more "inactives" indulged. See *Human Female,* pp. 304-7.

31. *Human Female,* p. 427. Rates for males are also correlated with premarital experience, in that lower-educated males have more premarital and extramarital experience than higher-educated males. See *Human Male,* pp. 586-90. However, this relation holds only in early marriage. In later marriage, the college males have the highest rates of adultery. Kinsey believes that there is no causal relation here between pre- and extramarital coitus. Terman, *op. cit.,* p. 340, also found a correlation for husbands and for wives, although the relation between pre- and extramarital coitus was lower for the wives.

32. *Human Female,* p. 437.

Kinsey lists several reasons for adultery, such as desire for revenge to raise social status, to assert independence, and so forth.[33]

It may be that part of the reason people who have had premarital coitus also engage in extramarital coitus is that they are more liberal; when they fall out of love with their mates, they are more likely to commit adultery before obtaining a divorce. Thus, lack of conservatism may explain some of this behavior. One need not look for a full causal connection, by any means, between all premarital and extramarital coitus.

A person whose premarital standard is the double standard generally believes that men should be allowed greater sexual freedom; thus, this standard may be extended to apply to extramarital coitus also.[34] Some wives tolerate their husband's episodes, and some husbands engage in these episodes, believing that they are all right for men, although unforgivable for women.[35]

Women often find it difficult to understand how a man who loves his wife can engage in extramarital coitus. For a double-standard man, this is not difficult. For such a man, the trite saying "I love my wife, but oh you kid!" seems to have much meaning. These men separated sexual behavior and affection in their premarital coitus; it is therefore not difficult for them to engage in extramarital coitus purely for pleasure. Such a man could love his wife but engage in coitus

---

33. *Ibid.,* pp. 431-36. Burgess and Wallin, *op. cit.,* pp. 400-2. The conditions under which their respondents would accept adultery are listed here.

34. Paddy Chayefsky's 1957 movie, "The Bachelor Party," shows clearly how the double standard can lead to adultery. Some empirical evidence for this notion can be obtained from the excellent study: William F. Whyte, *Street Corner Society* (Chicago: University of Chicago Press, 1955).

35. *Human Female,* pp. 434-36. Males rated their wives' adultery as important in divorce twice as often as the women so rated the man's adultery. An almost identical finding was made by Burgess and Wallin, *op. cit.,* p. 399.

with another woman without lessening his feelings for his wife.[36]

Many double-standard males engage in sexual activity with "bad" girls while going with a "good" girl. They want to avoid intercourse with the "good" girl so they relieve themselves with the "bad" girl. Some girls tell their boyfriends or fiances to engage in this type of coitus in order to keep themselves chaste. Here are verbatim reports from some engaged couples:

> FIANCEE: We talk about sex frankly. I don't think it's straining him not to have intercourse. There are other methods of relief. There are other women. The only objection I have is that he might contract some sort of disease.
>
> FIANCE: She believes it's the prerogative of the girl not to have sexual intercourse until she is married. Although I agree with her, I would have intercourse if she wanted to. It hasn't been a strain because I go out and get what I want, and she knows it. She doesn't mind. Her attitude is that men have to have it.
>
> FIANCE: It was not only with her knowledge but permission. I was rather emotionally and physically wrought up, and we realized that intercourse was the only outlet. It was impossible for her, so with her permission I went to a prostitute.[37]

This sort of training may well be conducive to double-standard extramarital intercourse in later years. Orthodox double-standard men and women engaged to be married are in a real dilemma. If the man has intercourse with his fiancee, he may lose respect for her, and she may feel quite guilty; if they abstain with each other, the man may seek satisfaction else-

---

36. Many conflicting customs, such as the double standard and abstinence, are allowed to co-exist by virtue of the effects of other customs, i.e., other customs, such as adultery, act as compensatory customs and enable us to live with our contradictions. See paper by the author entitled: "Functional Narcotics: A Compensatory Mechanism for the Social System."

37. Burgess and Wallin, *op. cit.*, p. 386.

where and provide a basis for later infidelities. Once again the conflict generated by this standard evidences itself.

Finally, one may note that when the double-standard man engages in extramarital coitus, he may thereby disrupt his marriage, and his wife may look for another sexual partner in order to get revenge. Revenge was one of the important reasons that women gave to Kinsey for adultery. Thus the double standard may encourage both male and female to seek extramarital coitus.

Since permissiveness without affection, like the double standard, separates sexual behavior and affection, it fails to build up a self-control structure based on the higher worth of person-centered coitus. But this standard does avoid many of the above difficulties of the double standard. Adherents of this standard may believe that body-centered coitus and its attendant pleasures need not be given up because of marriage and, therefore, they may accept extramarital intercourse for both husband and wife. In its extreme form, this may come out as a "wife-swapping club."[38] Of course, this need not be the case. Such adherents could accept a code of marital fidelity for both husband and wife, thereby altering their older and freer premarital sexual standards.

There are many aspects of permissiveness with affection which work against adultery. This standard builds up a respect for a monogamous, meaningful heterosexual relation. It helps a person develop self-control and self-respect in the

38. For a novel which deals with a modern day "wife-swapping club" and its consequences, see Philip Wylie, *As They Reveled* (New York: Avon Publications, 1935). One of the major insights of this book is the ease with which individuals can accept adultery for themselves but not for their mates. Kinsey backs up Wylie on this point, for although only 14 per cent of the women and 18 per cent of the men thought their own adultery led to divorce, 27 per cent of the women and 51 per cent of the men felt the *other person's adultery* was a major factor in divorce. Wylie points out that such reactions may well be based on the added "unexpectancy" which adultery entails. Adultery involves a loss of personal element in a marriage and it accordingly involves less mutual dependency.

sexual sphere, due to its person-centered nature and its association of intercourse with qualities of affection. Theoretically, such sexual behavior should lead to better marital sexual adjustment; therefore, there should be less reason for one to desire extramarital coitus.[39] Nevertheless, by emphasizing love, this standard may make one feel that when love has gone out of a marriage, adultery is permissible, even if the divorce is not yet final.

In summary, I would hypothesize that although any of these permissive standards *may* lead to adultery, I would expect that permissiveness with affection would do this least often in a marriage where love was still involved. Finally, I would reiterate that there are many other reasons for adultery which must be examined to fully understand this behavior.

c) *The End of Marriage?* In a time of rapid change, there are always people who forecast the end of civilization and other major disasters as the inevitable result of rapid change. One very common assertion made in regard to premarital coitus is that, as our society accepts sexual permissiveness, it is, at the same time, destroying our marriage institution.[40] Why will people marry if they can obtain sexual intercourse outside of marriage?—so the reasoning goes.

This assertion assumes that people marry predominantly to satisfy their sexual appetites. This is a rather naïve view of marriage. If one only desires sexual intercourse, that can quite easily be obtained outside of marriage, as most young people today have proven by their own behavior. The Greeks gave full endorsement to the double standard and allowed their men to have premarital intercourse and extramarital

---

39. Some evidence on this comes from Sweden, where the liberal attitudes towards premarital coitus are coupled with very stern attitudes toward adultery. See Kalvesten, *op. cit.*, pp. 67-68.

40. For such a critical view, but one which is not documented, see Pitirim Sorokin, *The American Sex Revolution* (Boston: Porter Sargent Publishers, 1956).

intercourse, and still their marriage institution remained well intact. In our own country, most men have had the privilege of premarital coitus for several centuries, and yet they continue to marry. Many non-literate cultures allow extensive sexual freedom and continue their marital institution.

What occurred to marriage when premarital coitus increased so rapidly in this country? Did marriage decline— did people marry later or less frequently? No; in fact, just about the opposite situation occurred. In 1890, the proportion of the population, over the age of fifteen, which was married at any one time was about 55 per cent; by 1940, it had risen to over 60 per cent, and by 1955, to about 70 per cent.[41] Over 92 per cent of our population who were between the ages of 45 and 54 in 1955 had been or were married.

Since the turn of the century, there seems to have been a general trend toward earlier marriages rather than later marriages. This trend was accelerated after 1940, but shows definite signs of stopping at the present time. As of 1955, about 50 per cent of the men that do marry were married by the age of 23, and about 50 per cent of the women that do marry were married by the age of 20. This earlier marriage trend is largely responsible for the increases in the number of people married at one particular time. We marry on the average about three years earlier than we did in 1900. This information should make it clear that the vast increases in premarital coitus do not seem to have lessened the number of marriages nor encouraged later marriages.[42] If, in time, pre-

41. See *Statistical Bulletin of the Metropolitan Life Insurance Company,* XXXVII (May, 1956), 4-5—probably the best brief account of recent marriage statistics. Since the recession in 1957, the marriage rate has slightly declined. See *Statistical Bulletin of the Metropolitan Life Insurance Company,* XXXIX (May, 1958), 1-4. The most complete source of statistics on marriage and divorce can be found in one volume: Paul H. Jacobson, *American Marriage and Divorce* (New York: Rinehart and Company, 1959).

42. The age at marriage may have remained the same rather than

marital coitus were to encourage later marriages by removing some of the purely sexual impulsion, it might well increase marital adjustment. Such later marriages would be between more mature people who might have better chances for achieving marital success.[43]

Premarital intercourse may be related to marriage, in the sense that it weakens the "frustrated" sexual motive for marriage.[44] Thus, the only cases wherein premarital coitus could eliminate marriage would be in those instances where there were only sexual motives for marriage. The "reward" would be granted before the price was paid, and if this "reward" were the only thing desired, why should one pay the price of marriage after engaging in intercourse? This attitude, however, involves the type of relationship most Americans would want disrupted. Our social norms do not approve of marriages between people who are only sexually interested in each other or who are being rushed into marriage by their impatient desire for coitus.

Sexual intercourse before marriage does not destroy the major motives for marriage.[45] It is interesting to note that

fallen as most statisticians report. It all depends on the sources and statistical methods. For a defense of this position, see Thomas P. Monahan, "One Hundred Years of Marriage," *American Journal of Sociology,* LVI (May, 1951), 534-45. Other statistics are unquestioned.

43. Terman, *op. cit.,* p. 181. Terman did some investigation of the correlation between age at marriage and marital happiness. His results indicated a slight correlation showing more happiness for later ages at marriage. The correlation, however, was too small to be significant. The high divorce rates of teen-age marriages is relevant here. Burgess and Wallin, *op. cit.,* p. 521, summarize the findings on relating age of marriage to marital success. It seems that marriages of above average aged couples tend to be more successful.

44. For a position which emphasizes the power of sex, see Sylvanus M. Duvall, *Men, Women and Morals* (New York: Association Press, 1952). On p. 295, Duvall states his position that if premarital coitus is allowed at all, it will occur promiscuously. However, psychologists seem to disagree and hold that emotional enslavement to sex, alcohol, etc. is not a sign of what will happen to *all,* but rather a sign of the great emotional needs of *some* people.

45. The increase in the divorce rate in the last 60 years cannot be

very often the same people who fear premarital coitus will do away with marriage also state that they think permissiveness will encourage early marriage, by involving people with one another at early ages. They fail to see the conflict in these two views and use each whenever desired. People marry in our culture predominantly because they are in love. This love feeling is supposed to be a blending of personalities[46] and not just a union of bodies. Most people, not all, need other people to complete themselves. Marriage in our culture enables two people to help each other fulfill their potentialities. Perhaps the highest reward of love is the intimacy and the resultant self-knowledge which it affords. Marriage gives one a chance to reveal to another human being his innermost thoughts and feelings. It affords the opportunity of entering into such a mutually fulfilling relationship for life. It contains the added security of social approval and many other satisfying features, such as bearing and rearing children. The point here is that it is the incompleteness of the individual, and his desire for a secure, socially supported, permanent relationship with someone he or she loves, which still is the main motive for marriage in America. Marriage will surely exist in America whether or not premarital coitus is allowed.

---

blamed on the increase in premarital coitus. Divorce is most high among teen-agers and poor people—several times as high as the rates for higher classes and older people. Jacobson, *op. cit.* The most accepted reason for divorce is that we now marry for love and not out of duty, so when love fails, we divorce. Related to this, is some slight evidence that those people who have premarital coitus have slightly lower marital success scores. However, the evidence is far from conclusive. See: Burgess and Wallin, *op. cit.,* chap. xv; Terman, *op. cit.,* chaps. iv and xiv; Clifford Kirkpatrick, *The Family* (New York: The Ronald Press, 1955), chap. xv; Albert Ellis, "The Value of Marriage Prediction Tests," *American Sociological Review,* XIII December, 1948), 710-18. For additional evidence see Harvey J. Locke, *Predicting Adjustment in Marriage* (New York: Henry Holt and Co., 1951), chap. vii.

46. Some people believe that premarital experience may be so enticing that marital sex will be dull by comparison. Were marital sex purely physical this might be the case, but it has a very important psychic element also.

SUMMARY OF THE
NEGATIVE-VALUE CONSEQUENCES

In examining these negative-value consequences, one can see how the likelihood of a consequence occurring varies with the three permissive standards. In other words, some of these standards are more closely integrated or associated with these aspects of our culture than others. More information is vitally needed, regarding the evidence of these associations, to see just what causal relations do exist. There is also a need for further knowledge as to how social variables (education, income, ethnic group, etc.) are associated with these three standards. One would expect each standard to be strongest among those groups who are most willing to accept the kind of consequences which go along with the standard. The existing evidence indicates that permissiveness with affection is more of a middle- and upper-class standard, while the double standard is stronger at lower educational and occupational levels. Permissiveness without affection also seems to be strong at these lower levels, but the evidence here is more ambiguous and it may also be powerful at a few very high social levels. What has been said here concerning the association of consequences and standards in our urban-industrial society is more suggestive than conclusive.

Chapter Eight

Ꮘermissive Standards and Ꮘositive-Value Ꮯonsequences

To COMPLETE THIS PHASE OF OUR ANALYSIS
of the three permissive standards, it is necessary to see how
and to what degree each standard results in consequences
which Americans generally evaluate as good.[1] It is hypothesized that these positive consequences will vary in their
closeness of association with each of our three permissive
standards. There is no systematic treatment of such relationships in sociological literature; it is needed if we are to gain
better understanding of premarital behavior.

PHYSICAL SATISFACTION

Physical satisfaction is seemingly the most obvious of the
consequences of premarital intercourse. Some degree of physi-

---

1. It is believed that the consequences examined here are the major
positive consequences of premarital intercourse. Of course, others may
well be brought out by future research. I am including here the ones which
I now feel are most important. Such a list is always tentative.

cal satisfaction or physical pleasure is present in almost all premarital coitus. It should be quickly added, however, that the nature of that pleasure varies considerably. For one thing, the physical satisfaction would be closely related to the guilt feelings which one might experience. If one feels he is doing something wrong, then whether his judgment is correct or not, he will probably find that his ability to enjoy himself is somewhat lessened.[2] Many girls achieve orgasm only after they have been able to lose their qualms about their action. The initial engagement in coitus frequently causes nervousness or fear because the activity is new, and it is unlikely that full enjoyment can always be obtained.[3]

Thus, it may be said that a believer in abstinence, engaging in coitus in violation of his belief, would probably not enjoy it as much as possible because of his guilt feelings. Also, because of the conflict with the formal standard of abstinence which the double standard involves, double-standard males may feel qualms and disgust which would tend to somewhat lessen the physical pleasure involved in coitus. In both of the single permissiveness standards, although the adherents deny guilt feelings, there may still be some vague, nebulous qualms. At times, the physical pleasure of the present relationship may not be altered despite guilt feelings, but such a situation, in extreme cases, could lead to the guilt feelings being carried over to marital coitus.[4]

Since physical satisfaction is one of the main goals of both permissiveness without affection and the double standard, perhaps these standards will afford more pleasure in the "thrill" sense of the term than permissiveness with affection. For those who fully accept permissiveness without affection

---

2. Kinsey, *Human Female,* p. 306.

3. Terman, *op. cit.,* p. 344. About half of the females in this study were bothered by physical pain at initial intercourse. There also would be psychological qualms, for many others.

4. Burgess and Wallin, *op. cit.,* chap. xx.

or the double standard and do not miss any deeper satisfaction, body-centered behavior may well yield a great deal of physical pleasure. On the other hand, permissiveness with affection may be the best means of achieving physical satisfaction, since, in this standard, the affection may increase the desire to give the other party pleasure and a long acquaintanceship may increase the knowledge of how to satisfy the other party.

Kinsey reported that men almost always reached orgasm during coitus, although some men become impotent if they feel too guilty about their behavior. About two-thirds of the females in Kinsey's sample, engaging in premarital coitus, reached orgasm at least part of the time.[5] Most of the females engaging in premarital coitus intended to continue such behavior. Kinsey presented evidence to indicate that the more the female thought the act was wrong, the less likely she was to achieve orgasm.[6]

Ehrmann's study contains some interesting and relevant information concerning sexual pleasure. He found that among his female college students, being in love did enhance the pleasure involved in sexual behavior. For men, Ehrmann found, being in love increased the pleasure most in light petting and only slightly in heavy petting or coitus. Of course, it is possible that these students were not separating psychic and physical pleasure and were speaking of both together; thus, these findings cannot fully settle the issue of which standard yields the most physical pleasure.[6a]

The question of the effects of inhibitions and the nature of sublimation, as well as the relation between premarital and marital orgasm, will be discussed later in this book. It should

---

5. *Human Female*, p. 288. This is the same rate of orgasm which married women achieved.

6. *Ibid.*, pp. 306, 343.

6a. Ehrmann, *Premarital Dating Behavior*, pp. 251-66; Ehrmann, did not find significant differences in the pleasure reactions by sex codes.

be merely noted here that it is undeniable that most people who participate in premarital coitus feel the satisfaction of releasing nervous energy and of achieving certain pleasurable activities. This release often enables a person to carry on in other areas of life in a more relaxed and regulated fashion. This seems largely true for all three of our permissive standards when guilt is not present.[7]

PSYCHIC SATISFACTION

Psychic satisfaction is one of the most significant consequences of premarital sexual intercourse, and yet it is largely ignored in the present-day literature on sexual behavior before marriage. The lustful, promiscuous, selfish aspects of intercourse have been accented, causing the psychic factor to be lost sight of. But it is this fact that, to many people, is most important.

I am using the term "psychic satisfaction" to refer to the non-sexual, lasting, emotional rewards a sexual relationship yields, such as the security, warmth, and emotional satisfaction which one can derive from sexual intercourse. Such psychic satisfaction seems dependent on the presence of strong affection in the relationship. This means that the double standard and permissiveness without affection are unlikely to yield such psychic consequences to any significant degree.[8] Only permissiveness with affection and the few love relations in the

---

7. The last chapter showed evidence for the small percentage of guilt feelings present in premarital coitus. Burgess and Wallin show the high value of physical release to 143 of their subjects. See Burgess and Wallin, *op. cit.,* p. 375.

8. Psychic satisfaction, of course, could be expanded to include the status rewards a double-standard male achieves for his "conquests." But the term is not being used in this sense here. I previously spoke of such other consequences when dealing with social condemnation in chap. vii and with the double standard in chap. iv.

transitional double standard could lead to full psychic satisfaction. Only with such standards could the participants experience lasting feelings of warmth, security, and satisfaction that are not purely physical. With a person one is fond of, psychic pleasure can be gained by conversation and expressing affection and by mutual contentment. In this situation, such psychic consequences indicate that the relationship is deepening—that the two people are now closer for having shared something so intimate and valuable as sexual intercourse. This is somewhat the feeling experienced by over 90 per cent of the engaged couples in the Burgess and Wallin study who engaged in sexual intercourse.[9]

To fully achieve psychic satisfaction, a couple must, of course, believe their relationship to be right. Guilt feelings would mar psychic satisfaction. Also, the condemnation the double-standard male often feels for his partner limits psychic satisfaction, since it limits any growth of affection. The emphasis on purely physical pleasure in the permissiveness-without-affection standard may similarly make the development of a stable, affectionate relationship less likely. Adherents of this standard may be more interested in finding new partners than in developing deep affection for old ones.

Some people seem content with the body-centered sexual relationship and its low level of psychic satisfaction. But for many others, it appears that the lack of greater psychic satisfaction is felt, for our culture stresses its value. In double-standard males, this lack may be partly responsible for the frequent feelings of disgust following coitus. When the sexual act is over, there is nothing left, and it is precisely then that psychic satisfaction is desired and its absence most sharply felt.[10]

---

9. Burgess and Wallin, *op. cit.,* pp. 371-74.

10. It is important to note that these last two consequences (physical satisfaction and psychic satisfaction) are the only *intended* (manifest) consequences of all the positive and negative consequences which will be

It should be clear that the presence of psychic satisfaction does not necessarily mean that the over-all relationship will be strengthened. It is possible that with increased insight and closeness to another person, one may come to see that he is not suited for that person. Sexual intimacy is not the only factor responsible for strengthening an existing relationship. Of course, if coitus occurs *after* a couple is in love, the chances of its strengthening the relationship are much higher, as evidenced by the engaged couples in the Burgess and Wallin study. But it should be kept in mind that psychic satisfaction from coitus is but one kind of reward, and other aspects of the "wheel relationship" may cancel out such a consequence.[11]

AID TO MARITAL SEXUAL ADJUSTMENT

The last major consequence of premarital coitus focuses on the connection between premarital sexual intercourse and marital sexual adjustment. In the past, the assertion was frequently made that premarital coitus hindered marital coitus.[12] The available evidence indicates that such an unqualified assertion is not valid. There is not complete causal proof of this, but it is known that people who experience orgasms in premarital

---

examined. The other consequences are *unintended* (latent) but are causally related to coitus. Future research will likely reveal other unintended consequences of coitus.

11. The more intimate a relationship, the more one would expect pain at its break. However, a study of college students indicates that they recover from most broken love relationships with remarkable speed. Over two-thirds of the boys and girls "recovered" in a matter of weeks. See Clifford Kirkpatrick and Theodore Caplow, "Courtship in a Group of Minnesota Students," *American Journal of Sociology,* LI (1945), 114-25.

12. This is at times asserted today. See the 1958 edition of Landis and Landis, *op. cit.,* p. 304. See also chap. xi of that book. Landis feels that having premarital coitus may fix the couple's attention too much on sex. This is a common view and it would be interesting to gather evidence on this. It is possible that the reverse is true, and that by abstaining one thinks more of sex because it is forbidden fruit.

coitus are much more likely to experience orgasms when married. This fact was brought out in many of the major studies.[13] More research is needed to see if the correlation here is due to the more sexually stimulated females having premarital coital orgasm and also marital orgasm—both as a result of their sexual desires—or if the premarital coitus actually aided their sexual development and made orgasm in marriage easier. Causal relations are very difficult to establish.

The chart on the following page shows some evidence in this area. Kinsey found that only 3 to 8 per cent of the females who experienced premarital coital orgasm failed to achieve orgasm in the first year of marriage. Forty per cent of the virgins who experienced no premarital orgasm failed to achieve marital orgasm in the first year of marriage. Ten years after marriage, 25 per cent of these virginal women had not yet reached orgasm. Those virgins who experienced premarital orgasm from other sources, such as petting or masturbation, fared much better than their more chaste, virginal sisters. About 15 per cent of this group did not experience orgasm in the first year of marriage. It should be noted that those females who engaged in premarital intercourse and failed to reach orgasm had a most difficult time reaching orgasm in marriage. Between 38 and 56 per cent of this group failed to reach orgasm in the first year of marriage. It is believed that much of this group is composed of abstinence believers who experienced inhibitions due to strong guilt feelings concerning their behavior. It may also be that some of these women only experienced coitus a few times or had partners whose ineptness or lack of concern prevented orgasm. Some may have engaged in coitus for other than sexual reasons, i.e., to obtain certain privileges. This group is over a third of

---

13. See Kinsey, *Human Female,* p. 406; Burgess and Wallin, *op. cit.,* p. 362; Terman, *op. cit., p.* 383. For more recent evidence on this point, see Kanin and Howard, *op. cit.*

the total number of women engaging in premarital coitus. Thus, the over-all figures show a high correlation between premarital orgasm, *from any source,* and marital orgasm. Nevertheless, those adherents of the three permissive standards *who achieve premarital orgasm,* have the best chance of marital orgasm.

Chart I—Percentage of Women Failing to Reach Orgasm in 1st Year of Marriage, by Various Sexual Backgrounds*

VIRGINS	
No Previous Orgasm	Orgasm in Petting or Masturbation
40	15

NON-VIRGINS			
No Orgasm	Orgasm only in Petting or Masturbation	Orgasm in Coitus —24 Times	Orgasm in Coitus +25 Times
56	38	8	3

* Kinsey, *Human Female,* p. 406. The virginal females were about 50 per cent "without previous orgasm" and 50 per cent with "orgasm in petting or masturbation." Forty-three per cent of the non-virginal females failed to achieve coital orgasm, and 57 per cent succeeded.

This does not mean that all three permissive standards are equally likely to lead to marital orgasm, nor to total sexual adjustment in marriage. There are factors relating to the interaction of *both* husband and wife which must also be considered. The individual's orgasmic history may have different consequences, depending on what standard underlies his experience and depending on the standard and experience of his mate.[14]

---

14. Burgess and Wallin, *op. cit.,* chap. xx. This chapter contains one of the most recent and most extensive researches into the sex factor in

In the Burgess and Wallin study, many of the couples (married on the average about four years) were sexually maladjusted. Three out of four husbands and about one of every six wives said they had seriously contemplated extramarital coitus. About a fourth of the men and a third of the women stated that their sexual desires were definitely not being satisfied. Two out of every three wives said their husband's sex drive exceeded theirs. Over a fourth of the women rarely or never reached orgasm in all their years of marriage. Seven per cent of the men likewise rarely or never experienced orgasm. Love between the husband and wife seemed to help in achieving sexual adjustment, but there were many couples who were in love but who were maladjusted sexually. These love couples did not often divorce, thus indicating that, although sex is a vital part of marriage, there are so many other important parts that it is quite possible for the sexual factor to be outweighed.[15]

One cannot say for sure why these married couples and many others find sexual adjustment in marriage so difficult. Surely it cannot be explained solely by the lack of orgasm on the part of wives. Reasoning from the data possessed, it would seem that the type of premarital standard held by these people may be one important factor. Burgess and Wallin mention that the double standard encourages men to develop their sexual desires and women to inhibit their desires.[16] This combination may be the crucial explanation of much of the

marriage adjustment. Terman, *op. cit.,* chaps. x-xiii. Terman found an even greater amount of sexual maladjustment in marriage than Burgess and Wallin did. Perhaps couples in the early 1940's (Burgess and Wallin sample) were happier than the couples in the 1930's (Terman sample).

15 Burgess and Wallin, *op. cit.,* chap. xx, p. 696. These authors found a moderate relation between marital success and sexual adjustment. It is, however, difficult to say whether the marital success was the cause or the effect. Also many marriages with poor sexual adjustment were good in other ways.

16. Burgess and Wallin, *op. cit.,* pp. 695-97.

sexual maladjustment in marriage. Men are made more desirous of sexual intercourse, women are inhibited, and then they are united in marriage. Sexual difficulties are thus most likely to occur. If people were trained more equally, a great deal of this could be avoided. Let me elaborate on this hypothesis and try to demonstrate why, in agreement with Burgess and Wallin, it is felt that the double standard in premarital intercourse is responsible for much of the sexual maladjustment in marriage.

A double-standard man develops certain strong attitudes regarding sexual relations, as a result of his own experiences. Most likely his sexual behavior was aimed at self-satisfaction. Such a man builds up self-centered methods of sexual gratification and associates sexual relations with "bad" women, thereby disassociating sex and affection.

Sexual relations in marriage, in our culture, are usually expected to involve mutual satisfaction with a woman respected and loved. The marital situation, then, is nearly as diametrically opposed to double-standard sexual relations as possible. The old double-standard attitudes and habits must be forgotten and new habits built up to replace them. The husband must learn to respect his wife; he must learn to associate sexual intercourse with tenderness and affection, rather than with disgust and lack of affection, and he must learn how to satisfy both his wife and himself and not only himself. This is an extensive change, and, in many cases, it may cause difficulty. No doubt some men find the change too difficult to make and continue to practice self-centered, affectionless, sexual intercourse which leaves their wives unsatisfied and emotionally disturbed.

Orthodox double-standard women (women who accept chastity for themselves but permissiveness for men) often feel that a double-standard man, because of his experience, is an asset. They prefer to marry such men and believe that this kind of husband would be able to teach them about sexual intercourse. Kinsey found that 32 per cent of the girls preferred non-virginal men for husbands, 23 per cent preferred to marry virginal men, and 42 per cent had no special preference.[17] The above statements, concerning premarital intercourse of the double-standard type and its effects on marital sexual adjustment, bring such views into serious question. Double-standard men may be quite ignorant about person-centered coitus. Furthermore, such women often bring their own handicaps to the marital bed, and, combined with a double-standard male, there would seem to be a good chance of sexual maladjustment.[18]

An orthodox double-standard woman must live up to a rather strict code. Not only must she avoid sexual coitus, she must not allow herself to be too free in the area of petting. She may be in the group of women who have never experienced premarital orgasm in any fashion. The average girl marries in her twenties, after about five to ten years of dating. It takes a considerable amount of control, and probably inhibition, to abide by such a strict standard for all those years. Such strict behavior could be accomplished with greater ease in a more ascetic culture, but in our culture with its accent on sex and young people, it is most difficult for a female to so sharply curtail her sexual behavior. After learning to restrict behavior for many years, it is often difficult to lose inhibitions. As one married woman in the Burgess and Wallin study stated in her interview:

> You develop inhibitions before marriage. There's a stone wall
> then, and after marriage it's a little hard to get over the stone

---

17. *Human Female*, p. 323. 3 per cent of the girls were undecided.

18. For an excellent literary example of this sort of maladjustment, see Maupassant, *op. cit.* See also: Burgess and Wallin, *op. cit.*, pp. 659-60, for evidence that over 25 per cent of the women said their premarital sex attitude was one of disgust, aversion, or indifference. Almost 10 per cent of the men said the same. Terman, *op. cit.*, p. 248, found 34 per cent of the women and 13 per cent of the men with such attitudes.

wall. I like to go as far as the stone wall. After that I don't respond.[19]

A woman like this can no more lose her inhibitions on the wedding night than the man can lose his self-centered sexual habits. At the very least, it will take time and understanding to chip away the veneer of culturally-imposed inhibitions. Such a woman would need a husband with a great deal of patience and love, in addition to an understanding of how to change his wife's sexual behavior. Even if the woman were an experienced female, she might still have difficulties due to the double-standard male's self-centered sexual attitudes.

Finally, it should be added that a double-standard male may carry over his behavior and accept extramarital coitus. This may further disrupt the over-all marital relationship and, in particular, the sexual relationship. Such extramarital coitus may remove much of the personal, unique, stable, and affectionate aspects of marital coitus, making it all the more difficult to reach a satisfactory sexual adjustment in marriage.

It is apparent that the double standard may set the stage for marital sexual maladjustment in a multitude of ways. Even the double-standard male who adheres to the transitional subtype will have had most of his sexual experience in a traditional double-standard body-centered way. His affectionate experience may help somewhat, but by and large, what has been said of the orthodox adherent should hold true for the transitional male also. It may well be the double-standard male who is responsible for some of the non-virginal women failing to reach orgasm. If the male is predominantly concerned about his own pleasure, he may not help his partner to achieve orgasm.

It is hypothesized that the single permissive standards are

_____
19. Burgess and Wallin, *op. cit.,* p. 677.

not so strongly involved in marital sexual maladjustment. Since permissiveness without affection involves mutual satisfaction, it avoids inhibitions on the part of the female or selfishness on the part of the male. There may, however, be some adjustment difficulties here due to the habitual body-centered, thrill-centered type of premarital coitus which these people have experienced. It may well be difficult to adjust to the stability of marital coitus.

It is further hypothesized that permissiveness with affection, because of its accent on mutual satisfaction and affection, is well integrated with marital sexual relations. This standard builds up attitudes favorable to stable, affectionate relations, and prepares one for the kind of coitus involved in marriage. Person-centered coitus is the easiest for both men and women to accept without qualms, and thus it should lead to a high rate of orgasm in premarital copulation. Such premarital orgasm is correlated with marital orgasm.[20]

In summary, I should mention that although there is a very high correlation between premarital orgasm and marital orgasm, there may well be more to sexual adjustment than reaching a climax. Although it could be said that chances for reaching orgasm in marriage are higher if orgasm is experienced before marriage, this cannot be recommended as a cure-all. Many people are so strongly opposed to premarital coitus that the attempt to achieve orgasm in premarital intercourse may lead to strong guilt feelings and greater sexual difficulties than formerly existed. Chart I shows clearly how some experienced women had a more difficult time than the virginal women in achieving marital orgasm. Such women

---

20. Kinsey, *Human Female*, p. 345 shows 91 per cent of girls having coitus with fiance only, had no definite regrets. This is highest of all groups. Of course, there are other factors in a marital relationship which may affect the sexual adjustment, besides one's past standards. However, in this section, only the relation between premarital standards and marital sexual adjustment is being examined.

may be in part those who felt guilty about their premarital behavior. Furthermore, orgasm alone is no guarantee of adjustment, as can be seen in the above examination of the double standard. It is my hypothesis that it is the *combination* of male and female premarital sexual standards that is most important in marital sexual adjustment. Finally, it must not be clear that such sexual adjustment occurs in the context of a total marital relation and can affect and be affected by that relation.

CONCLUSIONS ON ALL
EIGHT CONSEQUENCES

I have not gone into great detail to show how the subtypes of our three major permissive standards would vary. There is, of course, a great deal of similarity, but the consequences will vary in some crucial areas. This was touched upon only briefly during the analysis, because the research information is not yet precise and thorough enough to explain fully such subtype variations.

It should also be noted that within any one subtype there is a range of individual variation. Here again, there is not full research information as to what variations in the consequences may occur because of such specific positional differences.

I have tried to present what I feel is as complete an account as is objectively possible at the present time. The broad theoretical assumption that standards would be differentially integrated with consequences has been supported by the evidence of the last two chapters. In summary, it can be said that the particular association of standards and consequences which exists in a society depends on the nature of that society—that the associations I have discussed exist because of the kind of society America is. The picture of

America, developed in all the earlier chapters, provides the context of the discussion on standards and consequences.

On an over-all basis, permissiveness with affection is the permissive standard most closely integrated with the positive value consequences, such as psychic satisfaction, and most weakly integrated with the negative-value consequences, such as guilt feelings. This standard, on this account, seems to be well knit into modern society—particularly in middle- and upper-class groups, where such consequences seem most highly valued.

The person-centered coital behavior which goes with permissiveness with affection, and the affection which also is involved in such behavior, seem to be of vital importance in explaining the resulting integration. The evidence indicates that, in our kind of society, it is affection which helps insure that one can avoid the negative-value consequences and achieve the positive-value consequences. Another feature of person-centered coitus is the monogamous aspect of the affair. The more affection present, the more monogamous the affair; in American society, this, too, increases the likelihood of achieving the positive-value consequences and avoiding the negative-value consequences. The women who accept the transitional double standard also have person-centered behavior. However, because these women allow men greater sexual freedom, the consequences of this behavior may not be the same as those for the permissiveness-with-affection women.

Conversely, those affairs lacking in affectionate feelings and which are not monogamous, namely, those entailing body-centered coitus, seem to be more likely to lead to some of the negative-value consequences, as well as fail to achieve many of the positive-value consequences. Such body-centered affairs are those which largely follow from the double standard and permissiveness without affection, as well as those which are in violation of a person-centered standard. Even here, such negative-value consequences are simply more likely—they are by no means inevitable. The Puritan view of our standards is thus often erroneous, i.e, many people who disapprove of premarital intercourse try to paint all such behavior as disastrous in its consequences and are particularly prone to exaggerate the risks of body-centered coitus. Body-centered coitus does seem to have higher risks, but in many cases the difference is slight, and in other instances caution can control much of the risk involved.

As noted previously, these sexual standards seem differentially distributed by education and occupation classes—the lower classes having more adherents to the double standard, and the middle and upper classes leaning more toward permissiveness with affection.[21] Permissiveness without affection is more difficult to locate in terms of its dominant focus in our social structure. There is evidence of adherents in both the very high and very low segments of our class system. In any case, it is interesting to note that although all classes probably have adherents of all our major standards, some of these standards are stronger in some classes than in others. This means that premarital intercourse is not the same, in its social and cultural significance, in the different sectors of the social structure. Future research is needed to discern the exact distribution of standards and, equally important, the reasons for such distribution. At present, it may be suggested that since social classes differ as to their knowledge, and evaluation of the eight consequences we discussed, one would

---

21. It should be noted that Kinsey found that female sexual behavior did not vary as much by education or occupation classes. There were some differences such as lower-educational girls having coitus and petting at earlier ages and marrying earlier. However, Kinsey's data do not enable one to check whether, although the rates of coitus were similar, the lower-class group included more permissiveness without affection adherents. Kinsey, *Human Female,* chap. viii.

expect the popularity of these three permissive standards to differ accordingly.

Now that we have analyzed our three permissive standards we will turn in the next chapter to our formal standard of abstinence and see what characteristics and consequences are associated with this, our final premarital standard.

Chapter Nine

Our Formal Single Standard of Abstinence

CHASTITY FOR WOMEN IS AN ANCIENT CUS-
tom, practiced for many millenniums before Christianity.
Christianity was unique only in that it tried to introduce into
a predominantly double-standard Western world the notion
of abstinence for *both sexes*—a single standard of abstinence.
Christianity did not fully succeed in this attempt, but through
its efforts, we have inherited a certain amount of respect for
our formal sexual standard of abstinence.

People who accept abstinence believe that sexual intercourse is too important an act, too valuable and intimate to
be performed with anyone besides one's marriage partner.
They thus want to save sexual intercourse for marriage, which,
they feel, is the most secure setting for sexual relations. About
half of the women in the Kinsey, Burgess and Wallin, and
Terman studies were virginal at marriage. Since our culture
holds this standard up as an ideal, these people are reinforced
in their beliefs by our formal norms.[1]

---

1. What is said about the single standard of abstinence here applies

One fact which is certain is that a great many of the adherents of abstinence accept forms of sexual intimacy which would never have been permissible two or three generations ago. The female virgins in Kinsey's sample, born 1910 or later and who had at least been kissed, behaved as follows: Three of every four had experienced breast caresses, and between a quarter and a third of them engaged in masturbating their dates or in being masturbated, while about one in six engaged in the genital apposition form of petting. I am using the term "petting" to mean sexually exciting behavior usually involving the mammary and genital areas.[2]

One cannot be certain if these virgins all accepted their behavior as right and proper. There is evidence that many girls suffer from doubt over the correctness of their petting behavior; possibly because it clashes with the more conservative parental codes.[3]

What are the various subtypes of the standard of abstinence which regulate this behavior? Our present-day abstinence standard can be divided into (a) petting without affection, (b) petting with affection, (c) kissing without affection, and (d) kissing with affection.[4]

---

logically also to the orthodox double-standard female who believes only in female virginity. Many such females prefer abstinence but tolerate the double standard. There is very little information on male virgins. Many such males seem to be circumstantial virgins; they desire coitus but have not had the proper opportunity yet. Among female virgins, Kinsey found about 22 per cent, and among males, 35-52 per cent, who said lack of opportunity kept them virginal. Kinsey, *Human Female,* p. 332.

2. Kinsey combines both petting and kissing behavior under the rubric of petting. I have separated these two types. *Human Female,* pp. 280-81. Ehrmann, *Premarital Dating Behavior,* p. 46, also shows over half the females with petting experience.

3. Kinsey, *Human Female,* p. 261.

4. See comments below Chart II, in chap. x for an elaboration of these subtypes.

PETTING WITHOUT AFFECTION

The data cited above on petting make it clear that there are some people, both male and female, who accept abstinence but feel that as long as coitus is avoided, they can pet heavily with most people who physically attract them. This is the definition of the subtype, petting without affection. There are some distinctions beyond physical attractions made so as to preserve their reputations among more conservative people. For example, if such a girl feels that the boys in her own neighborhood are not as "liberal" as she, then she may try to preserve her reputation by not petting heavily with these boys and petting heavily with other out-of-town dates. This result is very similar to the "mobility effect" of the double standard. The less generally accepted the activity, the more likely a girl will have to go outside her neighborhood to find partners if she wants to keep her hometown reputation.

The men and women I interviewed who accept petting without affection tend to think of virginity in a strictly physical sense. They defend their beliefs by contending that as long as a person remains physically virginal, he or she is morally pure and will probably, therefore, make a more faithful marriage partner. This view is somewhat questionable as we shall see later on in this chapter.

A further look into this standard will reveal its similarity to our permissiveness without affection standard. Both of these beliefs involve a casual attitude towards sexual relations —a lack of association between sexual behavior and affection. Both are standards which encourage body-centered behavior. The female in the petting standard is still technically virginal, but she is also a sexually experienced female. Such a paradoxical woman is best defined as a "promiscuous virgin."

Our religions are opposed to petting without affection; in fact, they are opposed to any petting standard. Many of our more orthodox religions even forbid kissing if such behavior arouses one sexually. The casual and indiscriminate view towards sexual relations which goes along with petting without affection arouses perhaps the strongest religious opposition outside of opposition to actual coitus. Nevertheless, since this standard still technically requires virginity, it gains prestige and more acceptance than the non-virginal permissiveness without affection. Both these body-centered standards, however, probably have only moderate followings among the middle and upper classes. Although such people pet frequently, they seem to accept such behavior much more easily when a stable affectionate relationship is involved.

Petting without affection is a relatively new standard. It, of course, is not new behavior, but as an accepted subtype of abstinence, it is quite recent. Widespread dating without chaperonage only goes back to about the turn of the century, and such unchaperoned dating is a prerequisite for this type of sexual freedom. This standard appealed to those men and women who desired to obtain more sexual pleasures than the old abstinence standards would allow, but who did not want to fully lose their virginity. The added freedom insured by the end of chaperonage and the new economic independence and anonymity which the city afforded greatly encouraged more sexual freedom; petting without affection was one of the many new sexual standards to arise from these conditions.[5] This standard is further evidence of the sexually permissive direction we in America have headed toward during the last few generations. Petting without affec-

---

5. As an example of the vast increases here, see Kinsey, *Human Female*, p. 275. Only 15 per cent of those women born before 1900 petted to orgasm by age 25, while between 30 per cent and 43 per cent of the newer generations petted to orgasm by age 25. Some of this increase would be due to the growth of petting without affection.

tion would have been unthinkable in the nineteenth century. It is still somewhat extreme in America today—extreme, that is, for an abstinence subtype. It is not, however, the sexual intimacy which seems extreme to many Americans, but the indiscriminate fashion in which it is carried on. It violates our older Puritan feelings about body-centered behavior, and it does not have our newer justification of love.

PETTING WITH AFFECTION

My own informal questioning over the last several years with college students and others leads me to strongly believe that the most widely accepted subtype of abstinence is petting with affection. Ehrmann's study has perhaps the best evidence in support of the popularity of this standard, at least among girls. He states that "going steady added respectability to petting. . . ."[6] Petting with affection accepts petting only when strong affection or love is present. This standard is, in many ways, similar to permissiveness with affection. Both standards involve a strong association of sexual behavior and affection, of monogamous affairs, of mutual satisfaction and loyalty. Just as permissiveness with affection tends to build up psychic satisfaction, emotional maturity and other positive-value consequences, so one would expect this subtype of abstinence to do somewhat the same. Of course, all of these effects are usually on a smaller scale, since the amount of intimacy involved in a petting standard is less than that involved in coitus. The petting which the adherents of this subtype allow also varies a good deal, making some of these adherents more intimate than others.

Petting with affection has also greatly expanded in recent decades due to the previously discussed vast socio-economic

---

6. Ehrmann, *Premarital Dating Behavior,* p. 141.

changes which have occurred in our country. Those individuals not willing to go as far as full intercourse nor to be as indiscriminate as was required by petting without affection found a happy medium in the petting-with-affection standard. This standard was more in line with the older notions of virginity, as it held the idea of discrimination and faithfulness to one's partner. However, it did toss away that aspect of traditional virginity standards which held that women should enter marriage virtually "untouched." Furthermore, even though it is a person-centered standard, it is unacceptable to our present-day religions, since petting involves erotic arousal outside of marriage. Despite such disapproval, it seems to be a very popular standard among young people today.[7] The positive value our culture places on affection and discrimination in regard to sexual relations makes this standard appealing to many girls who do not yet feel ready to go further than petting.

KISSING WITHOUT AFFECTION

This subtype accepts only kissing but permits this whenever one desires. In my interviews, these adherents were young people in their early and middle teens who are too conservative to go beyond kissing but too much enamoured with kiss-

---

7. *Human Female,* pp. 240-41. Males seem to differ in the percentage who pet to orgasm. Of the men who attended college, 59 per cent petted to orgasm before marriage, 30 per cent of the men whose education stopped in high school petted to orgasm before marriage, and of those whose education stopped in the eighth grade, only 16 per cent experienced premarital orgasm from petting. These lower education groups make up for this difference in that they have the highest percentage in coitus. Girls presented a different picture in the Kinsey study. There did not seem to be any difference in educational level in petting to orgasm except that the lower-educational group began petting earlier. In response to a questionnaire I distributed to college girls, about two-thirds of 50 abstinent females said they accepted and preferred petting with affection.

ing to restrict it. Some of these adherents desire some sexual activity in order to keep their dates interested but fear to go beyond kissing.

This standard meets similar opposition in our culture and has similar characteristics to its "big sister," petting without affection. The key difference is that the opposition is much less than in the case of petting, because most Americans view indiscriminate kissing as of less consequence than indiscriminate petting. However, kissing without affection, because of its lack of discrimination, still seems to clash with the older notions of virginity.

KISSING WITH AFFECTION

This is the fourth and last subtype of abstinence. It is the most restrictive of all the abstinence standards. Those girls brought up by very conservative parents would be most likely to become adherents of this subtype. Probably more people in the younger age groups accept this standard. The older age groups would tend to be less restrictive. There seems to be a progression through which many girls proceed —kissing only while in high school, petting after high school and often accepting full coitus in their twenties. My own research supports this view, and Kinsey found that the number of non-virgins doubled between the ages of twenty and twenty-five.[8] It would be most worthwhile to see if this hypothesized age-sex progression is generally valid and to spell out the details of its functioning.

The restraints are too great and the actual intimacies too small for this standard to yield much psychic satisfaction as a direct result of the sexual behavior accompanying it. How-

8. *Ibid.,* p. 339. See Table 2 of this book, p. 224.

ever, many adherents do romanticize and glory over their kissing experiences. One unique characteristic of this standard is that it comes closer than any of the other standards to being acceptable by our organized religious groups. Accordingly, it is closer to the orthodox, traditional meaning of virginity. It stresses the almost complete lack of sexual experience before marriage and thus is in line with the "untouched" and discrimination notions of virginity.

If Kinsey's data is at all indicative, it would seem that about a quarter of those who accept abstinence limit themselves to kissing.[9] Other girls perhaps would like to, but fail to achieve this goal in practice. In any case, it would seem fair and conservative to say that the American female virgin belongs about half to the kissing standards and half to the petting standards. The petting standards probably are increasing in adherents and seem to be more popular with the older females.

VIRGINITY AND FAITHFULNESS

One of the reasons often put forth by abstinence believers in support of their views is the relation which they feel pertains between their standard and faithfulness in marriage.[10]

Just what does premarital chastity entail? Technically, it means that a person has not engaged in behavior involving the penetration of the vagina by the penis. In the case of the female, it also means that the woman is expected to possess a hymen, i.e., the fold which partially blocks the opening to

9. *Ibid.,* pp. 254-55. Ehrmann, *Premarital Dating Behavior,* chap. ii. Ehrmann found about one-third of all his females limited themselves to kissing.
10. There is some empirical evidence for this belief. Kinsey found that only one-third of the adulterous females entered marriage virginally. See *Human Female,* pp. 427-28, and my discussion in chap. vii.

the vagina. These physical conditions of virginity can and are met by persons who have engaged in genital apposition, mutual masturbation, and mutual oral-genital stimulation, to mention but a few of the heavy petting practices fairly common among our virginal groups. Moreover, one could have indulged in these practices with scores of partners and still be considered virginal. Now, does such a definition of virginity delineate those who are likely to be faithful?

In the last century, there were men like the Italian Lombroso who believed that one could tell criminals by their physical characteristics.[11] Lombroso felt that left-handed men were swindlers, men with scanty beards were highly inclined towards crime, as were men with slanting foreheads or large canine teeth. Today such a "physical" view of criminality is laughed off by the general public as well as by almost all professional criminologists.[12] It is known only too well that character cannot be judged by physical features. But what is being done when a girl who possesses a hymen is classified as a "good" girl and probably a faithful wife? Is not character being judged by physical characteristics?

The "promiscuous virgins" of petting without affection do not seem especially likely to be faithful in marriage. Such females have not built up a standard of discrimination; they have not controlled their sexual activity according to the affection they felt, nor have they discriminated on any other basis besides physical attraction. It is true that such a female has avoided sexual intercourse, but in a technical sense only. Orgasm experienced by bare genital contact is quite close to

11. Cesare Lombroso, *Crime: Its Causes and Remedies,* trans. H. P. Horton (New York: Little Brown and Company, 1911).

12. I say "almost all" for Sheldon and Eleanor Glueck have recently written a book entitled *Physique and Delinquency* (New York: Harper and Brothers, 1956), in which there is an attempt made to show correlation of body build with criminal activity. However, the Gluecks take a more sophisticated approach.

orgasm experienced by actual coitus. How much difference in her character would it have made if such a female had actually copulated? This sort of promiscuous virginity brings to mind the story of the man who, while ill for an entire month, was being fed by intravenous injections instead of by mouth. The man later claimed he had not really eaten for that month because no food entered his mouth. In a technical sense, he was right. But in a more meaningful sense, this man and a promiscuous virgin are both more accurately classified as "experienced."

There is a certain contradiction in being sexually promiscuous and being virginal in the traditional sense. The fault lies with the "physical" definition of virginity which is used. Some females are born without a hymen and thus would never be virginal in the physical sense, and other females may lose their hymens through masturbation. Thus one cannot rely upon the hymen as a sign of virginity. The hymen at times has great elasticity and there are cases of prostitutes who still possess their hymens.[13] Thus, if a physical definition of virginity is desired, it must be redefined as precluding the entrance of the penis into the vagina. But even this sort of definition involves difficulties. How far into the vagina must the penis enter before it is considered intercourse? Many females pet in a fashion allowing partial entry of the penis. These females still consider themselves as virgins. Are they? Where shall the line be drawn? The narrowness of the physical criteria of virginity becomes more and more obvious.

Such a physical definition might not be so faulty if our interest were only in a physical state, but most people are interested in what they believe such a physical state symbolizes

13. Dickinson, *Atlas of Human Sex Anatomy,* p. 68. An excellent illustrated discussion of the female virgin, the hymen, and other relevant topics can be found in this volume. See in particular pp. 60, 61, 62, 68, 103, 104, and 105. Also figures 55, 71, 73, 89, 95, and 100. For general reference, note the excellent diagrams in figures 15, 45, and 142.

—the presence of a "pure" female or male; one who will be faithful in marriage. In order to see if this connection necessarily exists, compare a promiscuous virgin female with a non-virginal female who accepts permissiveness with affection. Who is more likely to be faithful in marriage—everything else being equal—a woman who has experienced a few affairs involving coitus with men she loved, or a woman who has experienced scores of relationships involving heavy petting with men for whom she did not care. It seems probable that the non-virginal woman will have built up habits of associating sex with affection, of monogamous affairs, of emotional maturity, which all may tend toward faithfulness in marriage. The petting without affection adherent does not seem so likely to have developed such attitudes and habits. I think we can all agree that, in this case, the virgin, from a theoretical point of view, certainly seems to be more likely to be unfaithful than the non-virgin.

It seems more reasonable to determine faithfulness by an examination of a person's attitudes and beliefs rather than by an examination of physical characteristics. As shown previously, a female who is non-virginal physically may be virginal mentally, i.e., her attitudes may be discriminatory and likely to lead to faithfulness in marriage. The adherents of petting without affection have lost sight of the attitudes which the physical state was supposed to evidence. They have concentrated so much on one means that they, like the miser who hoards money, have forgotten why they have been saving themselves.

The above reasoning would seem to most clearly apply to the petting-without-affection adherents, but it also seems to have some validity for the other abstinence subtypes. In all cases, it would seem that a purely physical criteria for faithfulness is insufficient. Discrimination and emotional maturity are the crucial determinants, and one must see which standards are likely to develop these characteristics. In conclusion, it may be well to add that even these premarital coital attitudes are not sufficient bases for determining future behavior. As was pointed out in chapter seven, there are many other motivations to adultery.[14] Nevertheless, the fact remains that Kinsey did find more virginal women faithful to their husbands. As I noted in chapter seven, this may be due to the fact that more liberal people engage in coitus before a divorce is final or when love has left a marriage. Also some standards, such as the double standard, may encourage casual adultery. In short, I would still contend that in abstinence, as in the permissive standards, one has to examine the particular standard to see if and how it is related to faithfulness in marriage.

SEXUAL DESIRES AND INHIBITIONS

a) *Psychological Difficulties.* Nineteenth-century Victorianism put forth the doctrine that to inhibit oneself was a good in itself. The Victorians held that one must learn to control all impulses and can only become a mature adult if this task is fully accomplished. Then a Viennese doctor caught the breath of the world, and the nineteenth-century emphasis on restriction was stopped with a tremendous start and reversed with equal force. Sigmund Freud and his popularizers began to tell their doctrines to the world—declaring that to inhibit oneself was to invite neurosis and psychosis. They held that man's animal instincts, his "id," were constantly at war with society.[15] Society repressed man, and if man was to avoid

---

14. *Human Female*, pp. 427-28. The virginal woman may in part commit adultery because she is more subject to having romantic illusions of marriage and may be less well-adjusted sexually.

15. Sigmund Freud, *Civilization and Its Discontents* (London: Hogarth Press, 1930). This book affords one insight into Freud's views concerning the inherent conflict between society and the individual.

serious mental illness, he had to minimize these repressions and act freely in accord with his impulses. This was held to be particularly true in regard to sexual impulses. These ideas became most popular around the 1920's and have lasted until the present day, even though they do not quite accurately reflect Freud's own position or that of the present-day neo-Freudians.[16]

Psychologists today seem in general agreement that one must learn to regulate his emotions, but that one cannot be a complete dictator even to himself—to attempt to do so is to invite psychological troubles.[17] Freud saw the oppression and conflict in the Victorian approach, but like so many reform movements, at the beginning, his went all the way to the opposite extreme in a wide pendulum sweep. Freud failed to fully understand that man can accept society's customs, and, if he does, they need not be oppressive to him; rather they can become part of him. Freud did not fully appreciate that the part of man that may find "society" oppressive may be a part which was developed by that same society. It may be that there are parts of every society in conflict with each other; people, brought up in these societies, are likely to reflect this conflict within themselves.[18] This being the case, giving vent to impulses, ids, instincts,[19] and so forth would merely be giving vent to one type of learned behavior, and

---

16. For a brief summary of Freudianism, see Charles Brenner, *An Elementary Textbook of Psychoanalysis* (New York: International University Press, Inc., 1955).

17. For a modern-day development of this point of view, see Flanders Dunbar, M.D., *Mind and Body: Psychosomatic Medicine* (New York: Random House, 1947).

18. For elaboration of this, see Merton, *op. cit.,* chap. iv, "Social Structure and Anomie," pp. 131-60.

19. The term "instinct" was most effectively delineated and defined by the late Luther Lee Bernard, *Instinct* (New York: Henry Holt and Company, 1924). Bernard found over 14,000 different human traits which had been called instinctive, and he tried, therefore, to clarify the term so that it would be more than just an unknown name for the unknown. See also Shaffer, *op. cit.,* chap. ii.

such action, rather than leading to freedom, might lead to conflict with other learned forms of behavior. Thus, giving into one's impulses often will create as many problems as it solves. It seems that neither Victorianism nor Freudianism had the full answer to the consequences of inhibition.

The amount of inhibition (restraint of sexual desire)[20] should vary directly with the difference between the amount of desire the individual has and the amount of restriction involved in the standard. One might think that our two "kissing" standards would be held by those people who have developed the strongest inhibitions. Nevertheless, this must be qualified by adding that these people may not have strong desires. A girl sheltered and kept from experiences and friends which might arouse and develop her sexual desire may abide by a kissing standard and not inhibit herself greatly, since she does not desire very much else.[21] Since many parts of our culture stress sexual desire, it would be difficult to grow up without at least partially coming into contact with these forces via literature, movies, or friends. Thus, most people should feel some inhibition, although not necessarily a severe degree.

What are the results then for the females who do feel sexual desires but who contain themselves? There is a price to pay for all inhibitions. A woman will feel a certain amount

---

20. Inhibition is not lack of desire, but restraint of desire. It differs from sublimation which is transference or removal of desire via other activity, and differs also from frigidity which is lack of desire. For a good discussion of the difficulties of sublimation see: *Human Male*, pp. 205-13. For the classical discussion of these concepts, see Havelock Ellis, *Psychology of Sex* (New York: Mentor Books, 1954). Men like Havelock Ellis and Kraft-Ebing and others are pioneers in sex, but they are not too relevant in this book due to the psychological approach they used. For other purposes their work would be of first importance.

21. In Kinsey's sample, sexual unresponsiveness was checked as a definite reason for restraint by 32-45 per cent. *Human Female*, p. 344. This is probably most valid for younger females. Ehrmann, *Premarital Dating Behavior*, p. 229. Ehrmann found that about half the girls listed "no desire" as a restraint when a non-lover was involved but only 11 per cent said this when a lover was involved.

of pain if she tries to stop herself from doing what she wishes. This pain, however, can be counterbalanced by the feeling that one is doing right. It is only when the distance between one's sexual desires and one's sexual standards becomes quite great that the danger of serious emotional conflicts arises. In such a case, a person is torn between his or her strong desire for sexual relations and the powerful feelings concerning the wrongness of the act. Such a situation, if it continues for a length of time, can lead to serious psychological disturbances. Be it clear—the ordinary feeling of pain due to self-denial of a minor sort is not harmful psychologically; it may be helpful in that it aids in integrating behavior with values. Avoiding every bit of pain in life is avoiding life itself; this leads to naught but a spoiled and neurotic and unfulfilled individual. The serious situation is the one involving a wide gap between desire and standard.[22] The solution to conflict of this kind is easy to state but difficult to achieve. One must either change his desires or change his standards—or change both so as to bring them closer together, thereby lessening the intensity of the conflict.

The solution is not in indulgence any more than it is in chastity. The answer is in lessening the gap between desire and standard, and this can be accomplished either by indulgence or chastity depending on what the individual can accept and achieve. Some people feel so strongly about remaining chaste that the only workable solution is to try to lessen their sexual desires by avoiding certain kinds of situations. Others find it impossible to lessen their desires but are able to change their standards to allow themselves more sexual freedom. Others are unable to change either desires or standards and end up with strong emotional disturbances.

---

22. For two world-famous "case studies" of such deep conflict, see St. Augustine, *The Confessions of Saint Augustine,* trans. F. J. Sheed, (New York: Sheed and Ward, 1942), and Jean Jacques Rousseau, *The Confessions of J. J. Rousseau* (New York: Pocket Books, 1957).

b) Marital Difficulties. But what about those people who are able to control their desires without such severe difficulty? What about those whose desires are not too strong due to their restrictive upbringing? Will they become overly inhibited wives and husbands? Again there is no yes or no answer to such a question. If these people are engaging in either of the two "petting standards," it seems there is less likelihood of being unable to let "go" in marital coitus.[23] Such people will probably have developed their sexual emotions to a much greater degree than those adhering to the "kissing standards."

According to three of the major studies (Terman, Kinsey, and Burgess and Wallin), roughly ten out of every one hundred wives never in all their years of marriage achieved orgasm, and an additional twenty out of every one hundred wives achieved orgasm rarely and only after the first year or so of marriage.[24] The evidence of the association between premarital and marital orgasm has already been given.[25] From this evidence, it would seem that those abstinence women who lack premarital orgasm would be more likely to have orgasm difficulty in marriage. The kissing standards would more likely be involved here. Some of these people would be frigid women who did not desire orgasm.[26] Nevertheless, 60 per cent

---

23. Kinsey, *Human Female,* pp. 266-67.

24. Kinsey, *Human Female,* chap. ix, especially pp. 383, 393. Kinsey found that 10 per cent of the wives never reached orgasm and 15 per cent took over a year to reach their first orgasm, while about 50 per cent reached their first orgasm in the first month of marriage. The vast majority of this 50 per cent had experienced orgasm of some kind previous to marriage. Burgess and Wallin, *op. cit.,* p. 670. These men found that 5.1 per cent of the women never experienced orgasm in marriage and that an additional 21.5 per cent only experience orgasm sometimes. These women had been married on the average of four years. Terman, *op. cit.,* p. 300. He found that 8.3 per cent of the wives never experienced orgasm and an additional 25.1 per cent experienced it only sometimes. More wives reach orgasm in the more recent generations. See: *Human Female,* pp. 356-65.

25. See my Chart I, p. 185. I cannot stress enough that all that is known here is a correlation, and thus there may not be a direct causal relationship. Please keep this in mind throughout this section.

26. I use the term frigidity here to mean lack of sexual desire. For a

of this group of unexperienced virgins did achieve orgasm in the first year of marriage.[27] Thus, the prognosis for inexperienced virgins is not as poor as one might suppose.

The other group of women who have marital orgasm difficulty is composed of individuals who have engaged in coitus but failed to ever reach orgasm. Many of the guilt-ridden people in this group would be adherents of abstinence who had violated their beliefs. Thus the believers in abstinence, in particular those who violate this belief and experience guilt feelings and those who follow their belief but lack premarital orgasm experience, probably supply the bulk of those females who are unable to achieve orgasm in marriage. This situation is likely aggravated by the fact that these females are often mated with double-standard men who, as has been discussed in the last chapter, often make losing inhibitions even more difficult.

Many of the believers in abstinence are caught in a dilemma in our culture. They must walk a tightrope between guilt and serious inhibitions. If they go too far, they are bothered by guilt; if they do not go far enough, they are bothered by the risk of inhibitions which may be difficult to break. Were our culture less sensate, were it to accent the desirability of sexual behavior less than it does, it might be easier to be abstinent. But our culture, as it is now, merely aggravates the over-all situation by its allegiance to abstinence, while in our movies, songs, television, and books,

---

brief discussion of frigidity, see Lena Levine, M.D. and Mildred Gilmer, *op. cit.* For an article which states that clitoral orgasm is more typical than vaginal orgasm, see Albert Ellis, "Is the Vaginal Orgasm a Myth?", chap. xii in Alyappin Pillay and Albert Ellis, *op. cit.* For another psychiatric opinion, see Karl A. Menninger, M.D., "Impotence and Frigidity," in Aron Krich (ed.), *Men.*

27. *Human Female*, p. 406. For a discussion of female and male potency, see Mead, *Male and Female,* chap. x, "Potency and Receptivity." For a more conservative discussion of marital sex adjustment, see Allan Fromme, M.D., *Sex and Marriage* (New York: Barnes and Noble Company, 1955), chap. v, "Sex in Marriage."

sexuality is provoked in a multitude of forms. Americans find it difficult to digest both offerings. Let me hasten to add that, despite this situation, there are many girls who seem able to walk this tightrope and adjust quite well to marital coitus.

SECURITY, RESPECT, AND SAVING

The abstinence subtypes are, in one major respect, much more protective than the permissive standards. The general opinion in America favors abstinence; a female who abstains from intercourse is much less likely to run into social condemnation. It is this added security or acceptance element which encourages many girls to forego the desirable consequences of premarital sexual intercourse.

The over-all view as to security feelings is not easy to portray. As many abstinence females know, there are numerous aspects of their standard which make them feel insecure and unsure of themselves. Nevertheless, abstinence does afford the very comforting feeling of abiding by the formally accepted standard.[28]

Abstinence adherents, as a rule, feel that a boy will not make sexual advances unless he lacks respect for the girl. They believe the boy agrees with them that one should "save something for marriage." Thus, they believe they are in a better position—one which affords more respect from others than the position of the female who goes further in her sexual intimacies. This is a very common line of reasoning and deserves some comment here.

Such reasoning is somewhat vague and general. It is true that double-standard males will make their most aggressive

---

28. Many of these assertions concerning abstinence women are derived from my interviews. The importance of "respectability" to abstinence women was documented by Ehrmann, *Premarital Dating Behavior,* p. 239.

sexual advances with females they classify as "bad." But it is equally true that these males and single-standard males (which one must remember exist also) will make sexual advances of some sort with girls they like. As shown earlier, some person-centered coital relations are carried on by adherents of the transitional subtype of the double standard. Many other double-standard males feel that, although they would lose respect for a girl if she engaged in coitus, they would not lose respect for a girl who engaged in petting with men she liked a great deal.

Less than one-half of the men in the Kinsey study stated they would require virginity in their wives while less than a quarter of the females had such virginal requirements for their future mates.[29] Of course, many other men may prefer virginity even though they do not require it. Nevertheless, this is strong evidence that virginity is not as important to many groups of men as it once was.[30]

Thus it seems that many boys—double standard as well as single standard—accept petting when affection is involved, and many others accept coitus when love or engagement is involved.[31] These boys would not lose their respect for a girl who complied with such standards. They might very well pass up a girl whose standards were much stricter than their own.

29. *Human Male,* p. 323. Ehrmann's findings are quite similar. For a summary of findings from various researches on what percentage of men desire virginal mates see: Ehrmann, *Premarital Dating Behavior,* p. 190.

30. My own studies and Dr. Ehrmann's work in Florida indicate that about half of the college men accept coitus where love and engagement is present. The transitional subtype of the double standard and permissiveness with affection is probably quite popular with college men. *Ibid.,* pp. 185-86.

31. Many of the engaged couples in both the Terman and the Burgess and Wallin studies were indulging in coitus. Almost all of the men involved felt they were doing the right thing and their relationship was being strengthened. Thus there seems to be many men who accept coitus under these conditions.

In that sense, such men might "lose respect" for abstinence females because they were too strict or old-fashioned.

It is important to note that a great many abstinence women would lose respect for themselves if they engaged in petting or coitus before marriage, and they abstain for these reasons. Such women may feel they want sexual activity to be something sacred, and they, therefore, must avoid it until they marry and can associate it with a sacred union in marriage. This certainly is a widely accepted position.

The desire to save something for marriage is indeed one which most Americans look upon favorably. Marriage is of great importance, and most all people want to enter it under the best possible circumstances. Nevertheless, there is a dilemma present here. As in other things, if we wait too long, often our ability to perform the action decreases, and the notion of the action tends to lose contact with reality.[32] Thus it seems that the female who adheres strictly to the abstinence code may involve herself in disillusionment or sexual inhibitions, while the more liberal abstinence adherent may feel that the little she is saving is not meaningful enough.

Permissive individuals feel that in a larger sense, we all save something for marriage. We save a feeling of love for our mate which we have never exactly felt before and never will exactly feel again. Every love affair is new and unique in this sense and always involves something which was never present before. To the abstinence believer, however, such saving is not sufficient.

Part of the reason for the dilemma of abstinence "saving" lies in our conflicting social expectations. We demand that a female restrain herself and avoid developing sexual desires before marriage, and yet we expect that in marriage a magic

---

32. Maupassant, *op. cit.* This is a classic account of the experiences a young innocent virgin encounters when she meets and marries a dashing young double-standard man. I highly recommend this book to all for insight into both the double standard and abstinence in their orthodox forms.

transformation will occur to make this same restrained female passionate and well versed in the art of sexual gratification. The two roles of "pure virgin" before marriage and "good sexual partner" in marriage are difficult to combine.[33]

FINAL EXPLANATIONS OF
CHARACTERISTICS AND CONSEQUENCES

Some mention should be made that this standard, like our three other major standards, varies by education and occupational classes. Exact statements are not possible, but Kinsey's evidence indicates that among college-educated males, about one-third are virgins before marriage, while among grade-school-educated males, only about 2 per cent are virgins before marriage. Thus abstinence is likely much stronger among college males. However, 35-52 per cent of the virginal males stated that lack of opportunity kept them from losing their virginity; these men are likely "circumstantial" virgins rather than believers in abstinence.

Among females in Kinsey's sample the picture is somewhat different. Between the ages of 16 and 20, 38 per cent of the grade-school-educated girls and about only 18 per cent of the college-educated girls have intercourse. Since the grade-school-educated girls marry several years younger, eventually the college girls achieve the highest premarital intercourse rates (60 per cent). It is difficult to tell if the girls with a grade school education accepted abstinence, or whether they just married before they had the opportunity for coitus. Twenty-two per cent of the female virgins stated that they

---

33. Mead, *Male and Female,* chap. xiv. This chapter is a most interesting discussion of this and other incompatibilities in our courtship and marriage institution. For evidence of the greater sexual role of the female in marriage today, see: Kinsey, *Human Female,* pp. 356-65.

lacked the opportunity to have coitus and were just "circum-stantial" virgins.

So, in abstinence, too, one finds some variance by social classes, such as educational class. As stated, it is difficult to do more than make some general distinction, for most of the evidence focuses on behavior rather than standards.[34]

From this over-all discussion of abstinence, it should be clear that, although the social acceptability of abstinence may add to one's feelings of security, there are other parts of this standard which add insecurity and conflict. How restrictive should one be? How much should one save for marriage? Will one be able to enjoy marital coitus? Should one go "all the way" when in love? These are the questions which frequently arise and make the security of abstinence far from an unmitigated blessing.

As in most social beliefs, the major reason for adherence to abstinence is the fact that one was brought up to believe in it, and is thus emotionally attached. Other "reasons" given for such a belief are often shared rationalizations. Kinsey, Burgess and Wallin, and Ehrmann, all found that most of their women said that "moral objection" was a chief reason for restricting one's behavior. Such moral objection is verbal-ized as "a feeling that abstinenece is right or best." This feel-ing is what I mean here by emotional attachment due to one's upbringing.[35]

Most of the younger abstinence females are probably quite content with their standard. A good number of the older abstinence women, however, tire of always having to draw

---

34. For a discussion of the above points see *Human Male,* chap. xvii; and *Human Female,* pp. 295, 332 *passim.*

35. *Human Female,* p. 316; Burgess and Wallin, *op. cit.,* p. 344; Ehr-mann, *Premarital Dating Behavior,* pp. 91, 232. Ehrmann found that for non-lovers the chief reason for restraint was lack of desire, with morals second. All three studies found morals a strong, but less important, reason for restraint among men.

a line.[36] The possible bad consequences of coitus seem to have lost some of their fearfulness, and the good consequences seem to have become more attractive. Many of these people are torn between these two sets of consequences— wanting one set and yet still fearing and respecting the other set. Nevertheless, the traditional teaching of abstinence still has a grip on a great number of our young people. They very often feel as the following individual:

> We have discussed sexual relations and we both decided we'd rather not. It's not because we don't want to, but because we don't think it is worth it. And it's not because of any risk involved. I thought I would cheapen myself in my eyes and hers. I love her too much to have that relationship a furtive one.[37]

The above quote illustrates the basic feeling of wrongness that training has instilled—the act would "cheapen" oneself because it is viewed as immoral.

---

36. Many of my interviewees expressed these feelings of discontent, although they intended to remain chaste.
37. Burgess and Wallin, p. 347.

Chapter Ten

Future Trends in
Premarital Sexual Standards

THE KEY EVENTS OF THE LAST FEW CEN-
turies were the numerous revolutions which were dealt with
earlier in this book—the urban-industrial, romantic-love, and
feminist revolutions. These three revolutions were really one.
A mighty change was occurring in Western society—a change
more significant than any since the great discovery of agriculture ten thousand years ago. America and the Western
World were changing into a new type of society, an urban-
industrialized society. Because of this change, premarital
coitus is not the same today as it was one hundred years ago.
Its consequences and meaning today are quite different. Many
people have not yet realized this, for the old beliefs about
coitus tend to become reified.

Many of our problems in America today are due to the
fact that we are operating, in certain respects, with our ancient
rural customs in an urban-industrialized society. There is nothing wrong with these customs as such, but many of them do

not fit our present-day society. The early agricultural societies ten thousand years ago must have faced somewhat the same sort of conditions. In those times, it would have been the older hunting-society norms which would be hanging on and causing problems. This emerging type of society is quite new, less than four centuries old, so we still remember quite a bit about our agricultural-rural past. We have, however, forgotten mostly everything about our hunting-society past. In a few centuries, the same may be true of much of our agricultural past. We will have devised many new norms, kept some of the old, and reshaped many others to fit our changing needs. The customs which are still capable of maintaining society, of helping to keep our culture unified and strong should last. In many areas of behavior, such customs are lacking, and new ones will have to be developed if we are to maintain cohesion. In the area of premarital sexual activity, many of our older customs can no longer do their job of maintaining our courtship institution, and new customs, such as permissiveness with affection, the transitional double standard, and petting with affection, are evolving. When one looks at these changes in the setting of the totality of events which have occurred in our society, they are not at all surprising.[1]

THE DOUBLE STANDARD
AND ABSTINENCE

The revolutions have all tended towards equalitarian relations between men and women and were thus opposed to

---

1. For an informative account of our agricultural revolution 10,000 years ago see V. Gordon Childe, *Man Makes Himself* (New York: Mentor Books, 1953). For an equally insightful view of the changes which have occurred with the advent of civilization see Robert Redfield, *The Primitive World and Its Transformations* (Ithaca, N.Y.: Cornell University Press, 1953).

the double standard. It is unlikely that these revolutions will stop altering our society in this direction. Our society is too much a part of these revolutions. A rural society with its close-knit groups and strong social controls, with its non-rational approach and its lack of pragmatism is the ideal setting for the double standard. But that way of life is disappearing in America, and, as it departs, it is taking with it the double standard. The transitional double standard developed in the attempt to somewhat liberalize the double standard to make it fit better into our society. At present this subtype seems to be growing rather than decreasing. However, it is possible that as people become more aware of the typical double standard inequalities still within it, it may lose some of its popularity to a single standard, such as permissiveness with affection.   ,

Our way of life today emphasizes the full enjoyment of life by both men and women. We have a hedonistic approach to living, not an ascetic one. We are a nation of people who value rationality quite highly. We are so imbued with the scientific ethics of our time that we seem to demand that one be able to defend his views, whether they be in politics, religion, or in sexual morality.[2] The inequality of our traditional sexual customs and the many inconsistencies in them make them a good target for rationalism. The asceticism of these sexual standards is opposed by our hedonism and secularism.

However, the orthodox double standard is still very much with us. The fact that many millions of people reject it and would prefer another standard does not in itself remove this ancient belief. It has five or more millenniums of tradition to support it and it has the usual fear of the unknown to prevent

2. For a most insightful analysis of these characteristics and others of our society, see Robin M. Williams, Jr., *American Society* (New York: Alfred Knopf, 1956). See especially chap. xi, "Value Orientations in American Society," pp. 372-442.

people from leaving it. Many people probably have other preferences over and above the orthodox double standard, but most of these people are afraid to step out of line and they still have some amount of sympathy for this standard.[3]

This sort of attitude seems to be a frequent prelude to social change. The present-day situation indicates that the social supports of this way of life are greatly weakened, and more and more people are finding it distasteful. It is just a matter of time, then, until the reaction becomes somewhat stronger and people move more openly in other directions. The first innovators, in fact, have already appeared in the form of the adherents of the two single permissive standards, and in the supporters of the transitional double standard. In the meantime, do not be fooled; the "monster" is not dead. He is very much alive in the sexual customs of America—but the signs of his incurable illness are equally undeniable.

The trends in the standard of abstinence are quite similar to those in the double standard, as I have somewhat indicated in our previous discussion. Abstinence has lost adherents because its ancient supports have been greatly weakened, e.g., the risk of pregnancy, venereal disease, social condemnation, and guilt feelings are quite different in present-day society. Also, the emphasis on the desirability of physical and psychic satisfaction is higher today. The concept of behavior which is acceptable to this standard is changing also. Our petting standards are mainly outgrowths of the unchaperoned dating period starting before World War I and are clear reflections of the more liberal, less controlled form of behavior among young people, which was and is a reflection of the new type of society which is developing. In this sense, it may be said that as the

3. In 1956, I asked one hundred of my students how they felt about the double standard, and over 90 per cent of them said they would prefer another standard, but many added that they would go along with the double standard since they did not want to try to "change the world." This is evidence of both the strength and the weakness of this standard.

total number of adherents of abstinence decreased in the last fifty years, the relative number of adherents who accept petting as part of their standard of abstinence increased greatly.[4]

This sort of change in abstinence is what one would expect to occur in a society which was becoming much more open in its attitude towards sexual behavior and was also becoming freer and more equalitarian in its treatment of young people.[5] Such a change fits in perfectly with the over-all movement towards more sexual freedom for young people. It is in accordance with the tremendous increases in premarital coitus. In short, allowing increased sexual freedom to those who accepted abstinence was necessary if that standard was to continue to be significant in our culture. If the abstinence standards continued to allow only discriminate kissing, the number of adherents of such standards would probably have been drastically reduced. Such an event would have forced many people to choose coitus in preference to such rigid restrictions. This, however, did not occur, because there was an alternative; one did not have to choose between kissing or coitus; one could compromise and engage in petting. This is the choice many young people made. In this way they could gain increased sexual behavior and still keep their virginity. There have been suggestions made that we accept petting to orgasm for young people, as a compromise solution to our premarital sexual problems today:

> It seems that the solution most in accordance with modern knowledge lies in an intelligent giving of advice to adolescents, through the parents and through the ordinary channels of sex

---

4. Kinsey and Ehrmann found that well over half of all virgins petted. Thus, our estimate of about half acceptance of petting seems to be a conservative one. Furthermore, some of the petting rates, such as petting to orgasm have doubled and tripled with those born after 1900, indicating the trend about which we are speaking. See Table 1 in this chapter.

5. An interesting study of the sexual behavior of ministerial students today can be found in Austin L. Porterfield and H. Ellison Salley, *op. cit.*

education, about the forms of sexual play that are most likely
to lead to orgasm for both parties, and least likely to result in
conception or an undesirable carryover into adult practice,
coupled with a definite social tolerance of such equivalents as
will enable them to be open and not clandestine.[6]

Nevertheless, there are many aspects of such a compromise which make it precarious. One quite obvious one is that
petting is close enough to actual coitus so that it may easily
tempt one to cross the line in behavior and eventually in belief also. This would be particularly true for those who accept
heavy petting. These petting standards may be only stopping-
off points on the way to a fully permissive standard. Many
women, upon falling in love, seem to leave their petting
standard and accept permissiveness with affection or the transitional double standard. There is some evidence to support
this transitory view of the petting standards. Between the
ages of twenty and twenty-five, Kinsey found that the number of non-virgins virtually doubled. Most of these women
seem to accept their changed behavior without regret. It is
probable that this is the time when the majority of the con-
versions from abstinence to permissiveness with affection
or the transitional double standard occur. The transitional
double standard is another subtype which, like petting, developed in response to the liberal, permissive pressures of
the twentieth century. This standard may also be only a
temporary compromise on the road to a single standard of
permissiveness, such as permissiveness with affection.

The following tables list some of the evidence for increased heavy petting and for the rapid rise in both petting
to orgasm and actual coitus, between the ages of twenty and
twenty-five.

Many people may be bothered by such a prediction of the

---

6. Alex Comfort, *Sexual Behavior in Society* (New York: The Viking
Press, 1950), p. 99. Needless to say, Mr. Comfort is an Englishman.

increasing decline of the double standard and, more importantly, abstinence. But it cannot be denied that abstinence has declined since 1900, and there has been a strong shift in the direction of more sexual liberty for virgins. Furthermore,

Table 1—Accumulative Incidence of Petting to Orgasm among Females

AGE	DECADE OF BIRTH			
	Before 1900	1900-9	1910-19	1920-29
14	1 per cent	1 per cent	1 per cent	1 per cent
16	3	5	6	6
18	6	10	13	18
20	10	17	22	28
25	15	30	34	43
30	24	39	45	—
35	26	44	53	—

Source: Kinsey, *Human Female*, p. 275. The younger generation of males experienced a small increase in petting to orgasm. Kinsey, *Human Male*, p. 406. For the college-educated males, by ages 20 and 25, the respective percentages experiencing petting to orgasm are 37 per cent and 53 per cent for the older generation; 48 per cent and 62 per cent for the younger generation.

Accumulative incidence is *not* the same as cumulative percentage figures. The accumulative incidence percentage shows "the number of experienced persons in each age group, in relation to the number of persons in each group who are eligible for such experience." *Human Male*, pp. 115-18. Thus, in this table, at age 20, for those born before 1900, the rate is 10 per cent. This means that of all the women born before 1900 who were 20 years of age or over and who were unmarried at age 20 (this is the total eligible population), 10 per cent had experienced petting to orgasm by age 20.

Table 2—Accumulative Incidence of Premarital Coitus for Females

AGE	DECADE OF BIRTH			
	Before 1900	1900-9	1910-19	1920-29
13	1 per cent	1 per cent	1 per cent	1 per cent
15	2	2	3	4
20	8	18	23	21
25	14	36	39	37
30	26	53	48	—
35	35	56	54	—

Source: Kinsey, *Human Female*, p. 339. The percentage with experience goes even higher at older ages, but for our purposes, the most significant changes are the vast increases in the twenty to twenty-five age group. This is the time when many girls fall in love or become engaged. Such experiences appear to change their attitudes toward sexual intercourse. The younger generation of males, at the younger ages, had a small increase in the amount of coitus. See Table 5 in this chapter.

it cannot be denied that our society, with its lack of chaperonage, its anonymity, its rationality, its freedom for young people, and its equalitarian aspects, is not conducive to chastity. The main support today for both abstinence and the double standard is the emotional backing these standards derive from being taught as acceptable or proper behavior. People will think up reasons if they are asked why they behave a certain way, but emotional habit seems to be the valid explanation. Such emotional backing is potent and difficult to change regardless of other factors. One can see this in the reaction of American smokers to the lung cancer "scare." Although the American Cancer Society has come out against heavy cigarette smoking, most people continue to smoke and make up rationalizations for their behavior. The habits of years are hard to change. This is probably the major reason why abstinence and the double standard are still powerful despite all the forces which are slowly weakening them.[7]

As the double standard weakens, the choice more clearly becomes abstinence or permissiveness for both men and women. The double standard protected abstinence from this choice in the past, by affording a means of "evading" or "compensating" for full abstinence. Thus, although abstinence believers may dislike the double standard, it has been the main support of at least female chastity and of at least a formal allegiance to full abstinence. As equalitarian pressures weaken the orthodox double standard, it becomes more

---

7. One area of the double standard which would likely repay investigation is that of pregnancy. It is in our folklore (witness, *Streetcar Named Desire*) that often it is during a woman's pregnancy that her husband commits adultery. The lack of sexual relations during late pregnancy and the lack (at times) of desire on the part of the pregnant female may be responsible here if this is a valid pattern. Such a situation seems to support the double standard unless love becomes a factor which helps control the man and encourage the woman to be more satisfying to the man.

obvious that full abstinence for both men and women is not attractive to many Americans, and when forced to choose between full abstinence or greater female permissiveness, these people often choose permissiveness.

But one may ask—cannot something be done to reinstate, to strengthen abstinence and the double standard? These standards are still quite strong and are likely to remain so for many generations even though they are gradually weakening. Bertrand Russell has made some penetrating and sarcastic remarks concerning the possibility of reversing this process:

> If, on the other hand, the old morality is to be re-established, certain things are essential; some of them are already done, but experience shows that these alone are not effective. The first essential is that the education of girls should be such as to make them stupid and superstitious and ignorant; this requisite is already fulfilled in schools over which the churches have any control. The next requisite is a very severe censorship upon all books giving information on sex subjects; this condition also is coming to be fulfilled in England and America, since the censorship, without change in the law, is being tightened up by the increasing zeal of the police. These conditions, however, since they exist already, are clearly insufficient. The only thing that will suffice is to remove from young women all opportunity of being alone with men. Girls must be forbidden to earn their living by work outside the home; they must never be allowed an outing unless accompanied by their mother or an aunt; the regrettable practice of going to dances without a chaperon must be sternly stamped out. It must be illegal for an unmarried woman under fifty to possess a motor-car, and perhaps it would be wise to subject all unmarried women once a month to medical examination by police doctors and to send to a penitentiary all such as were found to be not virgins. The use of contraceptives must, of course, be eradicated, and it must be illegal in conversation with unmarried women to throw doubt upon the dogma of eternal damnation. These measures, if carried out vigorously for a hundred years or more, may perhaps do something to stem

the rising tide of immorality. I think, however, that in order to avoid the risk of certain abuses, it would be necessary that all policemen and all medical men should be castrated, with the exception of ministers of religion. (Since reading *Elmer Gantry*, I have begun to feel that even this exception is perhaps not quite wise.)

It will be seen that there are difficulties and objections whichever course we adopt. If we are to allow the new morality to take its course, it is bound to go further than it has done, and to raise difficulties hardly as yet appreciated. If on the other hand, we attempt in the modern world to enforce restrictions which were possible in a former age, we are led into an impossible stringency of regulation, against which human nature would soon rebel. This is so clear that, whatever the dangers or difficulties, we must be content to let the world go forward rather than back. For this purpose we shall need a genuinely new morality. I mean by this that obligations and duties will still have to be recognized, though they may be very different from the obligations and duties recognized in the past. So long as all the moralists content themselves with preaching a return to a system which is as dead as the Dodo, they can do nothing whatever to moralize the new freedom or to point out the new duties which it brings with it. I do not think that the new system any more than the old should involve an unbridled yielding to impulse, but I think the occasions for restraining impulse and the motives for doing so will have to be different from what they have been in the past. In fact, the whole problem of sexual morality needs thinking out afresh.[8]

THE SINGLE PERMISSIVE STANDARDS

The revolutions were much kinder to the single standards. As urban living, reinforced by contraceptive knowledge and feminist pressures, began to move society into a more equali-

8. Bertrand Russell, *Marriage and Morals* (New York: Horace Liveright, 1929), pp. 90-92. This is an excellent and stimulating book in many ways.

tarian position, the permissive standards began to grow. After all, if society is changing in the direction of greater equality among the sexes, it is natural to expect the development of such single standards allowing equal sexual rights to both men and women.

It was in the iconoclastic environment of the 1920's that the permissive standards took root. The generation of people born between 1900 and 1910 revolutionized our sexual customs. The generations born since that time have somewhat continued these changes, but for the most part, they have only consolidated the inroads that this older generation perpetrated. Those born in the 1900-09 decade vastly increased our former sexual rates in almost all areas when they came to maturity in the 1920's—the decade of the sexual revolution. For the first time in history, women were given a chance for a third choice, i.e., it no longer was the Greek choice of Hetaerae or wife, or the nineteenth-century choice of pleasure-woman or wife; women could now choose to accept premarital sexual behavior, not as prostitutes or pleasure-seekers but as lovers.

Let there be no misunderstanding about the 1920's. Many people were just enjoying prosperity and bootlegging and having a fling. These people were not looking for a new sexual standard; many lacked any strong standard. The rapid changes in our society had uprooted these people and left them somewhat disillusioned or indifferent to sexual standards. Many were armed with the new freedom ideology of Freud and were waging war against the Victorian restrictions still present in our culture. They had no clear-cut standard—they were simply against repression of any kind.[9] Nevertheless, these people

---

9. The situation in the 1920's seems to fit Merton's description of anomie or normlessness. There was great pressure to engage in sexual relations and yet no acceptable way. The result was that rebellious and innovating responses occurred and we had the great sexual explosion of the 1920's. Merton, *op. cit.,* chaps. iv and v.

started the changes which eventually led to the growth of these standards. People do not like to feel guilty about their behavior. Thus as time went on, many of these iconoclasts began to accept and formulate more liberal standards which would tolerate their behavior.

The following tables present evidence from our major research studies which documents this vast increase in premarital coitus and indicates the direction of these increases.

Tables 3, 4, and 5 contain much valuable information, but please bear in mind that the most that can be obtained from these studies is an indication of general behavior for certain segments of our population. The vast increase in sexual behavior, brought about by those people born between 1900 and 1909, is clearly illustrated in the tables. The male non-virginity figures are low on Table 3 because of the high number of male college graduates involved in this particular study. As mentioned previously college men seem to have

Table 3—Premarital Coitus of Men and Women by Decade of Birth

HUSBANDS:	DECADE OF BIRTH		
	Before 1890	1890-99	1900-9
None	50.6 per cent	41.9 per cent	32.6 per cent
With Fiancee Only	4.6	7.6	17.2
With Fiancee and Others	9.2	23.0	33.7
With Others Only	35.6	27.5	16.5
	100.0	100.0	100.0
Number of Cases	(174)	(291)	(273)
WIVES:			
None	86.5	74.0	51.2
With Fiance Only	8.7	17.7	32.7
With Fiance and Others	2.9	5.8	14.0
With Others Only	1.9	2.5	2.1
	100.0	100.0	100.0
Number of Cases	(104)	(277)	(336)

Source: Terman, op. cit., p. 321. The fiance(e) referred to here is the person eventually married.

the least amount of premarital coitus. This can also be seen in Table 5. Unfortunately, the part of Table 3 on men and Table 5 are not comparable, since Table 3 has no men in the birth category of the "younger generation." However, the general average of all the men in Table 3 and the college-educated men in the "older generation" in Table 5 are comparable. The males in Table 5 (older generation) are not broken down to check for trends within this group. In Table 3, such a breakdown is made into three decades and sharp trends are evidenced. Later increases in male non-virginity, as in the "younger generation" are slight and at certain ages only.

Table 4—Premarital Coitus of Women by Decade of Birth

| | DECADE OF BIRTH | | | |
	Before 1900	1900-9	1910-19	1920-29
None	73.4 per cent	48.7 per cent	43.9 per cent	48.8 per cent
With Fiance Only	10.4	24.4	23.3	27.3
With Fiance and Others	10.4	21.0	25.6	17.4
With Others Only	5.5	5.4	7.0	6.5
Incomplete Data	.3	.5	.2	.0
	100.0	100.0	100.0	100.0
Number of Cases	(346)	(610)	(896)	(627)

Source: The data for this table were furnished the author by the Institute for Sex Research, thanks to the kindness of Dr. Gebhard and Dr. Martin. It was contained in a letter to the author dated February 23, 1960. The word fiance here means the man eventually married. The table is based on 2,479 "ever married" women. Part of the data can be found in Kinsey, *Human Female,* chap. viii, and all of the cases are from this volume. Table 5 presents what data are available on males. Precisely comparable data are not available.

There are more recent data from the Terman study that could have been added to Table 3. These data indicate that 86 per cent of the men and 68 per cent of the women born between 1910-19 were sexually experienced before marriage, but this information was based on only 22 men and 60 women, and I have not included it.[10] The Burgess and Wallin study is

10. For a statement of this finding, see Terman, *op. cit.,* p. 321.

composed almost exclusively of couples born between 1910-19 and they report no such rapid rise in non-virginity.[13] Further, evidence for doubting this part of the Terman study can be obtained by examining Tables 4 and 5 which shows that Kinsey, like Burgess and Wallin, found no sharp rise in this decade.

In what kind of intercourse have these people engaged? In Table 3 the number of female virgins decreased from the "before 1890" to the "1900-09" birth group by a considerable amount, from 86 per cent to 51 per cent. Better than two-thirds of this decrease was due to increases in the number of women who had intercourse with their fiances only; the other one-third of the increase was due to women who had intercourse with their fiances and also with others. Kinsey's findings in Table 4 are somewhat more indicative of an equal growth in the "fiance and others" category as well as the "fiance only" category. But both of these categories indicate that there has been a tremendous increase in the number of women who are engaging in premarital coitus with their future spouses. Some of the "others" would be love affairs, while some would be more casual affairs.

Table 3 affords information on men over the course of several decades. An interesting set of changes appears to have occurred in this group of young men. Going from those born before 1890 to those born between 1900-09, we find there is an extraordinary reduction in the number of men who have premarital coitus of the "only with others" type. The percentage of men engaging in such behavior was more than cut in half. In the same period, the number of men who had experience only with their fiancees increased almost fourfold. The increase in the number of men who experienced coitus

13. Burgess and Wallin, *op. cit.,* p. 330. The general findings here were in accord with the tables presented. Roughly 46 per cent of the females and 68 per cent of the males were non-virginal in this study.

with their "fiancee and others" was almost as great. Kinsey also notes this decrease in "only with others," when he mentions that about 10 per cent of the total premarital coitus of all the men in his study was with prostitutes, and, although the total amount of coitus did not decrease, the frequency of coitus with prostitutes seemed to have been cut in half in the younger generation described in Table 5.[11]

The over-all evidence from Terman clearly indicates that men, too, have experienced a most radical increase in the amount of sexual intercourse with their future spouses. The great decrease in the number of men who experienced coitus "only with others" is evidence of a significant change, i.e., the decline of the double standard. Men who formerly would not have coitus with their fiancees because they were "good" girls were now altering their standards and indulging with their fiancees. This probably meant that these men were either accepting the transitional subtype or were rejecting the double standard altogether and accepting permissiveness with affection in its place. Here, then, was a general movement in which men stopped being so strictly double standard and women ceased being so strictly abstinent.[12] Person-centered coitus was coming of age.

The similarity between these tables, composed of data gathered from people from different parts of the country, in studies separated in time by about fifteen years, lends support to the belief that these findings reflect a genuine trend in our culture. One should, however, be aware of the high percentages of college graduates and urban people in these studies. Although these are the best studies available, they are not

---

11. *Human Male,* pp. 300, 416, 599, 603, and chart on p. 410.

12. Another study of similar age groups which also found the tendencies shown here is Harvey J. Locke, *op. cit.;* see especially pp. 136-37 and chap. vii *passim.* Note that in the Terman and Kinsey studies, although there have been vast increases in non-virginity, the percentage of non-virgins who indulge only with their future spouse remains almost the same.

fully representative and are subject to criticism on several levels, as was pointed out previously. They are, however, accurate enough to indicate general trends among large segments of our over-all population.

The lack of any sharp upswing in these trends since the peaks were established in the 1920's is hypothesized as due to a consolidation process. It might well be that, since the 1920's, what has been occurring is a change in attitudes to match the change in behavior of that era. The actual behavior may thus be very much the same, but a much larger percentage of these people today are people who no longer look upon their behavior as wrong and have more fully accepted person-centered coitus and petting.

It is worth noting that, although rates for coitus do not seem to have sharply increased since the twenties, the rates for petting have increased notably since then. (See table 1.)

Table 5—Accumulative Incidence of Premarital Coitus for Men by Generation and Education Level

Age	EDUCATION LEVEL: 13 YEARS OR MORE		EDUCATION LEVEL: 0-8 YEARS	
	Older Generation (Born before 1910)	Younger Generation	Older Generation (Born before 1910)	Younger Generation
12	.5 per cent	1.1 per cent	2.5 per cent	10.1 per cent
14	6.3	5.9	20.8	34.8
16	14.9	15.6	48.1	66.8
18	27.0	31.4	73.3	81.9
20	38.8	45.4	82.2	86.6
22	48.2	55.8	83.3	85.9
25	62.0	65.9	90.3	88.9

Source: Kinsey, *Human Male*, pp. 400, 404. Data on those males whose education stopped after 9-12 years of schooling, are not available for these generations. *Ibid.*, p. 550, shows over-all data for these high-school-educated groups which indicates that their frequency fall in-between the above two groups, e.g., by age 16, 58 per cent were experienced, by age 20, 75 per cent and by age 25, 84 per cent.

The older generation here refers to those males who came to maturity between 1910-25 and thus were born before 1910. This table only goes to age 25 in each generation but the rates for older unmarried males goes up only slightly. There is no data on the males type of partner comparable to the female data.

As has been mentioned, this increase in petting adherents may well lead, in time, to an increase in people who accept full coitus. It seems plausible to expect the change from abstinence to occur gradually and for individuals to accept petting before they fully accept coitus. This is one of the senses in which the time from the 1920's to the 1960's can be viewed as a consolidation process, a consolidation of the changes made and a preparation for further changes. In addition to the number of people who accept petting there seems to have been an increase in the transitional double standard, which also seems like a step toward a single standard of permissiveness with affection.

The 1920's were unusual times. Women were being arrested for wearing too-short bathing suits, men were being put on trial for teaching evolution, and bold girls were accepting the new ideas concerning petting and discussing sexual behavior with their dates. Out of this setting came the people who were to smash the sexual idols of Victorianism beyond repair. Compare our attitudes today to the 1920's and one can see immediately that, although our coital behavior is not radically different, we have consolidated our ideas and accept our behavior with a more natural, normal, air. We are more sure of our beliefs.[13] There is still much confusion in the area of sexual beliefs today. But there are strong signs that the air is clearing, and, as the "clouds" move away, one can see the battered orthodox double standard and abstinence structures alongside the new edifices of the standards allowing person-centered petting and coitus.[14]

---

13. Kirchwey, *op. cit.*, chap. by Leavenworth. This chapter was written in the 1920's, and one can see how chaperonage and the "evils" of divorce were much more current then. For an article written in the thirties on the changes in the twenties, see: Theodore Newcomb, "Recent Changes in Atitudes toward Sex and Marriage," *American Sociological Review,* II (December, 1937), 659-67.

14. The most recent evidence on the growth of person-centered coitus is in the before-mentioned study by Winston Ehrmann. Ehrmann found

My impression from my informal questioning of college and non-college people lends strong support to the research evidence quoted here.[15]

QUO VADIS?

This hypothesis concerning trends is supported by the authors of the major studies. They stated that a new, more permissive and equalitarian sex code is evolving.[16] None of of these authors, however, have spelled out in detail the specific nature of that code nor the vital reasons for such a change.

a) The 1960's and the Next Fifty Years. The changes which have occurred in the last few generations have been so extreme that no one could have fully foreseen them. The

---

that about one-half of the males and a smaller, though significant number of females accept intercourse when engaged. Ehrmann also found that if a girl was in love with her date, the chances of intercourse occurring were over three times what they were if no love was present. Ehrmann, *Premarital Dating Behavior,* chaps. v and vi.

15. Of course, a person's attitude cannot be discovered by simple direct questioning such as "What do you believe in?" Many people have not analyzed their own beliefs and do not fully know in what they believe. Others would answer differently depending on how well they knew the interviewer. The person who is asked "Is it right to go to church on Sunday mornings?" may well answer "Yes" because he has been taught that this is the proper answer, but he himself may only attend a few times a year and feel no qualms about it. So it is with people answering sexual questions. Most of them will give a recital of norms they have been taught. One must probe deeper and possibly use "projective" techniques such as asking their opinion of a hypothetical case of sexual behavior. This projective approach was used in my questionnaire study of high school and college students. For a most interesting discussion of interviewing see: Kinsey, *Human Male,* chap. ii.

16. *Human Female,* chap. viii, especially pp. 321-24; Burgess and Wallin, *op. cit.,* chap. xii, especially pp. 387-90; Terman, *op. cit.,* chap. xii, especially pp. 321-23. For additional support, see Locke, *op. cit.,* Ehrmann, *op. cit.,* Foote, *op. cit.,* and Ditzion, *op. cit.* For a review of research done in this area and all other areas in sociology from 1945-55, see Joseph B. Gittler (ed.), *Review of Sociology* (New York: John Wiley and Sons, 1957), especially chap. xi.

changes which will occur in the next few generations may be equally as extreme, and no one can fully predict them. In the light of the evidence and reasoning covered in this book, however, I will venture to say that the next fifty years, like the last fifty years, will witness an increasing acceptance of person-centered coitus and petting. Accordingly, it is hypothesized that there will be increasing numbers of double-standard people who will accept the transitional double standard and increasing numbers of abstinent people who will accept petting with affection. Finally, I believe Americans will increasingly move from the transitional double standard and petting with affection to full acceptance of permissiveness with affection.[17] This will occur because permissiveness with affection seems most fully integrated with our over-all society, and its cultural trends. It is such cultural trends which, in the long run, affect changes in attitudes. An analogous situation is the school integration issue in the South today. Although many southerners oppose such integration, many of them admit, and social scientists agree, that cultural factors, such as industrialism and urbanism, will eventually make school integration a reality in the South and in time will even make it acceptable.[18] It is by means of similar very powerful forces that our sexual standards are changing. Now, let me spell out in more detail the nature and speed of these trends as I see them.

Within the next decade, we should increasingly approach

17. Several years ago an anthropologist from Harvard made a prediction in this area. He said that in three generations America would be sexually permissive, but he did not spell out the type of permissiveness nor the other features of such a change. See George P. Murdock, "A Comparative Anthropological Approach," *Journal of Social Hygiene,* XXXVI (April, 1950), 133-38.

18. For understanding of this issue see: Harry S. Ashmore, *The Negro and the Schools* (Chapel Hill, N. C.: University of North Carolina Press, 1954); Harry S. Ashmore, *An Epitaph For Dixie* (New York: W. W. Norton and Co., 1958).

a clarification of our sexual beliefs and a concomitant increased consolidation of the changes begun in the 1920's. The post-war baby crop should finish off the consolidation process and make new inroads in the direction of the three standards which have been shown to be increasing most rapidly (petting with affection, transitional double standard, and permissiveness with affection). This post-war generation is being brought up in all sorts of permissiveness—it is being allowed freedom which previous generations were denied. This is so in part because, since World War II, we have been living in an era of prosperity, a time when we have had the leisure to worry about what is right and wrong and how to better bring up children. Even more important than our prosperity is our higher level of education and our favorable attitudes towards pragmatic, rational improvement of our lives.[19] The vast increases in the percentage of people going to college evidences this trend. One-third of the high school graduates attend college and with scholarships, this percentage may go even higher.[20] Such leisure, education, and pragmatic trends weaken the traditional order of our society and tend to strengthen the newer aspects in our way of life, especially among the upper and middle-class-educated group. Since our older way of life is not well integrated with our present society, these trends are very likely to continue regardless of our economic conditions.

There are other vital reasons why I believe this post-war

---

19. For an interesting forecast of our economic future, see Peter F. Drucker, "America's Next Twenty Years," *Harper's Magazine*, March, April, May, and June issues of 1955.

20. The opening fall college enrollment in 1959 was 3,402,297. This is degree-credit enrollment. See: U. S. Department of Health, Education, and Welfare, *Opening Fall Enrollment in Higher Education* (Washington, D.C., 1959). As of 1960, there were over eight million college graduates in America and about an equal number of people who had been to college but never finished. Each year about 300,000 people graduate from college. For predictions on education up to 1980, see: *Current Population Reports, Series P-20*, January 12, 1959, U. S. Bureau of the Census.

generation, even more so than the previous generations, will find person-centered behavior to its liking. The generation of the roaring twenties was a generation in revolt, a generation more busy breaking down old idols than building new ones.[21] The children of these idol-breakers, the parents of the present post-war generation, were born during and immediately before these iconoclastic twenties, and by the time they grew up, permissiveness in sexual behavior was becoming more acceptable due to the revolutionary behavior of their parents. These youngsters grew up in the depression times of the 1930's. People were liberal then—they were looking for new ideas to get out of the depression and, because of their own plight, many were more tolerant of others' behavior in all areas.[22]

Then came World War II, and these same parents, both men and women, went into the armed services in unprecedented numbers and traveled all over America, Europe, and Asia. This situation offered the opportunity to gain a broader perspective on our own American customs. After the war, as this generation settled down to family life, the good times continued, and this was the atmosphere into which their children were born.[23]

The new post-war generation is far enough removed from the puritanical past, and deeply enough involved in the newer

---

21. For a recent account of the 1920's, see Frederick J. Hoffman, *The Twenties* (New York: The Viking Press, 1955). See also Frederick L. Allen, *op. cit.*, chap. v, "The Revolution in Manners and Morals."

22. For a recent coverage of this time period, see Arthur Schlesinger, Jr., *The Age of Roosevelt* (Boston: Houghton-Mifflin Company, 1957). See also John K. Galbraith, *The Great Crash, 1929* (Boston: Houghton-Mifflin Company, 1955).

23. In 1957, the median family income was $5,060. See Selma F. Goldsmith, "Size Distribution of Personal Income," *Survey of Current Business,* April, 1958, pp. 10-19. The median family income for 1958 was about the same as 1957—it was $5,050. This lack of increase was due to the recession of that year. See Selma F. Goldsmith, "Income Distribution by Size—1955-58," *Survey of Current Business,* April 1959, pp. 9-16.

permissive tradition to take it for granted. It is hypothesized that in the 1960's, they will complete the consolidation process started by their grandparents and also start a more overt, public, and formal acceptance of standards which allow person-centered petting and coitus. Instead of the present-day informal acceptance of these standards, we may well find more and more people being brought up from childhood in accord with these more liberal norms. Then these additional "advances" will take time to consolidate and increase. Each generation should be more securely rooted in these new standards than the last generation. This is the process that I believe will slowly move petting with affection, and the transitional double standard, and, ultimately, permissiveness with affection into increasing dominance. This over-all process occurred for several generations previous to the revolt of the 1920's and has been going on since then. It is probably irreversible, given our emerging society and the consequences and meaning of coitus in that society.

The spearhead of this liberal move may well contain a strong mixture of college graduates. There are several reasons for believing this to be the case. First, college men are noted for their low incidences of intercourse with prostitutes, as compared to other groups; they are greater adherents to more equalitarian activities, such as petting with affection and permissiveness with affection, rather than the heavy concentration of body-centered behavior found at the lower educational levels. College graduates are thus more equalitarian in their approach to coitus and in their thoughts about it. Despite their higher percentage of abstinence people, these qualities make them more likely to continue to increasingly accept person-centered coitus. The change in sexual standards not only involves the female becoming more permissive but it also involves the male becoming more discriminate—it is a dual change in which the male and female are approaching each other. In this sense, the discrimination of the college male makes him a likely member of the "avant-garde." Also, college women seem to have the longest periods of courtship due to their later ages at marriage. This means they have more time to become involved in a premarital love affair which would entail sexual intercourse. It also means that college people have more time to spend in clarifying and altering their sexual beliefs. This, coupled with the already high predisposition this group has for equalitarian, person-centered coitus, leads one to expect they will set the pace in sexual changes in the direction of person-centered sexual behavior.

There will, of course, be opposition to these changes. Our religious organizations may fight such liberal moves, especially our more orthodox religions.[24] The restrictive moves of such religious bodies may, in the long run, encourage the new standards by making the old standards more difficult to live up to. The college group most likely will hold a great deal of prestige and power and they should not have a difficult time defeating opposition such as this. The most serious opposition to these new standards will probably come from the older and more conservative element within the college group.[25]

Finally, one should note that the rate of change will

---

24. The orthodox religions seem somewhat unintegrated with our emerging type of society and may themselves, therefore, undergo change. See Parsons, *Social System* (Glencoe, Ill.: The Free Press, 1951), p. 516; and Paul B. Horton and Gerald R. Leslie, *The Sociology of Social Problems* (New York: Appleton-Century-Crofts, 1955), chap. viii, "Religious Problems and Conflicts." For evidence on more liberality in the religious view of sex, see McHugh and Moskin, *op. cit.* For a good over-all view of religion in America see: Thomas F. Hoult, *The Sociology of Religion* (New York: Dryden Press, 1958).

25. Some recent evidence on the power and influence of college graduates can be found in C. Wright Mills, *The Power Elite* (New York: Oxford University Press, 1956), and W. Lloyd Warner and James Abegglen, *Big Business Leaders in America* (New York: Harper and Brothers, 1955).

surely vary for different parts of the country—being the slowest in the more rural regions such as the South. Many southern states still do not allow women on juries.[26] The strong double-standard tradition of the South will be most difficult to change. On the other hand, the highly urbanized areas of the Northeast and West Coast will probably lead in this change of sexual codes. There will also, no doubt, be class differences. Permissiveness with affection will not likely be as popular among the lower-educational classes—especially not with the orthodox-double-standard men in these classes. Such men may be more favorable to the transitional double standard which would be a less radical change.

As for changes in other institutions, such as the family and our political and economic establishments, one can only say that they will probably continue to some extent in the equalitarian direction in which they have been headed for the last several generations.[27]

b) Female Erotic Imagery. The female in Western society has usually lacked in erotic imagery, i.e., in the ability to stimulate herself sexually by mentally referring to certain standardized images.[28] Men have had such erotic imagery for centuries due to our culture. The ancient Sumerians had the lipstick and perfume we still have. Silk stockings and high heels are erotic images for males today. The upright female bosom seems one of the key symbols of the present,

26. *The Legal Status of Women in the USA* (Washington: Government Printing Office, 1956), p. 99. Alabama, Mississippi, South Carolina, and West Virginia, as of 1956, did not allow women on juries. Kinsey also gives evidence for more sexual conservatism in rural areas. See *Human Male,* chap. xii.

27. It is interesting to speculate what reception America in 1900, or even 1920, would have given to the "hula hoop craze" of 1958. The hula hoop, in one humorous way, symbolizes best our period of change and permissiveness.

28. For a discussion of erotic imagery, see Lindesmith and Strauss, *op. cit.,* pp. 434-45. For a discussion of Kinsey's position on this point see chap. i in my book.

with the emphasis on protruding buttocks increasing.[29] Thus, in a myriad of ways, men have cultural symbols which, although they have no intrinsic connection with biological factors, are capable of arousing or strengthening desires. Because our history has been largely one of a double standard, the development of such erotic imagery for women has been neglected—women were to represent erotic imagery for men but the reverse relation was undeveloped. This is probably one of the major reasons why women are not, on the average, as quickly or easily aroused as men, why their concentration on sexual fulfillment is somewhat more difficult to maintain, and why they often need more manual manipulation[30]—they lack erotic imagery to help focus and intensify their desires.

There are indications that these things are changing and that we are slowly developing erotic imagery for women. Now, of course, even if one's culture does not stress such imagery, women can develop their own erotic images and have done so in the past. But today we seem to be developing shared, cultural erotic images.

Given our type of culture, one of the most common attributes of erotic imagery is forbiddenness. That is, an increase in sexual desire occurs, not because of the sexual

---

29. This emphasis on the buttocks can be seen in some of the Hollywood movies where the curve of a spinal column can bring immediate fame. Extreme protrusion of the buttocks can be found among the Hottentots in Africa and is called steatopygia. Among these people the buttocks may extend a foot or so out from the small of the back. For a picture of this see George P. Murdock, *Our Primitive Contemporaries* (New York: Macmillan, 1934), p. 478. The trend in this direction in American can be seen in advertisements which stress the ability of the girdle to "shape your derriere" with pads and "contour panels." See p. 30 of the *New York Times* magazine section of October 25, 1959. Should this fad catch on, we may witness a rivalry in falsies for the buttocks and for the breasts. For an advertisement for false buttocks pads see: Lawrence Langer, *The Importance of Wearing Clothes* (New York: Hastings House, 1959), p. 213.

30. This may also help explain why one of the few erotic images females may have is the male's hands. The hands may symbolize manipulation. Many of my female respondents reported this erotic image.

object or any other symbols of sexual desire, but predominantly because the sexual object is forbidden. This is behind the traffic in strip tease shows and the fantastic sales of banned books. However, just as people who read banned books find they have no interest in non-banned literature, people with a strong "forbidden" orientation to sexual behavior, find they lose interest when the act is not forbidden. Men, due to our culture, are likely to have many erotic images besides the forbidden symbol. In the case of women, one may be more apt to find situations where the lack of other erotic imagery leads to serious loss of interest in non-forbidden sexual relations, such as in marriage. As female erotic imagery develops, such women will have other images to fall back upon, and as sexual behavior becomes more acceptable, the forbidden may become less significant in motivation.

Perhaps the emphatic stress on women being less inhibited concerning the display of their figures in hula hoops, cha-chas, and beach and summer wear is part of the "freeing" of women's sexual impulses. Perhaps the popularity of Elvis Presley and his type is an indication of the willingness of women to watch men throw "bumps and grinds"— a growth of erotic imagery. The emphasis in movies, books, and song, on women who have developed sexual desires and, apparently, sexual imagery, fits into this same pattern. For example, the National Council of Churches of Christ, a relatively liberal organization, has protested against the kind of movies being released. It may well be that their protest is aimed at movies like *Anatomy of A Murder,* wherein the female lead frequently discusses her torn pair of panties; or *North by Northwest,* wherein the female lead successfully propositions the male lead to spend the night with her. Such displays of sexual interest on the part of females may be a step in the direction of encouraging the growth of female erotic imagery.

In the world of music, similar emphasis on female sexuality can be found in songs like "A Warm Hearted Woman and a Cold Hearted Man." In the area of books, there are many recent publications which openly purport to show the woman how to enjoy her sexual life in marriage and which instruct her that such pleasure is her right.[31]

The erotic imagery of men results in hundreds of millions of dollars being paid to the female cosmetic and clothing industries. The cosmetic and clothing industries for men are not as much affected by erotic imagery. However, the roles of men and women have changed to such an extent in this century that men can no longer be certain that it is only the female who must keep up her physical appearance. The independence of the female has probably made both the male and the female more concerned with the male's physical attractiveness. More importantly, as the male and female roles have changed, they have become more interdependent, i.e., men and women overlap more in what they do, and often they do the same thing. Women are more in business and men more in the home than before; this increasing familiarity with each other's roles may make the woman more able and desirous of developing a complementary type of erotic imagery.

Admittedly, many of the above details are speculative, but the general development of erotic imagery on the part of females seems very probable. Perhaps the most important factor in this development has not been mentioned, namely, the vast increase in female sexual behavior. Perhaps out of such increasing experience with sexual behavior comes the

---

31. See Jerome and Julia Rainer, *Sexual Pleasure in Marriage* (New York: Julian Messner Inc., 1959); Maxine Davis, *The Sexual Responsibility of Women* (New York: Dial Press, 1956).

most important erotic images which in time come to be shared and informally passed down.

c) *A Code of Their Own*. There is one very important aspect of the change in our sexual standards which should be noted before closing this book: As one looks at our past, particularly at the double standard, one finds that sexual activity was usually a divisive force—a force which kept men and women from really knowing and loving each other. The girl's role as controller of the sexual relation is becoming more and more difficult as her own experience makes her more sexually desirous of coitus.[31a] A "hungry" guardian is not very reliable, and in modern-day society, the frigid female is more and more a thing of the past.[32]

By forbidding premarital coitus to the female, the double standard makes premarital relations a forbidden fruit and sets up a barrier between men and women. Girls use sex as the bait, and men use lines to obtain the lure. Sex becomes a weapon between men and women.

Permissiveness with affection, together with petting with affection and the transitional double standard, are changing this situation. For the first time in thousands of years, we have sexual standards which tend to unify rather than divide men and women.[33] Especially in permissiveness with affection, coitus is no longer forbidden, and the motivation to deceive the opposite sex in order to obtain pleasure is greatly reduced.[34] For the first time in many milleniums, Western

31a. Ehrmann, *Premarital Dating Behavior,* pp. 58, 59, 215. Ehrmann found that girls initiated sex behavior about one quarter of the time. When in love this increased to one-third of the time.

32. Many people are concerned about how increased permissiveness will affect teenagers—how much permissiveness to allow to teenagers. But this is really a familiar problem for it exists in terms of drinking and driving too. Parents must decide how much autonomy to give in all these areas.

33. This equalitarian move is weakest in the transitional double standard, for this standard still maintains more rights for men in regard to body-centered coitus.

34. Since this is not a psychological study, I have not devoted much

society is evolving sexual standards which will tend to make men and women better able to understand and live with each other.

Past sexual standards were developed by parents—by those in authority. These standards were devised, consciously and unconsciously, so as to make the "best" match for off-spring. As has been shown, about the end of the nineteenth century, the balance of power in mating choice shifted to the young people themselves. Things changed quite rapidly. Love became the crucial basis for marriage. Still, the young people kept the older, adult-devised sexual code and tried to adjust to it. Now a new code is being fashioned and, for the first time, by young people themselves. Since they are the ones to choose their mates, they must also decide how to act in courtship.[35] Because this new code is being devised by young

---

space to non-sexual, psychological motivations to sexual behavior, e.g., neurotic tensions which leads to indulging in coitus as an outlet. Coitus, being pleasurable, can be used as a compensatory mechanism for many of our problems. When a culture makes coitus "forbidden fruit" and at the same time teases its members by activities all the way from burlesque to television, then such conflict may increase the amount of neurosis and also may make it more likely that non-sexual tensions will be relieved by sexual relations. Thus, our double-standard customs may well encourage conflict and non-sexual motivation to coitus. More psychological study is needed to fully document this position. A good illustration of it can be seen in the Brigitte Bardot movie, *And God Created Woman*. It is significant that most reviewers saw mainly the "sexy" element in this picture and missed entirely the deeper message concerning non-sexual motivations to sexual behavior. See *Time*, November 11, 1957, pp. 121-22. Were sexual behavior more naturally accepted, it might be less likely to be associated with neurosis. Some analogous evidence for this can be found in the very low rates of alcoholism for Jews and other groups which accept drinking. Alcohol is less likely to be neurotically used in these groups. However, the case of France requires explanation—France has free drinking and high alcoholism rates. For recent studies, see Robert Strauss and Seldon D. Bacon, *Drinking in College* (New Haven: Yale University Press, 1953), and Charles R. Snyder, *Alcohol and the Jews* (Glencoe, Ill.: The Free Press, 1958). See also Hunt, *op. cit.*, p. 107, for evidence on the repressive attempts of the early Christians leading to sexual obsessions.

35. It seems likely that, as industrialism spreads and individual choice of mate becomes more widespread, we shall witness in other countries the same growth of permissivenes in young people's interrelations. However,

people, it is concerned with their problems and desires. The situation today is most sharply distinguished from the past in that sexual behavior is now almost fully separated from pregnancy and marriage, if one so desires. That is, the chances of pregnancy occurring can now be controlled, and since marriages are arranged by young people themselves, they need not marry the person they have sexual relations with, and parents cannot force them to do so. In the past, the only time sexual behavior could be separated from pregnancy and marriage was when it occurred in a house of prostitution. This exclusive franchise no longer exists.

Our newer affectionate standards merely say "not all sex is bad," they do not say "all sex is equally good" or "all sex is good but some better." They have thus not fully lost their Puritanism.[36] Many of the believers in these newer sex codes think they are holding "individual" beliefs. In reality, their beliefs are social and are well rooted in our emerging society. Permissiveness with affection, for example, is based on our cultural blending of sex and affection and on our custom of allowing free choice of one's mate. Such a new code is no more an individual matter than was our older double standard or abstinence code which was rooted in parental choice of mate customs and the separation of sex and affection.

The transition to a newer code has occurred along with the change in marriage from a union of two families to a union of individuals. As this change took place, economic reasons for controlling one's children's sexual behavior lessened, and the balance of power moved from the parents to the young people themselves. This, of course, is not an all-or-none

---

the permissiveness will likely differ for the various social stratum, just as is the case in America.

36. For a good selection of readings on Puritanism and a good bibliography, see George M. Waller (ed.), *Puritanism in Early America* (Bostion: D.C. Heath, 1950). For a statement of some "shocking" Puritan behavior see: Oberholzer, *op. cit.*

matter—parents still have some say in mate choice. But, as parental controls diminished, new sexual codes were devised by the young people themselves—more liberal codes, to be sure, but codes which nonetheless were still rooted in our past. Permissiveness without affection and the strong-affection subtype of permissiveness with affection are, to a great extent, free of our older sexual taboos, but these are minority positions. Nevertheless, the newer affectionate codes are new in that, unlike the orthodox double standard, they have linked sex and love, and they are capable of generating understanding between men and women. This is indeed something new in Western society.

One dating custom which is relevant here and which has only come into its prime in the last twenty years is "going steady." Ehrmann's study contains one of the most thorough analyses of this pattern. He found that going steady did lead to more sexual privileges, predominantly because of the affection present. Such a person-centered courtship form seems to be a factor in the trends about which we are speaking. In addition, Ehrmann and others have noted the great tolerance young people have for other people's sex behavior. This attitude, too, should help speed up the prevailing trends.[36a]

d) Dangers of Prediction. Surely, all the above evidence is not perfect. As stated previously, the researches have not dealt with all segments of America. Many things may happen to throw off a prediction. The generation born around 1800 was thought by many to be the generation which would change the world in numerous respects. These people were a great disappointment and turned out to be more conservative than their parents. Perhaps the same thing will happen now.

Regardless of the liberalism of the next generation, it

36a. Ehrmann, *Premarital Dating Behavior,* pp. 132-43, 169, chaps. iv, v, vi, *passim.* Rockwood and Ford, *op. cit.,* p. 48.

does not take a prophet to deduce that permissiveness with affection, together with petting with affection and the transitional double standard, would rate highest on the criteria of general integration with at least the large middle and upper segments of our culture. It is such cultural integration which, in time, affects people's preferences. Even though many Americans may oppose these standards now, in time the cultural pressures will lead to more and more young people accepting them. Suppose, however, Americans decide not to make any choice—suppose they decide to leave things as they are? It is possible that the situation may remain somewhat the same for the next generation or two.

Such an event, however, would merely put off these changes to a future date. Sooner or later people in our country will have to choose. They cannot forever continue to be confused or to resist the pressures for change that emanate from many parts of our culture. Certainly, every culture has many contradictions and inconsistencies within it, just as every individual does.[37] But there is a limit to the number which a culture or an individual can tolerate. This is particularly true once people realize these conflicts. America is very close to the saturation point in terms of our sexual customs, and, therefore, change should come soon. We are too conscious of the problems in this area to be likely to do otherwise than make a choice. Unless our urban-industrial-equalitarian culture alters quite unexpectedly, as Americans change, the move will continue to be in support of person-centered premarital sexual behavior.

Such trends, of course, only determine what the dominant standard will be; there will always be groups who accept

---

37. All societies have compensatory and evasive mechanisms which prevent change from occurring even when conflicts exist, but in this area, such mechanisms seem to have been largely exhausted, e.g., the rationalizations supporting our orthodox standards are not as widely or strongly supported as formerly.

other standards. Our nation is much too heterogeneous to expect 100 per cent acceptance of any standard. It may well be that many of our grandchildren will accept person-centered coitus with the same vigor as our grandparents accepted chastity. A full switch will, of course, take more time. We can be sure that the orthodox double standard and abstinence will still exist and probably will be supported by sizable followings for many generations to come.

PRESENT-DAY STANDARDS

Many people have expressed their fears concerning the rapid growth of body-centered coitus. The evidence cited does not seem to support such views. There are, no doubt, many instances of body-centered coitus of the double-standard type; in fact, this is probably still the dominant type of coitus in America for males. But in the last century, there has been a constantly increasing proportion of person-centered coitus, despite the fact that permissiveness without affection and petting without affection have probably experienced a considerable, although smaller, growth. But our cultural opposition to such body-centered behavior is a strong obstacle to any rapid acceptance of such standards. It appears probable that person-centered coital and petting standards will continue to be the major direction of growth for quite some time to come.

Following is a list of all the major standards and their subdivisions. The evidence is far from complete. Many segments of our population need to be investigated, and more research in terms of standards as well as behavior is sorely needed. The distribution of sexual standards here applies only to the higher educational and occupational segments of our population, since it is predominantly those segments which are known through research.

Chart II—Sexual Standards in America*

ABSTINENCE
a) Petting without Affection
b) Petting with Affection
c) Kissing without Affection
d) Kissing with Affection

DOUBLE STANDARD
a) Orthodox
b) Transitional

PERMISSIVENESS WITHOUT AFFECTION
a) Orgiastic
b) Sophisticated

PERMISSIVENESS WITH AFFECTION
a) Love
b) Strong Affection

* Two other divisions should be made in Abstinence: (1) Separate the petting standards into those who accept only mammary petting and those who in addition accept genital petting; (2) Separate all these petting standards into those that are equalitarian and that are not. I did not make these divisions in my discussion for the sake of simplicity.

Chart III—Distribution of Sexual Standards in America for Higher Occupational and Educational Classes*

MAJORITY POSITIONS

Men: Most men adhere fairly closely to the double standard, but they often modify this belief by a slight feeling that abstinence is "really" the best standard and/or by believing that intercourse for women is acceptable if they are in love or engaged, i.e., the transitional subtype.

Women: Most women tolerate the double standard but feel that a single standard of abstinence would be preferable. The petting-with-affection subtype seems most popular.

MINORITY POSITIONS

Men: A full acceptance of abstinence and permissiveness with affection, strong affection subtype, are the two most popular minority positions for men. A very small number accepts permissiveness without affection.

Women: The most popular minority positions are the transitional double standard and permissivenes with affection, love subtype. A very small number accepts permissiveness without affection.

* The higher occupations referred to here would include white-collar jobs and especially the professions and the business executive positions. The higher educational groups include those who have graduated from high school and especially those who have been to college.

As this chart shows, for the higher occupational and educational classes, it is believed that of our three most rapidly growing standards, petting with affection and the transitional double standard are at present the most widespread. Permissiveness with affection also seems to have a sizable following but since it is further removed from our older standards, its greatest growth is probably yet to come.

CONCLUSIONS

This book's functional examination of the integration of sexual standards is merely a first step. Much of what has been stated here is hypothetical and must be further clarified and tested.[38] Sexual behavior is a constant process and one which has high potentialities for maintaining or disrupting the existing social organization. It is imperative that more work be done to ascertain how our sexual standards are related to such important socio-cultural variables as values, ethnic groups, and social classes, and to investigate further the sociological reasons for such differences as may exist.[39]

---

38. We need more information on other socio-cultural determinants of sexual behavior besides standards—such as the desire to marry an upper-class male, the desire for money, etc., which can act as determinants of sexual behavior. Kinsey, *Human Male,* pp. 417-48, shows how the class one ends up in is more closely related to sexual behavior than is the class one presently belongs to. This indicates the importance of reference groups in determining both our standards and our behavior. The preliminary findings of my study of high school and college students tends to support this finding. This further stresses the importance of discovering how and when sexual standards are learned. Kinsey's evidence indicates that our sex standards are fairly fixed by age 16.

39. My current questionnaire research on college and high school students is aimed at obtaining more precise knowledge of standards. I am devising Guttman scales to measure degrees of permissability in sexual standards and also to measure equalitarianism. In this way I hope to add precision to the sexual standards we have examined.

The great increases in sexual behavior are not just violations of belief, but are predominantly signs of the new sexual standards which are emerging. One of the major aims of this book is to fill a gap in the literature on sexual behavior by putting forth an analysis of the integration of our sexual standards, by means of an examination of the characteristics, consequences, and trends of these standards. It is hoped that through the "four standards" functional approach developed in this book, additional insights into sexual behavior can be obtained and more knowledge gained of the conditions under which certain consequences and socio-cultural trends occur. This approach makes possible the distinction between patterns of sexual *behavior* and sexual *standards,* thus alerting us as to what cultural standards accompany what societal behavior patterns. Such distinctions are essential in order to understand social and cultural change. By means of our examination, it is hoped that we have shown how, as the meaning of sexual behavior changed in terms of its consequences and integration in society, the standards also changed. The values underlying our sexual standards have changed in their meaning for us greatly in the last century—some have become more important, some less, some have changed in their consequences, some remain constant. By focusing on such values, we can understand standards more objectively than by special pleading concerning the worth of a particular value or standard.

In our present state of affairs, the situation is such that, no matter which standard our young people abide by, there will likely be a goodly amount of conflict connected with it. Many Americans reflect our split culture by being partly in sympathy with the new and partly with the old. Our culture is in flux, and it is most important for social scientists as well as other persons to understand these changes and to do more research in this area. Only then, will we be better able to grasp the precise nature of these trends in the integration of our premarital sexual standards. This book is intended as a partial contribution to such understanding.

Bibliography

ABERLE, SOPHIE D., AND CORNER, GEORGE W. *Twenty-Five Years of Sex Research*. Philadelphia: W. B. Saunders Co., 1953.

ADLER, POLLY. *A House Is Not a Home*. New York: Popular Library Edition, 1954.

ALLEN, FREDERICK LEWIS. *Only Yesterday*. New York: Bantam Books, 1959.

ANSHEN, RUTH N. (ed.). *The Family: Its Function and Destiny*. New York: Harper and Brothers, 1949.

ASHMORE, HARRY S. *The Negro and the Schools*. Chapel Hill, N. C.: University of North Carolina Press, 1954.

————. *An Epitaph for Dixie*. New York: W. W. Norton and Co., 1958.

Automation and Technological Change. Hearings before the 84th Congress. Washington: U.S. Government Printing Office, 1955.

AXELROD, GEORGE. "The Seven-Year Itch," *Theatre '53,* ed. J. Chapman. New York: Random House, 1953.

BABER, RAY E. *Marriage and the Family*. New York: McGraw-Hill Book Co., 1953.

BAMBERGER, BERNARD J. *The Story of Judaism*. New York: Union of American Hebrew Congregations, 1957.

BARNOUW, ERIK, AND CLARK, E. GURNEY, M.D. *Syphilis: The Invader*. Public Affairs Pamphlet No. 24A, 1955.

BEALS, RALPH, AND HOIJER, HARRY. *Introduction to Anthropology.* New York: The Macmillan Co., 1953.

BECKER, HOWARD, AND HILL, REUBEN (ed.). *Family, Marriage and Parenthood.* Boston: D. C. Heath and Co., 1948.

BEIGEL, HUGO G. "Romantic Love," *American Sociological Review,* XVI (June, 1951), 326-34.

BENTON, WALTER. *This Is My Beloved.* New York: Alfred Knopf and Co., 1945.

BERG, LOUIS, M.D., AND STREET, ROBERT. *Sex: Methods and Manners.* New York: McBride Co., 1953.

BERNARD, LUTHER LEE. *Instinct.* New York: Henry Holt and Co., 1924.

BERRILL, NORMAN J. *Sex and the Nature of Things.* New York: Dodd, Mead and Co., 1954.

―――. *Man's Emerging Mind.* New York: Dodd, Mead and Co., 1955.

BIERSTEDT, ROBERT. *The Social Order.* New York: McGraw-Hill Book Co., 1957.

Birth Control U.S.A. New York: Planned Parenthood Federation.

BOULE, MARCELLIN, *and* VALLOIS, HENRI V. *Fossil Men.* New York: Dryden Press, 1957.

BOWMAN, HENRY A. *Marriage for Moderns.* New York: McGraw-Hill Book Co., 1954.

Breaking the Vicious Circle. New York: Planned Parenthood Federation.

BRENAN, GERALD. "Courtship in Granada," *Atlantic,* August, 1957, pp. 33-38.

BRENNER, CHARLES. *An Elementary Textbook of Psychoanalysis.* New York: International University Press Inc., 1955.

BRINTON, CRANE, CHRISTOPHER, JOHN B., AND WOLFF, ROBERT L. *A History of Civilization.* New York: Prentice-Hall Inc., 1955.

BROMLEY, DOROTHY D., AND BRITTEN, FLORENCE. *Youth and Sex.* New York: Harper and Bros., 1938.

BURGESS, ERNEST W., AND WALLIN, PAUL. *Engagement and Marriage.* New York: J. B. Lippincott Co., 1953.

―――, AND LOCKE, HARVEY J., *The Family.* New York: American Book Co., 1953.

BURTT, EDWIN A. *The Metaphysical Foundations of Modern Science.* New York: Doubleday Anchor, 1954.

CALDERONE, MARY S., M.D. (ed.). *Abortion in the United States.* New York: Paul B. Hoeber Inc., 1958.

CAPELLANUS, ANDREAS. *The Art of Courtly Love.* Translated by John J. Parry. New York: Frederick Ungar Co., 1959.

CASTIGLIONE, BALDESAR. *The Book of the Courtier.* Translated by Charles S. Singleton. New York: Doubleday Anchor, 1959.

CAVAN, RUTH S. *The American Family.* New York: Thomas Y. Crowell Co., 1953.

CHAMBLISS, ROLLIN. *Social Thought from Hammurabi to Comte.* New York: The Dryden Press, 1954.

CHESSER, EUSTACE. *The Sexual, Marital and Family Relationships of the English Woman.* New York: Roy Publishers, 1957.

CHIERA, EDWARD. *They Wrote on Clay.* Chicago: University of Chicago Press, 1938.

CHILDE, V. GORDON. *Man Makes Himself.* New York: Mentor Books, 1953.

CHRISTENSEN, HAROLD T. *Marriage Analysis.* New York: Ronald Press, 1958.

CLARK, E. GURNEY, M.D. "A Warning to America," *This Week Magazine,* September 2, 1956.

CLARK, WILFRED E. LEGROS. *The Fossil Evidence for Human Evolution.* Chicago: University of Chicago Press, 1955.

———. *History of the Primates.* Chicago: University of Chicago Press, 1957.

COCHRAN, WILLIAM, MOSTELLER, FREDERICK, AND TUKEY, JOHN. "Statistical Problems of the Kinsey Report," *Journal of the American Statistical Association,* XLVIII (December, 1953), 673-716.

COHEN, MORRIS R., AND NAGEL, ERNEST. *Logic and Scientific Method.* New York: Harcourt, Brace Co., 1934.

COLE, CHARLES W. "American Youth Goes Monogamous," *Harper's Magazine,* CCXIV (March, 1957), 29-34.

COMFORT, ALEX. *Sexual Behavior in Society.* New York: The Viking Press, 1950.

CONANT, JAMES B. *On Understanding Science.* New Haven: Yale University Press, 1951.

DAVID, LESTER. "The Controversy Over Swedish Morals," *Coronet,* XLI (December 1956), 126-32.

DAVIS, ALLISON. "Class Differences in Sexual and Aggressive Behavior among Adolescents," *Marriage and the Family,* eds. Winch and McGinnis. New York: Henry Holt and Co., 1953.

DAVIS, KINGSLEY. "The Sociology of Prostitution," *American Sociological Review,* II (December, 1938), 744-55.

———. *Human Society.* New York: The Macmillan Co., 1950.

———. "The Myth of Functional Analysis as a Special Method in Sociology and Anthropology," *American Sociological Review,* XXIV (December, 1959), 757-72.

DAVIS, KATHERINE B. *Factors in the Sex Life of Twenty-Two Hundred Women.* New York: Harper and Brothers, 1929.

DAVIS, MAXINE. *The Sexual Responsibility of Women.* New York: Dial Press, 1956.

DAY, DONALD. *The Evolution of Love.* New York: Dial Press, 1954.

DIAMOND, EDWIN. "Young Wives," *Newsweek,* LV (March 7, 1960), 57-60.

DICKINSON, ROBERT L. *Atlas of Human Sex Anatomy.* Baltimore: Williams and Wilkins Co., 1949.

———. *Techniques of Conception Control.* Baltimore: Williams and Wilkins Co., 1950.

DIETZ, FREDERICK. *The Industrial Revolution.* New York: Henry Holt and Co., 1927.

DITZION, SIDNEY. *Marriage, Morals and Sex in America.* New York: Bookman Associates, 1953.

DOBZHANSKY, THEODOSIUS. *Evolution, Genetics, and Man.* New York: John Wiley and Sons, Inc., 1955.

DOTEN, DANA. *The Art of Bundling.* New York: Farrar & Rinehart, 1938.

DRUCKER, PETER F. "America's Next Twenty Years," *Harper's Magazine,* March, April, May, and June, 1955.

DRUMMOND, ISABEL. *The Sex Paradox.* New York: G. P. Putnam's Sons, 1953.

DUNBAR, FLANDERS, M.D. *Mind and Body: Psychosomatic Medicine.* New York: Random House, 1947.

DUVALL, EVELYN M., AND HILL, REUBEN. *When You Marry.* New York: D. C. Heath and Co., 1953.

DUVALL, SYLVANUS. M. *Men, Women, and Morals.* New York: Association Press, 1952.

EDEL, ABRAHAM. *Ethical Judgment.* Glencoe: Illinois: The Free Press, 1955.

EDWARDES, ALLEN. *The Jewel in the Lotus*. New York: Julian Press, 1959.

EHRMANN, WINSTON W. "Influence of Comparative Social Class of Companion upon Premarital Heterosexual Behavior," *Marriage and Family Living*, XVIII (February, 1955), 48-53.

————. "Some Knowns and Unknowns in Research into Human Sex Behavior," *Marriage and Family Living*, XIX (February, 1957), 16-22.

————. *Premarital Dating Behavior*. New York: Henry Holt and Co., 1959.

ELLIS, ALBERT. "The Values of Marriage Prediction Tests," *American Sociological Review*, XIII (December, 1948), 710-18.

————. "A Study of Human Relationships," *Journal of Genetic Psychology*, LXXV (September, 1949), 61-71.

————. *The Folklore of Sex*. New York: Charles Boni, 1951.

————. *The American Sexual Tragedy*. New York: Twayne Publishers, 1954.

————. "The Effectiveness of Psychotherapy with Individuals Who Have Severe Homosexual Problems," *Journal of Consulting Psychology*," XX (1956), 191-95.

————. *Sex without Guilt*. New York: Lyle Stuart, 1958.

————, AND ABARBANEL, ALBERT (eds.). *The Encyclopedia of Sexual Behavior*. New York: Hawthorn Press, 1960.

ELLIS, HAVELOCK. *Psychology of Sex*. New York: Mentor Books, 1954.

Everyday Life in Ancient Times. Washington: National Geographic Society, 1951.

FAIRCHILD, JOHNSON E. (ed.). *Women, Society and Sex*. New York: Sheridan House, 1952.

FISHBEIN, MORRIS, AND KENNEDY, RUBY (eds.). *Modern Marirage and Family Living*. New York: Oxford University Press, 1957.

FOLSOM, JOSEPH K. *The Family and Democratic Society*. New York: John Wiley and Sons, 1943.

FOOTE, NELSON N. "Love," *Psychiatry*, XVI (August, 1953), 245-51.

————. "Sex as Play," *Social Problems*, I (April, 1954), 159-63.

————, AND COTTRELL, LEONARD S., JR. *Identity and Interpersonal Competence*. Chicago: University of Chicago Press, 1955.

FORD, CLELLAN S., AND BEACH, FRANK A. *Patterns of Sexual Behavior*. New York: Harper and Brothers, 1953.

FOSTER, ROBERT G. *Marriage and Family Relationships.* New York: The Macmillan Co., 1954.

FOWLER, H. W., AND FOWLER, F. G. (trans.). *The Works of Lucian of Samosota.* London: Oxford University Press, 1939.

FREUD, SIGMUND. *Civilization and Its Discontents.* London: Hogarth Press, 1930.

FROMME, ALLAN. *Sex and Marriage.* New York: Barnes and Noble Co., 1955.

GALBRAITH, JOHN K. *The Great Crash, 1929.* Boston: Houghton-Mifflin Co., 1955.

GARLAND, MADGE. *The Changing Face of Beauty.* New York: M. Barrows Co., 1957.

GEBHARD, PAUL H., POMEROY, WARDELL, MARTIN, CLYDE, AND CHRISTENSON, CORNELIA. *Pregnancy, Birth and Abortion.* New York: Harper and Brothers, 1958.

GEDDES, DONALD P., AND CURIE, ENID (eds.). *About the Kinsey Report.* New York: Signet Books, 1948.

GITTLER, JOSEPH B. *Review of Sociology.* New York: John Wiley and Sons, 1957.

GLUECK, SHELDON, AND ELEANOR. *Physique and Delinquency.* New York: Harper and Brothers, 1956.

GOLDIN, HYMAN E. *Universal History of Israel.* New York: Hebrew Publishing Co., 1935.

GOLDSMITH, SELMA F. "Size Distribution of Personal Income," *Survey of Current Business,* XXXVIII (April, 1958), 10-19.

———. "Income Distribution by Size—1955-58," *Survey of Current Business,* XXXIX (April, 1959), 9-16.

GOODE, WILLIAM J. "The Theoretical Importance of Love," *American Sociological Review,* XXIV (February, 1959), 38-47.

GORER, GEOFFREY. *Exploring English Character.* New York: Criterion Books, 1955.

GUYON, RENE. *The Ethics of Sexual Acts.* New York: Blue Ribbon Books, 1941.

———. "The Doctrine of Legitimacy and Liberty of Sexual Acts," in Pillay and Ellis (eds.). *Sex, Society and the Individual.* Bombay: International Journal of Sociology, 1953.

HALEVY, JULIAN. *The Young Lovers.* New York: Dell Publishers, 1955.

HALL, CALVIN, AND LINDZEY, GARDINER. *Theories of Personality.* New York: John Wiley and Sons, 1957.

HARPER, ROBERT A. (ed.). "Premarital Sex Relations: The Facts and the Counselor's Role in Relation to the Facts," *Marriage and Family Living,* XIV (August, 1952), 229-38.

HARTUNG, FRANK. "Cultural Relativity and Moral Judgments," *Philosophy of Science,* II (April, 1954), 118-26.

HENSHAW, PAUL S. "Physiologic Control of Fertility," *Science,* CXVII (May 29, 1953), 572-82.

HILL, REUBEN. *Families under Stress.* New York: Harper and Bros., 1949.

HILTNER, SEWARD. *Sex Ethics and the Kinsey Reports.* New York: Association Press, 1953.

HIMELHOCH, JEROME, AND FAVA, SILVIA (eds.). *Sexual Behavior in American Society.* New York: W. W. Norton and Co., 1955.

HIMES, NORMAN E. *Medical History of Contraception.* Baltimore: Williams and Wilkins Co., 1936.

———, AND TAYLOR, DONALD L. *Your Marriage.* New York: Rinehart and Co., 1955.

HIRNING, JACOB AND ALMA. *Marriage Adjustment.* New York: American Book Co., 1956.

HOCH, PAUL H., AND ZUBIN, JOSEPH (eds.). *Psychosexual Development in Health and Disease.* New York: Grune and Stratton, 1949.

HOFFMAN, FREDERICK. *The Twenties.* New York: Viking Press, 1955.

HORTON, PAUL B., AND LESLIE, GERALD R. *The Sociology of Social Problems.* New York: Appleton-Century-Crofts, 1955.

HOULT, THOMAS F. *The Sociology of Religion.* New York: Dryden Press, 1958.

HUNT, MORTON M. *The Natural History of Love.* New York: Alfred Knopf, 1959.

HUXLEY, ALDOUS. *Brave New World.* New York: Harper and Bros., 1950.

JACOBSON, PAUL H. *American Marriage and Divorce.* New York: Rinehart and Co., 1959.

JENSEN, OLIVER. *The Revolt of American Women.* New York: Harcourt, Brace and Co., 1952.

JOHNSON, GERALD W. "Dynamic Victoria Woodhull," *American Heritage,* VII (June, 1956), 44-47, 86-91.

KALVESTEN, ANNA-LISA. *The Social Structure of Sweden.* Stockholm, Sweden: University of Stockholm, 1953.

KANIN, EUGENE A., AND HOWARD, DAVID H. "Postmarital Consequences of Premarital Sex Adjustments," *American Sociological Review,* XXIII (October, 1958), 556-62.

KARPMAN, BENJAMIN. *The Sexual Offender and His Offenses.* New York: The Julian Press, 1954.

KELLER, WERNER. *The Bible as History.* New York: W. M. Morrow Co., 1956.

KEY, ELLEN. *Love and Marriage.* New York: E. P. Putnam and Sons, 1911.

KIEFER, OTTO. *Sexual Life in Ancient Rome.* New York: Barnes and Noble, 1953.

KINGSLEY, SIDNEY. "Detective Story," *Best Plays of 1948-1949.* New York: Dodd, Mead and Co., 1949.

KINSEY, ALFRED C., POMEROY, WARDELL B., AND MARTIN, CLYDE E. *Sexual Behavior in the Human Male.* Philadelphia: W. B. Saunders Co., 1948.

KINSEY, A. C., POMEROY, W. B., MARTIN, C. E., AND GEBHARD, P. H. "Concepts of Normality and Abnormality in Sexual Behavior," in Hoch, P. H., and Zubin, J. (eds.). *Psychosexual Development in Health and Disease.* New York: Grune and Stratton, 1949.

————, POMEROY, WARDELL B., MARTIN, CLYDE E., AND GEBHARD, PAUL H. *Sexual Behavior in the Human Female.* Philadelphia: W. B. Saunders Co., 1953.

KIRCHWEY, FREDA (ed.). *Our Changing Morality.* New York: A. and C. Boni, 1924.

KIRKENDALL, LESTER A. "Premarital Sex Relations," *Pastoral Psychology,* VII (April, 1956), 46-53.

KIRKPATRICK, CLIFFORD. *The Family.* New York: The Ronald Press, 1955.

————, AND CAPLOW, THEODORE. "Courtship in a Group of Minnesota Students," *American Journal of Sociology,* LI (September, 1945), 114-25.

KNOWLTON, CHARLES. *Fruits of Philosophy, or the Private Companion of Young Married People.* London: Bradlaugh, 1877.

KOLLER, MARVIN R. "Some Changes in Courtship Behavior in Three Generations of Ohio Women," *American Sociological Review,* XVI (June, 1951), 366-70.

KOOS, EARL L. *Marriage.* New York: Henry Holt and Co., 1957.

KRICH, ARON M. (ed.). *Men*. New York: Dell Publishing Co., 1953.
———— (ed.). *Women*. New York: Dell Publishing Co., 1953.

LANDIS, JUDSON T., AND LANDIS, MARY G. (eds.). *Readings in Marriage and the Family*. New York: Prentice-Hall Inc., 1952.
————, AND ————. *Building a Successful Marriage*. New York: Prentice-Hall Inc., 1953 and 1958.

LANGER, LAWRENCE. *The Importance of Wearing Clothes*. New York: Hastings House, 1959.

LAWTON, SHAILER U., M.D., AND ARCHER, JULES. *Sexual Conduct of the Teenager*. New York: Derby Press, 1951.

LEA, HENRY C. *The History of Sacerdotal Celibacy in the Christian Church*. New York: Russell and Russell Co., 1957.

LEAVENWORTH, ISABEL. "Virtue for Women," in Kirchwey, F. (ed.), *Our Changing Morality*. New York: A. and C. Boni, 1924.

LECKY, WILLIAM E. H. *History of European Morals*. New York: George Braziller, 1955.

LEMASTERS, ERSEL E. *Modern Courtship and Marriage*. New York: The Macmillan Co., 1957.

LEVINE, LENA, M.D., AND GILMAN, MILDRED. *Frigidity*. New York: Planned Parenthood Federation of America, 1951.

LEWINSOHN, RICHARD, M.D. *A History of Sexual Customs*. New York: Harper and Bros., 1958.

LICHT, HANS. *Sexual Life in Ancient Greece*. New York: Barnes and Noble, 1953.

LINDESMITH, ALFRED R., AND STRAUSS, ANSELM L. *Social Psychology*. New York: Dryden Press, 1950.

LINDSEY, BEN B., AND EVANS, WAINWRIGHT. *The Companionate Marriage*. New York: Boni and Liveright, 1927.

LOCKE, HARVEY J. "Changing Attitudes towards Venereal Diseases," *American Sociological Review*, IV (December, 1939), 836-43.
————. *Predicting Adjustment in Marriage*. New York: Henry Holt and Co., 1951.

LOMBROSO, CESARE. *Crime: Its Causes and Remedies*. Translated by H. P. Horton. New York: Little Brown and Co., 1911.

LOWIE, ROBERT H. *Are We Civilized?* New York: Rinehart and Co., 1929.

LUNDBERG, GEORGE A. "Science, Scientists and Values," *Social Forces*, XXX (May, 1952), 373-79.

MacIver, Robert M. *Social Causation.* New York: Ginn and Co., 1942.

McCary, James L., and Sheer, Daniel E. (eds.). *Six Approaches to Psychotherapy.* New York: Dryden Press, 1955.

McHugh, Gelolo, M.D., and Moskin, J. R. "What Ministers Are Learning About Sex," *Look Magazine,* November 25, 1958, 79-86.

McKeon, Richard (trans.). *The Basic Works of Aristotle.* New York: Random House, 1941.

McKinney, Fred. *The Psychology of Personal Adjustment.* New York: John Wiley and Sons, 1947.

Maddox, George L. "Occupational Prestige: Some Empirical Applications of the North-Hatt Rating Scale." *Southern Sociological Meetings,* 1958.

Magoun, F. Alexander. *Love and Marriage.* New York: Harper, 1956.

Maisel, Albert Q. "New Hope for Childless Women," *Ladies Home Journal,* August, 1957.

Maloney, John J. (ed.). *Great Love Stories.* New York: Bobbs-Merrill Co., 1952.

Maranon, Gregoria, M.D. "Climacteria: The Critical Age in the Male," in Krich, A. M. *Men.* New York: Dell Publishing Co., 1953.

Maugham, Somerset. *Rain.* New York: Doubleday Doran and Co., 1937.

Maupassant, Guy de. *A Woman's Life.* New York: Lion Books Inc., 1954.

Mead, George Herbert. *Mind, Self and Society.* Chicago: University of Chicago Press, 1934.

Mead, Margaret. *Coming of Age in Samoa.* New York: Mentor Book Co., 1949.

———. *Sex and Temperament in Three Primitive Societies.* New York: Mentor Books, 1950.

———. *Male and Female.* New York: William Morrow and Co., 1953.

Merton, Robert K. *Social Theory and Social Structure.* Glencoe, Ill.: The Free Press, 1957.

Mill, John Stuart. *The Subjection of Women.* Philadelphia: J. B. Lippincott and Co., 1867.

Miller, Lois M. "Mother of Planned Parenthood," *Readers Digest,* July, 1951, pp. 27-32.

MILLS, C. WRIGHT. *The Power Elite.* New York: Oxford University Press, 1956.

MONAHAN, THOMAS P. "One Hundred Years of Marriage in Massachusetts," *American Journal of Sociology,* LVI (May, 1951), 534-45.

MONROE, RUTH L. *Schools of Psychoanalytic Thought.* New York: Dryden Press, 1955.

Moral Aspects of Birth Control. New York: Planned Parenthood Federation, 1938.

MORLOCK, MAUD, AND CAMPBELL, HILARY. *Maternity Homes for Unwed Mothers.* Washington: Children's Bureau Publications No. 309, 1946.

MULLAHY, PATRICK (ed.). *A Study of Interpersonal Relations.* New York: Hermitage Press, 1949.

MURDOCK, GEORGE P. *Social Structure.* New York: The Macmillan Co., 1949.

————. "A Comparative Anthropological Approach," *Journal of Social Hygiene,* XXXVI (April, 1950), 133-38.

————. *Our Primitive Contemporaries.* New York: The Macmillan Co., 1954.

MURTAGH, JOHN M., AND HARRIS, SARA. *Cast the First Stone.* New York: McGraw-Hill Book Co., 1957.

MYRDAL, GUNNAR. *An American Dilemma.* New York: Harper and Brothers, 1944.

NATIONAL MANPOWER COUNCIL. *Womanpower.* New York: Columbia University Press, 1957.

NEWCOMB, THEODORE. "Recent Changes in Attitudes toward Sex and Marriage," *American Sociological Review,* II (December, 1937), 659-67.

NOVAK, EMIL, M.D. "Menopause: The 'Change of Life,'" in Krich, A. M. *Women.* New York: Dell Publishing Co., 1953.

OBERHOLZER, EMIL, JR. *Delinquent Saints.* New York: Columbia University Press, 1956.

OLSEN, ARTHUR R., MUDD, EMILY H., AND BOURDEAU, HUGO (eds.). *Readings on Marriage and Family Relations.* Harrisburg, Penna.: The Stackpole Co., 1953.

O'NEIL, EUGENE. *Anna Christie.* New York: Boni and Liveright, 1923.

OVID. *The Art of Love*. Translated by Rolfe Humphries. Bloomington, Ind.: Indiana University Press, 1957.

OWEN, ROBERT. *Moral Physiology*. London: E. Truelove, 1870.

PAINE, THOMAS. *Age of Reason*. New York: Willey Book Co., 1942.

PARKER, ROBERT A. *A Yankee Saint: J. H. Noyes and the Oneida Community*. New York: Putnam Co., 1935.

PARSONS, TALCOTT. *The Social System*. Glencoe, Ill.: The Free Press, 1951.

————, AND SHILS, EDWARD. *Toward a General Theory of Action*. Cambridge: Harvard University Press, 1951.

————, AND BALES, ROBERT F. *Family*. Glencoe, Ill.: The Free Press, 1955.

PETERS, SAMUEL. *General History of Connecticut*. London: J. Bew, 1781.

PILLAY, ALYAPPIN P., AND ELLIS, ALBERT (eds.). *Sex, Society and The Individual*. Bombay, India: International Journal of Sexology, 1953.

PINCUS, GREGORY, GARCIA, CELSO, AND ROCK, JOHN. "Effects of Three 19-nor Steroids on Human Ovulation and Menstruation," *American Journal of Obstetrics and Gynecology*, LXXV (1958), 82-91.

PLATO. *Apology*. (*Dialogues of Plato*, trans. Benjamin Jowett.) New York: Random House, 1937.

————. *The Republic*. Translated by A. D. Lindsay. New York: E. P. Dutton, 1950.

PORTERFIELD, AUSTIN, AND SALLEY, H. ELLISON. "Current Folkways of Sexual Behavior," *American Journal of Sociology*, LII (November, 1946), 209-16.

QUEEN, STUART A., AND ADAMS, JOHN B. *The Family in Various Cultures*. New York: J. B. Lippincott Co., 1952.

RAINER, JEROME AND JULIA. *Sexual Pleasure in Marriage*. New York: Julian Messner Inc., 1959.

REDFIELD, ROBERT. *The Primitive World and Its Transformations*. Ithaca, N.Y.: Cornell University Press, 1953.

REED, RUTH. *The Illegitimate Family in New York City*. New York: Columbia University Press, 1934.

REISS, IRA L. "The Double Standard in Premarital Sexual Intercourse: A Neglected Concept," *Social Forces,* XXXIV (March, 1956), 224-30.

——. "Sociology and Values: A Case Study." Paper delivered at Southern Sociological Society Meetings, April, 1956.

——. "The Treatment of Premarital Coitus in 'Marriage and the Family' Texts," *Social Problems,* IV (April, 1957), 334-38.

——. "Functional Narcotics: A Compensatory Mechanism for the Social System." Paper delivered at Eastern Sociological Society meetings, April, 1958.

——. "Toward a Sociology of the Heterosexual Love Relationship," *Marriage and Family Living,* XXII (May, 1960), 139-45.

——. "Personal Values and the Scientific Study of Sex." Paper delivered at the December, 1959, meetings of the Society for the Scientific Study of Sex.

——. "Changing Standards of Sexual Behavior," *Encyclopedia of Sexual Behavior,* ed. by Ellis and Abarbanel. New York: Hawthorn Press, 1960.

RILEY, JOHN W., AND RILEY, MATILDA W. "The Use of Various Methods of Contraception," *American Sociological Review,* V (December, 1940), 890-903.

ROBERTS, ALEXANDER, AND DONALDSON, JAMES (eds.). *The Ante-Nicene Fathers.* 10 vols. Buffalo: Christian Literature Co., 1886.

ROCK, JOHN, M.D., AND LOTH, DAVID, M.D. *Voluntary Parenthood.* New York: Random House, 1949.

ROCKWOOD, LEMO D., AND FORD, MARY E. *Youth, Marriage and Parenthood.* New York: John Wiley and Sons, 1945.

ROSE, ARNOLD. *Theory and Method in the Social Sciences.* Minneapolis: University of Minnesota Press, 1954.

——. (ed.). *The Institutions of Advanced Societies.* Minneapolis: University of Minnesota, 1958.

ROUGEMONT, DENIS DE. *Love in the Western World.* New York: Harcourt, Brace and Co., 1940.

ROUSSEAU, JEAN JACQUES. *The Confessions of Jean Jacques Rousseau.* New York: Pocket Books Inc., 1957.

RUSSELL, BERTRAND. *Marriage and Morals.* New York: Horace Liveright, 1929.

——. *A History of Western Philosophy.* New York: Simon and Schuster, 1945.

SANDERS, IRWIN T., *et al.* (eds.). *Societies around the World.* New York: The Dryden Press, 1956.

SCHAUFFLER, GOODRICH C., M.D. "It Could Be Your Daughter," *Readers Digest,* April, 1958, pp. 55-58.

SCHLESINGER, ARTHUR JR. *The Age of Roosevelt.* Boston: Houghton-Mifflin Co., 1957.

SERVICE, ELMON R. *A Profile of Primitive Culture.* New York: Harper and Brothers, 1957.

SHAFER, JAMES K., Sc.D., USILTON, LIDA J., Sc.D., AND PRICE, ELEANOR V. "Long Term Studies of Results of Penicillin Therapy in Early Syphilis," *Bulletin of World Health Organization,* X (1954), 563-78.

SHAFFER, LAURENCE F. *The Psychology of Adjustment.* New York: Houghton-Mifflin Co., 1936.

SHAPIRO, HARRY L. (ed.). *Man, Culture and Society.* New York: Oxford University Press, 1956.

SHAPLEN, ROBERT. *Free Love and Heavenly Sinners.* New York: Alfred Knopf and Co., 1954.

SHARP, MARGARET. *The Stone of Chastity.* New York: Avon Publications, Inc., 1955.

SHERWIN, ROBERT VEIT. *Sex and the Statutory Law.* New York: Oceana Press, 1949.

SIMPSON, GEORGE GAYLORD. *The Meaning of Evolution.* New Haven: Yale University Press, 1951.

SKIDMORE, REX, AND CANNON, ANTHON. *Building Your Marriage.* New York: Harper and Bros., 1951.

SMUTS, ROBERT W. *Women and Work in America.* New York: Columbia University Press, 1959.

SNYDER, CHARLES R. *Alcohol and the Jews.* Glencoe, Ill.: The Free Press, 1958.

SOROKIN, PITIRIM A. *The American Sex Revolution.* Boston: Porter Sargent Publishers, 1956.

Statistical Bulletin of the Metropolitan Life Insurance Company, XXXVII (May, 1956); XXXVIII (August, 1957); XXXIX (May, 1958); XL (September, 1959).

STOKES, WALTER R., AND MACE, DAVID R. "Premarital Sexual Behavior," *Marriage and Family Living,* XV (August, 1953), 234-49.

STOWE, HARRIET BEECHER. *Uncle Tom's Cabin.* New York: The Macmillan Co., 1926.

STRAUS, ROBERT, AND BACON, SELDON D. *Drinking in College*. New Haven: Yale University Press, 1953.

STRAUSS, ANSELM. "Personality Needs and Marital Choice," *Social Forces*, XXV (March, 1947), 332-35.

TAYLOR, HOWARD C. JR., M.D. *The Abortion Problem*. Baltimore: Williams and Wilkins Co., 1944.

TERMAN, LEWIS M. *Psychological Factors in Marital Happiness*. New York: McGraw-Hill Book Co., 1938.

THOMPSON, CLARA. "Changing Concepts of Homosexuality," in Mullany, Patrick (ed.). *A Study of Interpersonal Relations*. New York: Hermitage Press, 1949.

THOMPSON, WARREN S. *Population Problems*. New York: McGraw-Hill Book Co., 1953.

THORP, MARGARET F. *Female Persuasion*. New Haven: Yale University Press, 1950.

THORPE, BENJAMIN (ed.). *Ancient Laws and Institutes of England*. London: Commissioners on the Public Records of the Kingdom, 1840.

TRUXALL, ANDREW G., AND MERRILL, FRANCIS E. *Marriage and the Family in American Culture*. New York: Prentice-Hall Inc., 1953.

U. S. BUREAU OF THE CENSUS. *Current Population Reports: Population Characteristics*. Series P-20. Washington, D.C., January 12, 1959.

————. *Current Population Reports: Consumer Income*. Series P-60. Washington, D.C., January 15, 1960.

————. *Current Population Reports: Population Characteristics*. Series P-20. Washington, D.C., January 25, 1960.

————. *Statistical Abstract of the United States*. Washington, D.C., 1955. (Also 1956, 1957, 1958, and 1959 editions.)

U. S. DEPARTMENT OF HEALTH, EDUCATION, AND WELFARE. *VD Fact Sheet*, Issue No. 12. Washington, D.C., December, 1955.

————. *Earned Degrees 1954-55*. Washington, D.C., 1956.

————. *Statistics of Higher Education: Faculty, Students, and Degrees, 1955-56*. Washington, D.C., 1958.

————. *Milestones in VD Control*. Washington, D.C., 1959.

Selected References on Services for Unmarried Mothers. U. S. Department of Health, Education, and Welfare, 1959.

————. Mimeographed Material on Illegitimate Births. Washington, D.C., May 1, 1959.

————. *Opening Enrollment in Higher Education.* Washington, D.C., 1959.

U. S. DEPARTMENT OF LABOR. *Women As Workers.* Washington, D.C., 1955.

————. *The Legal Status of Women in the U.S.A.* Washington, D.C., 1956.

WAKEMAN, FREDERIC. *Mandrake Root.* New York: The Dial Press, 1953.

WALLER, GEORGE M. (ed.). *Puritanism in Early America.* Boston: D. C. Heath, 1950.

WALLER, WILLARD. *The Family.* Revised by Reuben Hill. New York: The Dryden Press, 1951.

WARD, J. "Don't Have an Abortion," *Readers Digest,* XXXIV (August, 1941), 17-21.

WARNER, W. LLOYD, AND ABEGGLEN, JAMES. *Big Business Leaders in America.* New York: Harper and Bros., 1955.

WEBER, MAX. *The Protestant Ethic and the Spirit of Capitalism.* Translated by Talcott Parsons. London: George Allen and Unwin, Ltd., 1930.

WHITE, ANDREW D. *The Warfare of Science with Theology.* New York: George Braziller, 1955.

WHITE, WILLIAM H. "Birth Control by Pill?" *Look Magazine,* October 7, 1952.

WHITEHEAD, ALFRED NORTH. *Science and the Modern World.* New York: Mentor Books, 1948.

WHYTE, WILLIAM F. "A Slum Sex Code," *American Journal of Sociology,* XLIX (July, 1943), 24-31.

————. *Street Corner Society.* Chicago: University of Chicago Press, 1955.

WIGHTMAN, WILLIAM. *The Growth of Scientific Ideas.* New Haven: Yale University Press, 1953.

WILLIAMS, JOSEPHINE J. "Patients and Prejudice: Lay Attitudes toward Women Physicians," *American Journal of Sociology,* LI (January, 1946), 283-87.

WILLIAMS, ROBIN M., JR. *American Society.* New York: Alfred Knopf Co., 1956.

WILLIAMS, TENNESSEE. *Streetcar Named Desire*. New York: New Directions, 1940.

WINCH, ROBERT F., AND MCGINNIS, ROBERT (eds.). *Selected Studies in Marriage and the Family*. New York: Henry Holt and Co., 1953.

WINCH, ROBERT F. *Mate Selection*. New York: Harper and Bros., 1958.

WOLLSTONECRAFT, MARY. *Vindication of the Rights of Women*. Philadelphia: Mathew Carey, 1794.

WYLIE, PHILIP. *As They Reveled*. New York: Avon Publications, Inc., 1935.

Index

Abarbanel, Albert, 84
Abegglen, James, 240
Aberle, Sophie D., 78
Abortion: estimated incidence, 154n; regret involved, 154n; variance by social class, 153n; *see also* Illegitimacy, Pregnancy
Abstinence: and inhibitions, 206-12; sexual advances and respect, 212-14; variation by social class, 215, 216; *see also* Christianity, Marital sexual adjustment, Petting, Virginity
Adams, John B., 42, 47, 49, 52
Adler, Polly, 71, 122
Adultery: reasons for, 169-70; relation to premarital coitus, 169-73; *see also* Sexual standards
Alexander the Great, 45
Allen, Frederick L., 238
Anthony, Susan B., 61, 62
Archer, Jules, 119
Aristotle, 44

Ashmore, Harry S., 236
Aspasia, 45
Astel, Mary, 59
St. Augustine, 209

Baber, Ray E., 73
Bacon, Seldon D., 246
Bales, Robert F., 69
Bamberger, Bernard, 42
Bardot, Brigitte, 246
Barnouw, Erik, 156
Beach, Frank A., 24, 25, 27, 28, 29, 30, 31, 32, 108, 109
Beals, Ralph, 27
Becker, Howard, 148
Beigel, Hugo G., 54
Benton, Walter, 134
Berg, Louis L., 34, 148
Bernard, Luther Lee, 207
Berrill, Norman J., 17, 18, 20
Bierstedt, Robert, 31
Blackwell, Henry, 62
Boule, Marcellin, 40
Bowman, Henry A., 73
Brenan, Gerald, 102